M000273811

Kamikaze Terror

Jeff Veesenmayer

Kamikaze Terror

Sailors Who Battled the Divine Wind

Jeffrey R. Veesenmeyer

Jeffrey Marketing & Publishing
Cambridge, Wisconsin
2017

First Published in 2017 by Jeffrey Marketing & Publishing
First Edition
Copyright 2017 by Jeffrey R. Veesenmeyer
Additional material copyright of named contributors.

The views expressed are solely those of the author.
ISBN-13: 9780692913468
ISBN-10: 0692913467
Library of Congress Control Number: 2017910328
JEFFREY MARKETING & PUBLISHING, Cambridge, WI

This book was designed, produced and published in the United States of America by
the
Jeffrey Marketing & Publishing
Cambridge, WI 53523
Email: JeffreyMktg@Gmail.com
Website: www.USSHadley.net
Facebook Pages: Kamikaze Destroyer, and USS Hugh W. Hadley (DD-774)
Jeffrey Marketing and Publishing publishes historical books, creates marketing news-
letters, develops direct mail marketing packages.
Front Cover: "Hell Over the Hadley" by Marc Stewart
Back Cover: "Kamikazes Over the Evans" by Marc Stewart, signed Kissing Sailor
photo, USS *Laffey* scoreboard, USS *Bunker Hill*, Kamikaze plane, Amphibious Training
Center patch.
Cover Design: Dianne Owens - Owen Graphics, Cambridge, WI

Contents

Dedication

SM1/c Robert W. Veesenmeyer and PFC James A. Horstman

Dedicated to the memory of my Dad and my Uncle Jim.

On the Covers

THE cover paintings are by Marcus W. Stewart. They depict an air/sea battle between 156 kamikazes and two radar picket ships at Okinawa on 11 May 1945. The destroyers portrayed on the front and back covers are the USS *Hugh W. Hadley* (DD-774) and the USS *Robley D. Evans* (DD-552).

"Hell Over the Hadley" (front cover) shows the *Hadley* in a full speed turn while evading kamikaze attackers and shooting down several planes. This painting won Best in Show at the 2006 National Museum of Naval Aviation Competition Exhibition.

"Kamikazes Over the Evans" (back cover) captures the *Evans* in a fierce battle with all guns blazing. This companion painting depicts another element of the action. Both ships battled wave after wave of kamikazes for 95 agonizing minutes.

Stewart chose these ships to honor their amazing gunnery record. *Hadley* was credited with destroying 23 planes, an all-time naval record for a single engagement. *Evans* gunners took credit for 19 more planes. Both ships were hit multiple times, fought fires and flooding, but survived.

Marc Stewart is a retired Navy pilot. His love of flying began as a teenager. He joined the Navy after college. He flew a half dozen different aircraft including the TA-4J Skyhawk. He rose to the rank of Lt. Commander while in the Naval Reserve. He always enjoyed art. His experience in the military influenced his love for aviation art, especially WWII planes.

Stewart's paintings and prints are on display in over 20 aviation museums worldwide, including the Imperial War Museum in Duxford, England. His work is also displayed at the National Marine Corps Museum in Quantico, Virginia. He has won a dozen awards at juried exhibitions and shows.

When asked why he chose to paint the *Hadley,* Stewart explained that the ship's legend became even bigger than the story. He lives in Newman, Georgia with his wife Robin. His paintings and prints are available directly through him and at many other military art websites.

AVIATIION ARTIST MARCUS W. STEWART, JR.

aviationart@att.net

www.AviationArtByMarcStewart.com

Acknowledgements

WHEN I discovered the USS *Hadley* website it was a life changing moment. I had Google searched for my great-uncle Louis Veesenmeyer. His name came up on a list of 30 shipmates killed in action on 11 May 1945. He was buried at sea near Okinawa after 156 kamikazes attacked his ship. I clicked on other pages to find more information for my family's genealogy records.

At the very bottom of a *Hadley* Reunion page I found an email address for Doug Aitken. He was co-chair of the *Hadley* Reunions. I emailed him. He emailed me back with an invitation to their next reunion. I attended that reunion in 2012.

My encounters with Aitken helped me author "Kamikaze Destroyer" and now "Kamikaze Terror." I'm webmaster of the www. ussHadley.net site; Facebook manager of Facebook/USS *Hugh W. Hadley* page and curator of the *Hadley* photo archives. I spend my days working on the website, the Facebook page, and communicating with relatives of *Hadley* shipmates. Researching the Battle of Okinawa has led me to a dozen other ships and their shipmates who also fought the kamikazes.

To learn more about destroyers I joined the Tin Can Sailors Association. I also joined the LSM-LSMR Association to learn about the ship my dad served on. I've attended their events, given presentations and provided articles in their newsletters. I've expanded the kamikaze stories in this book through contacts made with members of these organizations.

Hal Burke, who organizes annual Tin Can Sailor Bull Session meetings, introduced me to George Mendonsa, aka the Kissing Sailor. Mendonsa's VJ Day photo on Times Square (see back cover) is one of the most famous pictures of WWII. Burke also introduced me to Dick Lillie, a shipmate from the *Bunker Hill*. Lillie was rescued by Mendonsa and the crew of USS *The Sullivans*. I interviewed both sailors. I met Tom Blaszczyk at the same Chicago Area Bull Session. He is the newsletter editor for the USS *Bache* Association. Tom helped me contact the surviving WWII *Bache* shipmates. I interviewed six of them.

LSM-LSMR historian, Ron McKay Jr. referred me to several LSM(R) sailors. His book "The U.S. Navy's Interim LSM(R)s in World War II" became invaluable in understanding this unique class of ships.

Another author, Marty Irons, introduced me to several men he had interviewed. One of them is Marine pilot Phillip 'Pots' Wilmot. Pots provided me with detailed accounts of the kamikaze attack on the *Bunker Hill*. Irons' book "Phalanx of the Wind" will publish in 2017.

The National Museum of the Pacific War (NMPW) provided me with eight oral histories from shipmates serving at Okinawa. Reagan Grau, the NMPW archivist searched their extensive database for the ships or veteran's names I requested. The Wisconsin Veterans Museum maintains an online oral history archive. I obtained five oral histories through this source.

Some sailors kept personal diaries during the war. Diaries were in violation of war-time regulations. My brother-in-law, Mike Oswald, shared his dad's diary with me. Thomas Patrick Oswald risked punishment to record the valuable history of the USS *Bennington*. I'm so glad he did. His war-time diary is as detailed as a ship's daily log book.

My proofing crew members are all saints. Joy, my wife, has read this book four or five times. She corrects my dangling participles and past perfect tenses. I can read a sentence with a missing word a dozen times; but she'll spot it on the first pass. My hunting buddy Marty Ochs takes time from biking, hiking, fishing, volunteering, and his wife to read my early rough drafts. By the time he reads this finished product it will look like a different book.

My college roommate, Earl Bickett, enjoyed reading "Kamikaze Destroyer." So, I asked if he'd proof my next book. He took the project on like a professional proof reader. When a historical fact looked odd, he Googled it. He'd recommend more information that would enhance a story. Earl questioned my overuse of exclamation marks. He helped break me of a bad habit.

Tom English is gone but never forgotten. Tom was co-chair with Doug Aitken for most of the *Hadley* Reunions. He helped me get interviews with many *Hadley* shipmates and family members for my first book, "Kamikaze Destroyer." Before passing away in 2016 he gathered up 40 years of *Hadley* archives. He would send me a packet of photos, or cards or letters every month for about a year. I have a banker box of these memories. They were good resources for this book and made for memorable posts on Facebook and the *Hadley* blog.

A special thank you to all the men who shared their stories with me. The phone interviews, survey forms, newspaper articles and photos all helped make this book possible. This information is now preserved for their families. And the stories these men provided are a gift for future generations.

My uncle, James Horstman, was a voracious reader of military history. He joined the Marine Corps at the end of WWII and served again during Korea. He provided me with a library of books on

WWII, Okinawa and naval history. He was an accomplished writer and public relations professional. The encouragement and praise I received from him will never be forgotten.

The paintings of the *Hadley* and *Evans* on the front and back covers are by Marc Stewart. He is an award-winning aviation artist with a love for WWII aircraft. He graciously provided these historic paintings for "Kamikaze Terror." Graphic artist, Diane Owens of Owens Graphics in Cambridge, Wisconsin designed the dramatic covers.

Finally, I thank my dear mom. She salvaged a stack of letters from our flooded basement. They were letters my dad sent her while he was in the Navy. My dad had already tossed a whole box of letters sent to her from him. He thought they were the silly kid stuff from a home-sick boy. She was hurt. They were hers even if damaged by water. But he missed a batch of about 50 letters and postcards from 1945. Mom saved them in a box with his Navy memorabilia. A thin pink ribbon tied the letters together. It looked like the bow had remained tied for 70 years. She didn't need to read them again. When I found the box in her attic, I asked if I could have Dad's Navy stuff. She said sure. The letters were on top. She knew they were there. What a find.

My dad wrote to her almost every day. Each letter included details of his shipboard life. The return addresses and cancellations told me when and where he was writing from. I pieced together a more complete picture of his service history. They were also love letters from an 18 year-old boy to a 17 year-old girl. These kids had their whole future planned. They'd get married when he got home and live happily ever after.

I realize now, this is how these young men faced their fear of the war. Dad was worried and felt scared. Thinking of home and a future was an escape from the war. Thanks Mom and Dad for the letters.

Jeffrey R. Veesenmeyer
April 2017

Introduction

WAR news dominated newspaper headlines throughout WWII. During the spring of 1945 all the major battles were being reported. All except one. The Battle of Okinawa seemed mostly forgotten. It was partly due to military censors. The news from Okinawa was gruesome. Japanese ground troops were fighting to the death. Kamikaze pilots were crashing their planes into American ships with devastating results.

When writing my first book I researched Japan's kamikaze tactics. "Kamikaze Destroyer" was about the tin can sailors of the USS *Hadley*. They fought heroically against waves of kamikazes for 95 terror filled minutes. Writing that book raised many questions. Why were kamikazes targeting a destroyer 50 miles away from Okinawa? What effect did kamikazes have on other sailors serving at Okinawa? I wondered if the suicidal defense of Okinawa influenced our decision to use the atom bomb. My research led me to more sailors and airmen with incredibly heroic stories of their own. Through their stories I found answers to many of my questions. Another book was needed to complete the epic air/sea confrontation between men wishing to die and men praying to live. "Kamikaze Terror" is that book.

News coverage of Okinawa was minimal. The New York Times had bigger news stories to cover in April, May and June of 1945. The news from the home front and in Europe overshadowed Okinawa. President Roosevelt died on April 12, 1945. Vice President Truman had been sworn into office. American, British and Russian troops were racing for Berlin. The war in Europe was coming to a climax. Plus, Okinawa was so far away that few people in America had ever heard of the island.

The April 1 invasion of Okinawa involved an armada of over 1,400 ships and 183,000 ground troops. To men who survived the battle, the island would never be forgotten. The ground troops met the stiffest resistance American troops had ever encountered. The Navy faced relentless attacks from hundreds of kamikazes, day and night. Few people back home understood the horrors and terror at Okinawa. The kamikaze – meaning Divine Wind – was too unbelievable for people to comprehend.

I knew very little about Okinawa when I began researching the USS *Hadley*. Few books or movies had covered this last big battle of WWII. My initial interest was to learn how my uncle, Louis Veesenmeyer, died on the USS *Hadley*. I only knew Uncle Louis was killed by a kamikaze. His story led me to dozens of other sailors who faced the kamikazes. They are now part of this book. "Kamikaze Terror" takes the reader into the life and death struggle sailors faced daily.

After I published "Kamikaze Destroyer," more stories about the *Hadley* crew emerged. The most interesting discovery involved Japanese documents retrieved from a dead kamikaze pilot. A *Hadley* shipmate held on to this war memorabilia for 50 years. Now these Japanese documents are translated and archived in the Museum of the Pacific War in Fredericksburg, Texas. Photos of these documents are in Chapter 21 of this book.

Hadley family members contacted me and shared their relative's stories. My book tours for "Kamikaze Destroyer" opened additional doors into WWII veteran's groups. I was introduced to many other surviving sailors who fought kamikazes at Okinawa. I learned my family had two other sailors who were connected to Okinawa. Another uncle, Elmer Veesenmeyer was aboard the hospital ship USS *Bountiful*. His ship was stationed near Okinawa the same day his brother Louis was killed on the *Hadley*. If only wounded, Louis might have been transferred to his brother's ship for treatment. My dad, Robert Veesenmeyer, was on the rocket ship *LSM(R) 411*. He was headed for Okinawa when the war ended. This companion book expands the story of the USS *Hadley* and the involvement by many other ships and crews. It digs deeper into the terror unleashed by kamikazes on the entire Okinawa invasion fleet.

"Kamikaze Terror" is about all the sailors who faced kamikazes at Okinawa. It goes beyond destroyers on picket duty. The tin can sailors took the brunt of what kamikazes would dish out. Every sailor on every ship at Okinawa felt the terror and constant threat from any plane in the sky. All ships became targets. They included aircraft carriers, battleships, transports, amphibious ships, tug boats and even non-combat hospital ships. It made no difference what type of ship or how well it was protected, they were all vulnerable to kamikaze attacks.

I found one recurring theme from sailors who witnessed kamikaze attacks. They were all certain the plane was aiming directly at them. The terror made some sailors freeze. Others dove for cover. Many stood their ground until the end. I've tried to portray what sailors and kamikaze pilots experienced. At times they'd be eyeball to eyeball while facing death.

The USS *Hadley* crossed paths with many ships at Okinawa. She had connections to *Laffey, Aaron Ward, Bache, Shea, Curtiss, Bunker Hill* and others. I included stories and interviews from crewmembers of these ships as well as those of the *Hadley*. Their stories come from interviews, oral histories, articles, diaries, letters, websites and books. Personal narratives from crewmembers are indented and in italics.

They are not quotations. These are their thoughts written in first person that are edited for clarity.

Okinawa was the last battle of the war. It was the last stand for Japan. Their generals hoped a fierce defense would convince America to end the war without an invasion of Japan's homeland. Their do-or-die defense became fanatical. American naval losses at Okinawa exceeded the devastation at Pearl Harbor. The Army, Navy and Marines suffered over 49,000 casualties during the three-month battle. Japan did stop the invasion of their homeland islands; but not with the conditional truce they hoped to negotiate. The Battle of Okinawa convinced President Truman to use an alternative to invasion. He hoped America's atom bomb might end the war and save thousands of American lives. Each chapter of this book adds foundation to that decision.

Naval jargon and terminology can sound foreign to anyone who never went to sea. I've tried to clarify much of it throughout the book. I've also included several Appendices following Chapter 21. A glossary of naval terms and slang should help. These listings may improve understanding of the stories.

Shipboard life during WWII offered little entertainment. Sailors escaped boredom and the horrors of war in many ways. Letter writing, listening to music and keeping diaries were common pastimes. Quite a few sailors tested their poetic skills. The final three Appendices in this book offer a look within several sailor's thoughts. Their feelings show through their poems.

Writing these two books made me realize how important it was to preserve WWII stories. Capturing them in print or on tape is critical and needs to be done before all the participants are gone. Many of the shipmates and their relatives have thanked me for finally telling their stories. Much of this information has never been shared before. I received this note from a *Hadley* shipmate's granddaughter. It speaks for many families.

Granddaughter of a Hadley shipmate: Thank you for writing *Kamikaze Destroyer*. Everyone in my family has received a copy. It means a lot to us. My grandfather was a shipmate on the *Hadley*. I have heard some stories from him but not many. I wanted to pass on to you that he is not doing well. I wish that he could have met you to thank you for recreating the events for future generations.

The oral histories, interviews, letters, poems and diaries provide a view from WWII veterans not found in most history books. The Battle of Okinawa was a forgotten story after the war. There were no movies. It would be 30 years before any major books were published about the battle. It's my hope that this book will add more understanding and interest to the Battle of Okinawa.

Chapter 1

Patriots Point

TERROR helped end the war!

Japan's kamikaze units accomplished two things in 1945. The terror sailors felt when facing kamikazes was overwhelming. And kamikaze terror influenced Truman's decision to drop the bomb.

I'm standing on the deck of the USS *Laffey* (DD-724). The *Laffey* is the last *Sumner* Class destroyer in North America. The museum ship is preserved at Patriots Point in Charleston Harbor, South Carolina. Early morning sun is warming the harbor. The *Laffey* is docked in the shadows of the USS *Yorktown*. The massive air craft carrier, ten times her size, dwarfs the *Laffey*.

As I look up at the flight deck of the *Yorktown*, the 376 foot *Laffey* seems tiny. Yet her mission during WWII was to protect U.S. aircraft carriers, battleships and cruisers. A destroyer's speed, maneuverability, and firepower gives her a tactical edge. Radar and sonar provide defense needed to protect bigger warships and transports. The ability of US shipyards to produce destroyers at the rate of almost two per week during the war made these tiny ships more expendable.

Forty-two destroyers were either sunk or damaged while patrolling the radar picket line at Okinawa in 1945. *Laffey* was one of them. Destroyers provided early warning and a perimeter defense for the invasion fleet. I'm visiting here because my uncle's ship, the USS *Hugh W. Hadley* (DD-774) was one of those ships. Both *Laffey,* and *Hadley* fought off attacks by kamikazes while patrolling the most dangerous picket stations at Okinawa. Both ships took a beating from kamikazes, bombs, and strafing. They almost sank. Casualties were high and many were killed. My uncle died while manning a 40mm gun on the *Hadley.*

I wanted to learn more about these WWII destroyers. It's important to preserve their stories. I'm walking the decks of the *Laffey* – the identical ship design as the *Hadley* – to get a feel for life aboard a *Sumner* class destroyer. Many books have included battle history of these famous ships. I'm interested in the personal stories about the young men who faced kamikaze terror attacks. I want to know what my uncle, Louis J. Veesenmeyer, saw and felt on the last day of his life.

I head up to the bow of the *Laffey* and look up at the twin five-inch barrels of gun mount number one (51 mount). Each barrel extends 16 feet forward. Though small compared to the guns of a cruiser or battleship, they are versatile and accurate. They had a range of nine miles and could be used for shore bombardment, ship to ship battle or anti-aircraft (AA) defense. They were aimed by a Fire Control Computer that analyzed distance, speed, angles, wind velocity and even the roll of the ship. The standard AA shells were auto fused to go off in front of the approaching plane. They could also fire new variable time (VT) shells. These would explode when metal was detected on the targeted plane. Dual five-inchers with computerized fire control were the best AA naval guns of the war. *Laffey* has three of these mounts. Two of them on the bow and one back on the fantail.

The five-inch mounts have an enclosed turret that was manned by 14 men. The steel exterior is already warm from the morning sun. I'm wondering how they could work in such a cramped space. It had to be hot and loud in these sealed steel compartments. Ed Zebrow was gun captain on the 51 mount in 1945. His crew was well trained. They splashed the first two kamikazes on 13 May 1945. Each man's job was part of a choreographed operation requiring perfect timing from the entire gun crew. Every time the gun fired a hot shell was removed by a man wearing shoulder-high asbestos gloves, a powder man loads powder, the ramming shoe lever is pulled, a 55 pound shell is loaded, the breech was closed, the sight setter matches the cross hairs and the gun is fired...do it again. A well trained gun crew could keep each barrel barking every three seconds.

Kamikaze pilots would avoid bow attacks due to the massive fire-power from four 5-inch barrels, two 40mm gun mounts and several 20mm guns. There is a video that provides a dramatic depiction of what it was like inside these mounts during a kamikaze attack on the *Laffey*. The voice over begins..."You are inside the turret of a five-inch 38 caliber gun. Fourteen well trained men are working together in these tight quarters. They will fire 22 rounds per minute per barrel." I can only imagine what the constant da-thump, da-thump, da-thump sounded like from inside these turrets.

I continue my tour in a small room below *Laffey's* bridge. It's set up like a home theatre. Several other visitors are already seated. A quote appears on the screen that reads..."Whenever there is a mess, the de-stroyer runs first. She is expendable and dangerous." – John Steinbeck

The 44 minute film begins with the first USS *Laffey* hull number (DD-459). The ship I am touring today is the 2nd *Laffey* (DD-724). Both destroyers were named for Bartlett Laffey, a Medal of Honor recipient who piloted a Civil War stern wheeler against the Confederate Navy. In 1942, the brand new *Laffey* (DD-459) and her crew were rushed through training and a shakedown cruise to join the fight for Guadalcanal.

On the night of Friday, 13 November 1942 the *Laffey* (DD-459) was part of a squadron of eight destroyers, three light cruisers and two heavy cruisers. They were ordered to intercept a Japanese at-tack force that was going to bombard Henderson Airfield on Guadalcanal. The *Laffey* was second in the single line of 13 ships approaching Savo Island Strait. The Japanese task force included two battleships, one cruiser and 14 destroyers. The Japanese had the U.S. squadron greatly out gunned. The video's narrator pointed out that gun size and range was of little factor in this closely fought engagement.

The night was pitch black when the two forces met head on in a near collision course. The 2200 ton *Laffey* made emergency maneuvers to avoid colliding with the 31,000 ton battleship *Hiei*. Gunners on *Laffey* opened fire point-blank on *Hiei* as the massive ship missed her fantail by a mere twenty feet. It was so close they could hit the ship with a sling shot. In fact this was a "David and Goliath" encounter. David targeted the head of his enemy as did *Laffey*. Gunners on the five-inchers, 40mm and even 20mm guns targeted the ship's superstructure, the head of the enemy. This is the only location where they could inflict some damage from guns too small to penetrate the battleship's thick steel hull. Tracers and shells exploded on the upper decks and masts of the *Hiei*. Hot tracer shells started fires. The bridge was torn apart killing several officers and wounding the Task Force Commander. The *Laffey* and several other destroyers at the head of the U.S. column now found themselves completely surrounded by enemy ships.

While watching the film and taking notes, I realize I had read about this battle while researching the USS *Hadley*. Now I remember why I recognize the story. Lieutenant Patrick McGann, the Gunnery officer for the *Hadley* in 1945, had been on the *Laffey* (DD-459) in 1942. He was a young Ensign that fateful night. He witnessed one of the most chaotic naval battles of the war. Ships were firing torpedoes and shells in all directions. Some ships were hit by friendly fire. Search lights illuminated targets, star shells were bursting overhead, explosions sent geysers of water and fireballs of debris hundreds of feet up into the night sky. It was like a free-for-all dog fight in a dark alley.

Laffey was hit by a salvo of 14 inch shells. A torpedo took off *Laffey's* stern. Her magazine exploded. *Laffey* sank and Ensign McGann abandoned ship with over 200 surviving shipmates. Two and a half years later McGann – now a full Lieutenant - was the gunnery officer on the USS *Hadley*. He would face an even greater terror...the kamikaze.

McGann would be awarded the Navy Cross for directing fire and shooting down 23 kamikazes on the radar picket line at Okinawa.

During the six-month Battle of Guadalcanal, dozens of ships – both U.S. and Japanese – were sunk. A channel of water north of Guadalcanal was nicknamed "Iron Bottom Sound." During the next two years, nine new destroyers were named for ships or honored for sailors lost in the naval battles at Guadalcanal. A new *Laffey, Aaron Ward, Monssen, Little* and *Gregory* were commissioned with new hull numbers. Captain Cassin Young and Admiral Callaghan - both killed on the cruiser *San Francisco* - had destroyers, named in their honor. *The Sullivans* was named after the five Sullivan brothers who went down with the *Juneau*. And the *Hugh W. Hadley* was named for Commander Hadley who was killed on the *Little*. These ships would make history again on the radar picket line at Okinawa in 1945.

I look around at others in the room and wonder if we're all thinking the same thing…this is only the beginning of the *Laffey* story. It would already make a great movie. But the *Laffey* legend continued to grow when DD-724 was commissioned in February of 1944, just in time for D-Day. *Laffey* provided bombardment and screening along Utah beach. Then she was ordered to knock out harbor artillery at Cherbourg. *Laffey* (DD-724) would fire over 1,000 rounds during the first days of the D-Day invasion. She took a direct hit from an artillery shell that fortunately was a dud. The legend of *Laffey* (DD-724) was just beginning. The ship would be ordered back to the states and then sent to the Pacific. In March of 1945 she joined the task force headed for the invasion of Okinawa. I'm familiar with the rest of the *Laffey* story. I decide to leave the film room and continue my tour.

I head up a ladder to the bridge and pass a locked hatch door with Combat Information Center stenciled next to it. It was a top secret space in 1945 and apparently still is. But I know what it would have looked like inside. I had visited a replica CIC display at the National Museum of the Pacific War in Fredericksburg, Texas. The museum display is designed to look like the Combat Information Center

(CIC) on the USS *Hadley*. Doug Aitken, one of the *Hadley's* CIC officers, helped design the display for the museum's Okinawa room. The *Hadley* Reunion group toured the museum in 2012. Most of the *Hadley* shipmates attending the reunion were seeing what CIC looked like for the first time. To me - with a degree in photojournalism – it looked a lot like the photo dark rooms where I had developed and printed film.

It was dark inside the CIC. There were no portholes. The only light was provided by a couple of red bulbs and the illumination from radar screens. This was necessary for viewing the little green dots on radar screens that identified planes and ships. The new surface search and air search radar on the *Laffey* and other *Sumner* class destroyers was the most advanced radar of the war. Only radar operators and those with a need-to- know were allowed inside CIC. The screens and plotting boards in CIC could provide the location and movement of any ships or planes within a 50 mile radius. *Laffey's* Executive Officer Charlie Holovak was stationed in CIC. He was in constant communication with the bridge, the gunnery officer, the fleet anchorage at Okinawa and Combat Air Patrol (CAP) pilots. This was the nerve center of the ship. Destroyers patrolling the Okinawa picket line could provide the fleet with a 15 minute early warning of kamikaze attacks. CAP planes could be launched from carriers and land based airfields to intercept attacking planes. CIC teams would direct CAP pilots toward approaching targets. During General Quarters the XO would manage early warning and intercept from CIC. The Captain would manage the ship from the bridge.

Radar equipment and data inside CIC were top secret. Everything had to be destroyed in the event a crew was ordered to abandon ship. Sinking ships didn't always go down right away. They might be boarded by an enemy submarine crew or become grounded on a reef. CIC officers were required to "deep six" (six fathoms of water) everything but their swivel stools. Equipment would be placed in bags with lead weights and tossed overboard. This duty went to the junior officers – who became last to go over the side.

The Japanese realized destroyers on the picket line had advanced radar capabilities. These destroyers were taking away Japan's ability to launch surprise attacks on the fleet. Too few of their kamikazes were reaching Okinawa. The heavies – carriers, battleships, cruisers and tankers – weren't being sunk. This radar equipment made the *Laffey* and other destroyers on the radar picket line prime targets at Okinawa. Destroyers became the only targets for many kamikaze pilots. Japan's brass thought if they could eliminate the destroyers they'd take away their enemy's eyes and ears. Then they would be able to cripple the fleet that was supporting troops on Okinawa. But the U.S. fleet at Okinawa included 200 destroyers. The destroyers were expendable. Admiral Nimitz once made the sardonic comment that he could replace destroyers faster than the Japs could build planes.

I continue up to the bridge. There I find the ship's scoreboard. It shows the 20 Japanese planes *Laffey's* gunners were credited with shooting down. They also participated in shore bombardments at Normandy and the Pacific. The superstructure includes the captain's cabin, his office, a radio shack, the chart house, a signal bridge and the pilot house which looks out over the entire ship. The captain, the officer of the deck, the quartermaster, a signalman, phone talkers and assistants would be on duty here during General Quarters. Commander F. Julian Becton, was Captain of *Laffey* (DD-724). His previous command had been on the *Aaron Ward* at Guadalcanal. He had fought alongside *Laffey* (DD-459) the night when both ships were sunk by the Japanese task force.

The men up here on the bridge had a great view of the ship, the sea, and the airspace around them. A kamikaze pilot also had a great view of the superstructure. It was a very visible tall target. There was less chance of missing the ship when a kamikaze pilot aimed for the mid-ship area. And a hit on the superstructure would disrupt the command center for communications, navigation, gunnery and radar.

I step out on the port side wing-bridge. This is where the lookouts would scan the sky with binoculars for planes. They were trained to scan right, go up ten degrees, scan left, go up ten degrees, scan right...

it was tough on a man's eyes and nerves. Lookouts had to spot the planes that radar missed. A plane low on the water could slip in under the radar. Float planes made mostly of wood and cloth – no reflective metal - could totally fool the radar. The men with the binoculars had the lives of their shipmates in their hands. The wing-bridge served another valuable function. In rough weather a seasick sailor could hang over and heave without getting wet or messing up the deck.

I look back to the fantail. In 1945 this is where the torpedoes, depth charges, quad 40mm and 20mm guns were located. They are gone now. *Laffey* (DD-724) would serve the Navy until 1975. By that time smaller AA guns, depth charges and torpedoes were no longer effective weapons against modern ships or planes. They were replaced with a chopper pad for a drone anti-submarine helicopter. The U.S. Navy began using drones long before most people had ever heard of them. But the versatile five-inch number three (53) gun mount is still on the fantail.

At the start of the battle on 16 May 1945, *Laffey's* five-inch guns splashed the first five kamikazes. But one of those planes drew first blood on the *Laffey*. A port side 20mm gun crew became the first casualties when the Judy dive bomber released its bomb before crashing into the sea. The bomb exploded close to the ship. It sprayed shrapnel on the weather deck and wounded the gunners. At that point the 80 minute battle had just begun. The *Laffey* would survive despite taking hits from five kamikazes and four bombs. She earned the dubious honor of being hit by more kamikazes and bombs than any other ship. History would remember her "as noted" in Commander Becton's book title as "The Ship That Would Not Die."

I try to visualize how the battle looked to the lookouts standing where I'm at on the wing- bridge. I imagine what these young men were feeling and thinking as a 5,000-pound plane came screaming toward them at 300 miles per hour. It would be firing 7.7mm machine gun shells into the ship. Crewmembers could see an ugly bomb mounted below the plane, the wings disintegrating from exploding shells and plumes of burning fuel trailing behind. Still the plane got closer until the pilots ceremonial sash and aviator goggles were discernable in the cockpit. Nothing these young men had ever experienced could compare to the pure terror they must have felt waiting for the plane to explode... or crash into them. Which would it be?

Sailors on the *Laffey* had to be asking, "Who are these pilots? What are they hoping to accomplish by taking out one destroyer? Where did Japan find men willing to die in order to kill? Why would they send men to their certain death?" And finally, "how on earth do we stop these body crashers?"

USS LAFFEY (DD 724) launched on November 21, 1943 at Bath Iron Works, Bath, Maine. She was Commissioned February 8, 1944. She served at D-Day, the Philippines, Iwo Jima, Okinawa and Korea. Final Decommission March 29, 1975. Now she's proudly afloat at Patriots Point, Charleston Harbor, South Carolina alongside the aircraft carrier USS Yorktown and submarine USS Clamagore. Photo taken from the flight deck of the Yorktown. These museum ships are open to the public daily. (See Laffey scoreboard on back cover)

The five-inch 38cal. twin guns on Laffey's #52 mount. These guns were considered the most versatile weapons of the U.S. Navy. With fire control to direct aiming and radar range finders they were deadly accurate against aircraft, ships, or shore targets. Laffey has three five-inch mounts – two on the bow and one astern.

Chapter 2

One Man, One Ship

THOSE body crashers were young boys too!

The first volunteers for kamikaze service were young new pilots. By 1944 most of the experienced older pilots had already been killed. Those who were left were needed to fly fighter escort on bombing missions or to defend homeland airfields. When the call went out for volunteers, only unmarried pilots with siblings were allowed to join. The first 24 kamikaze pilots were eager. They felt there was little chance of surviving the war anyhow. They wanted their deaths to be of value to their country.

> ***Norio Okjomoto, Japanese Navy pilot:*** *I was a soldier of Japan and as such was taught to abandon any thought of coming home alive. I was trained to erase all home ties and think of selling my life for the Emperor. I actually felt a sort of relief when I joined the kamikazes. I had nothing else to worry about.*

Later recruits for kamikaze training were mostly college students. They were ill trained as pilots. A one week course taught them to take off, follow a navigator plane and attack using proven kamikaze tactics. Landing skills weren't needed. They were asked if they would be willing to die for their mother, father or sister. These young men felt the need to protect their homeland and families. Japan's cities were being fire-bombed by B-29 flying fortresses. This encouraged many young recruits to join kamikaze units. They considered the kamikaze to be an honorable way to die and did not think of it as a suicide mission. They believed in the seven virtues of the Bushido code...Courage, Benevolence, Honesty, Honor, Loyalty, Respect and Rectitude. This was part of the ancient Samurai warrior culture. These young men were ready to lay down their lives to honor their families and serve the Emperor. Most citizens of Japan had never seen or even heard Emperor Hirohito speak. He was like a god to them.

19 Year Old Student: I have been recruited as a Japanese Kamikaze pilot. How did I get to where I am and what will my life look like until my mission?

Initially, the idea for a kamikaze attack force was not welcomed by Japan's High Command. The loss of pilots plus a dwindling supply of planes was too high a price to pay. Only those fighter pilots whose planes had been hit were encouraged to crash into ships. If their plane was already going down the pilot's death would at least be meaningful by crashing into a ship instead of the sea. This type of heroism and sacrifice was not limited to the Japanese. Jimmy Doolittle had considered a suicide option too. After addressing his 80 volunteer raiders before their bombing mission on Japan in 1942, he was asked a question. What did he plan to do if his plane was going down over Japan? "I don't intend to be taken prisoner," he said. "I'll order the crew to bail out and then, full throttle into any target I can find that will do the most damage." He explained that he was 45 years old, but if he was in his twenties like most of his volunteer aircrews, he probably wouldn't make the same decision.

Bob Whitacre, USS Colhoun: The kamikazes gave their lives for their fatherland in a way that none of us understood. We were not trained that way.

In May of 1944 the first kamikaze attack against a U.S. ship was reported. The plane had made a conventional attack against a carrier. The wing was hit, engine damaged, smoke trailed; it was about to crash into the sea. The pilot crashed into the ship instead. Several more kamikaze attacks were reported that summer, but all involved planes that were already about to go down. These attacks caused damage and casualties but never sank a ship. Then in October of '44 one pilot with one plane sank one ship...the aircraft carrier USS *St Lo* in the Philippines. It was a planned kamikaze attack. Most conventional air attacks on carriers had been very costly to Japan. A dozen of their planes might be lost in an effort to score a single hit from a bomb or torpedo. But the idea of a piloted bomb gained some approval after the successful attack on the *St Lo*. That single kamikaze plane crashed through the wooden flight deck, its bomb exploded on the hanger deck below, and its burning gasoline ignited parked planes loaded with fuel, bombs and ammunition. The ensuing fires exploded the ship's ammunition magazine. The *St Lo* sank in just 30 minutes. This successful attack convinced Japan's General Staff of the merits of kamikaze attacks.

Another weapon was invented by Lieutenant Ota, a young aeronautical engineer, His design provided the impetus to move forward with a Special Attack force. His idea – a manned rocket - would save the high value bomber and fighter planes. Plus it did not require experienced pilots who were impossible to replace. It carried a more powerful payload than a bomb and traveled at a speed that would be impossible to intercept or shoot down. He was convinced his new weapon was guaranteed to stop the American advance.

Lieutenant Ota heard the Army had been working on rockets. Germany had shared the V-1 rocket design with Japan. The Army was trying to redesign the V-1 into a winged rocket that could be dropped by a bomber and guided by radio frequency. The rocket engines worked well but accuracy of the guidance system was a problem. Ota's idea was to substitute human pilots for the guidance system. He designed a small rocket propelled craft that was a pilot-guided missile. The warhead carried a ton of TNT inside an armor piercing shell. A firing pin would detonate time-lag fuses on impact. The bomb would explode only after it had penetrated the hull of a ship, causing maximum damage. The plane's speed would be 500 plus miles per hour. It would be built mostly of wood which saved scarce metal supplies. The rocket plane was relatively easy and fast to construct – compared to building a conventional plane. Its narrow wingspan allowed it to be delivered to the target underneath a bomber – same as a large bomb. The pilot would climb into the cockpit when ships were sighted and within range. His training only required enough piloting skill to keep the rocket aimed on target. His rocket only needed enough fuel to get it to a target. This new secret weapon would be called an Ohka which translates to "Exploding Cherry Blossom." Five pink petals were painted on each side of the Ohka bomb's nose. To the Japanese, in the secret language of flowers, the cherry blossom means gentle and kind. The delicate beauty of a cherry blossom would hide one of the ugliest weapons ever developed. This was the super weapon that Japan hoped would impact the outcome of the war.

On 16 August 1944 design and production began on 100 Ohka planes. They would be ready for deployment by the end of October. Technicians were shocked to learn they would be building human bombs. The project was kept top secret with the entire team confined to an off-limits building. Japan had produced other weapons that were considered suicide missions. They had manned torpedoes, crash boats and midget-submarines. But these all provided a chance for the user to escape. There was no possible escape from an Ohka rocket bomb screaming towards impact at 500 miles per hour. While success or failure of the plane depended on the design, many wondered if enough volunteers could be found to fly an Ohka to their death.

The initial call for volunteers ended that speculation. More trainees stepped forward than were needed to fill the unit. In fact, four groups that were designated as Very Eager, Eager, Earnest or Compliant were formed. Many signed their acceptance in blood. The Navy's fear of not having enough volunteers was dismissed. That shouldn't have been a worry at all. By 1944 suicide had become the preferred way to serve their country with honor. Japanese people had been told that the greatest glory they could achieve would be to die for the Emperor. They heard repeatedly that if men were captured by Americans they would be tortured to death. Women would be raped and killed. Children would be eaten. Servicemen were forbidden to surrender. This was an offense that was actually punishable by death. So why not just volunteer for the inevitable and go down a hero!

Itatsu-San (19 year old pilot): If Okinawa was invaded, then the American planes would be able to use it as a base to attack the main islands of Japan. So we young people had to prevent that. It was a normal thing to be a kamikaze pilot. All of us who were asked to volunteer did so.

The first Ohkas off the assembly line were used for test flights. Since these planes would never need to land, they had no landing gear. The test planes were fitted with a sled type apparatus that allowed the test pilot to crash land. A couple of test pilots were killed. Modifications were made, controls handled better and successful flights were made. Now they were ready for the real thing. The Ohka project went into full production. Pilots began their training and plans were made for attacks on the Philippines. The first fifty Ohkas were feverishly built in 30 days with workers putting in 72 hour weeks. These were shipped on the new super-carrier *Shimano*. The convoy hugged

Japan's southern islands en route to its base in the Philippines. On 28 November 1944 the U.S. submarine *Archerfish* was patrolling off southern Japan for downed B-29 crews. The convoy was spotted and the *Archerfish* attacked the *Shimano* with a spread of six torpedoes. Four torpedoes hit the ship. The ship rolled over seven hours later and all 50 Ohkas went down with it. Fifty U.S. ships had just escaped the same possible fate.

As 1944 came to a close, the once feared Japanese Imperial Navy was a mere shadow of what it had been in 1941. Naval battles at Midway, Guadalcanal and Leyte Gulf had left Japan with no naval offensive power and minimal defense for their supply convoys. At the beginning of the war the U.S. Pacific fleet had 73 submarines. Now they had nearly 300. Submarines had decimated Japan's merchant fleet. Japan relied on ships to supply their military at garrisons all across the vast Pacific. Those same ships would bring the needed raw materials back to the homeland for war production. Allied submarines were a key factor in crippling Japan's war effort. It wouldn't be learned until after the war just how crippling they were to the Ohka program. On 19 December 1944 the aircraft carrier *Unryu* was headed for Clark Field in the Philippines with another shipment of 30 Ohkas. The US submarine *Redfish* hit it with 2 torpedoes that exploded in the munitions room. The *Unryu* sank in 30 minutes. The Ohka program that was guaranteed to stop the American advance wasn't getting off the ground as planned.

Despite these setbacks Ohka production continued. There were 100 volunteer Ohka pilots in training and their special attack unit was formed. The Ohka pilots would be called "Thunder Gods." They had hoped to be hero worshiped as their unit name implied. The loss of the first 80 planes was devastating to them. The kamikaze pilots flying conventional planes had proven to be successful. Their name - Kamikaze – was chosen by Admiral Onishi. It translates to "Divine Wind" and is reference to the hurricane that saved Japan from the invading Mongols in 1281. Organized kamikaze attacks with fighter escorts were inflicting substantial losses on the ships supporting the Philippines campaign. Admiral Onishi had proven the worth of his kamikaze special attack units. He reported back to Japan's high command that his kamikaze units were a "crushing success" against the American warships. His overzealous report gave doubters of the suicide units hope that the invading Americans could be stopped. He now had full support to expand the program. The kamikazes were stealing the "Thunder Gods" thunder.

> *Admiral Takijiro Onishi: There is only one way of assuring that our meager strength will be effective to a maximum degree. That is to organize suicide attack units composed of Zero fighters armed with 250-kilogram bombs and crash-dive into an enemy aircraft carrier.*

There were now two very different special attack units of suicide planes. What they would both share in common is the ability to inflict pure terror among the sailors who faced them. In November of 1944, destroyers defending the fleet at Leyte Gulf were introduced to these new weapons. Deck logs and Action Reports contained references to suicide attacks. On 1 November USS *Bush* reported the maneuvers of a Zeke fighter plane appeared to be "an attempted suicide crash dive." USS *Laffey* (DD-724) faced off with the Divine Wind for the first time in December of 1944. The *Laffey* participated in a bombardment and beach landing at Ormoc Bay in the Philippines. The destroyers assigned to support the landing were attacked by wave after wave of kamikazes. The USS *Mahan* (DD-364) was the first to feel their wrath. Her crew fought off numerous attacks but three bomb laden kamikazes finally got through. *Mayhan* had to be abandoned and sunk. Then the aging USS *Ward* (APD-16) was hit by a kamikaze at the waterline, taking out her boilers and leaving her dead in the water. The whole mid-section of the ship erupted into an inferno of twisted metal and exploding munitions. She was also abandoned and sunk. This was the same ship that had fired the first shot of the war.

Ward had been on patrol outside Pearl Harbor on 7 December 1941. Her sonar picked up a submarine, and the visual sighting of a periscope confirmed the enemy sub. *Ward* fired her 5-inch gun, dropped depth charges and sank a Jap midget sub attempting to enter the harbor.

The kamikaze attacks continued at Ormoc Bay. *Laffey* was able to fight off any attackers that came her way. But what the men had witnessed was enough for a lifetime. As the crew was able to stand down from battle stations and line up for chow, they talked. Comments like "These Japs are crazy" and "I hope we never have face kamikazes again," were passed around the ship. Commander Becton heard the chatter. He assured some of the Chief Petty Officers that most of those pilots were being forced to be "body crashers" by fanatics. Once the fanatics were eliminated the others would change their minds. Becton knew his assurance to the chiefs would get around through the ranks even though he wasn't so sure it was true. He didn't want his entire crew to believe that every Jap plane was on a suicide mission aimed at the *Laffey*. That would have hurt morale and performance. Men need to believe they have a chance to win and survive to be an effective fighting force.

> **Shunsuke Tomiyasu (degree in Political Science):** *Dear Father, Mother, and Sister, I was suddenly ordered to sortie to a certain area, and must depart now, since from the beginning I gave my life for our country. I do not expect to return alive. I am determined to achieve excellent battle results.*

Seventeen ships were sunk by kamikazes as of 30 December 1944. Many more were damaged. As the Philippine campaign dragged on into 1945 the outcome was certain. There simply weren't enough kamikaze planes to crush the huge American fleet which supported the U.S. Marines on the Philippines. And most Ohkas had been destroyed before ever taking off. B-29 bombing raids on Japan's home airfields had further hampered the production and planning of the Ohka program. Some of the rocket planes had been destroyed in hangers. More importantly many of the bomber "mother planes" that were needed to deliver the Ohkas were destroyed on the airfields. Also, the fighter planes needed to protect bombers were being decimated while trying to defend Japan's airfields. The Ohka was becoming more folly than exploding flower. In frustration, some of the Ohka pilots volunteered for kamikaze missions instead.

Iwo Jima was the next target for U.S. war planners. The island's airfield was desperately needed for the support of the B-29 bombing campaign of Japan. It would provide an emergency landing strip for damaged planes returning from bombing runs on Tokyo. It was well within range of Japan's home airfields. The kamikaze was considered the number one threat to the invasion fleet at Iwo. Yet, surprisingly, few kamikazes, Ohkas or any other type of air attacks came during the 36-day campaign. Horrible weather might have been a factor. But more likely Japan was conserving their now limited air power for the final showdown at Okinawa. Allied ships at Okinawa would only be 340 miles from Japan's home-based airfields. Both kamikaze and Ohka attacks could be launched with fighter escorts. The Ohka pilots were told to visit their families. Their time for glory had finally come. A lieutenant addressed the unit when they returned. "All right you little gods. You've had the balls to come this far, now we'll see if you can go all the way!"

> **Kanichi, a kamikaze pilot's last letter home:** *I'll die between eight and nine this morning. As I have already sent some of my stuff in advance, please pick it up at Mitsu Station office. I've resolved to blossom at the end of my life. It's time. They are starting up. Sayonara dear Mother and Father.*

On 17 March, American air craft carriers launched a bombing raid on Japan's airfields. The purpose of the raid was to destroy aircraft and hamper the operational readiness of kamikazes that would be used against the Okinawa invasion fleet. After retrieving their planes the carrier force turned south for Okinawa. Two days later a Thunder God joint assault was launched. It included 18 Betty bombers with crews of eight, 18 Ohka planes and pilots, plus 60 fighter escorts. They took off at 9:45 a.m. to intercept and destroy the carrier task force that was speeding away from Japan. The 60 fighter escorts were only half the number of planes needed to support this mission. Many fighter planes had been damaged or shot down two days earlier while defending Japan's airfields. Most of the remaining escort planes were in very poor condition. About half of the fighter escorts turned back due to mechanical problems. The destroyers, providing rear guard screening for the U.S. convoy, spotted the approaching bombers on radar. Fifty carrier based Hell Cat and Corsair fighters were vectored to intercept the raid. The melee began when the Betty bomber group was still 60 miles from the carriers. The normal speed of the bombers was 272 miles per hour. But with a 4,000 pound Ohka plane hanging below the fuselage, their speed and maneuverability was greatly reduced. They were sitting ducks for the Hellcats and Corsairs. The outnumbered Jap Zero's and their pilots were no longer an equal match for very experienced Navy and Marine pilots in superior planes. The escorts were easily scattered and shot down. The bombers started going down in flames next. Three of the Bettys jettisoned their pilotless Ohkas and dove to evade the attackers. Only two Zeros were able to limp back to their base later that night. All 18 bombers with Ohkas and 162 crewmembers, were lost. The mission was a total disaster. U.S. pilots returned to their carriers and reported shooting down some kind of special bombers with a "winged gizmo" slung underneath. The Ohka Special Attack Corps had suffered another set-back.

Twelve days later the invasion of Okinawa began. The invasion fleet was met with very light resistance. A massive shore bombardment from 18 battleships, plus hundreds of cruisers, destroyers and gunships received no return fire from Japanese batteries. Army and Marine divisions landed unopposed and could walk ashore. Air attacks from Japanese bombers and kamikazes were very light. Two Japanese airfields were captured on day one. All the Okinawa based planes except two had been flown back to Japan. They were both captured in a camouflaged bunker on Yontan Airfield. The astonished Marines who first examined the strange little craft were dumbfounded as to how the thing would take off and fly. Aviation experts soon put the pieces of the puzzle together. They realized these were the silly looking "winged gizmos" attached to bombers, that had been shot down two weeks ago. There was nothing silly about the one ton armor piercing warhead and rocket propulsion. The little cockpit with limited controls and no navigational aids made them realize this craft was built to be a human guided bomb. The code name for this totally misunderstood aircraft became the Baka bomb. Baka translates to idiot in Japanese. Only an idiot would get in that cockpit.

Okinawa had been part of Japan's homeland for centuries. It was 70 miles long and up to 18 miles wide. It had a local population of over 400,000. This was to be Japan's "Do-or-Die" battle of the war. Most of Japan's military leaders now accepted that the war was lost, but by stopping the Americans at Okinawa they hoped for a conditional end of the war. The kamikaze had proven to be an effective weapon. The Ohkas might still be effective if not launched as the primary weapon in a main assault. They would now be part of mass attacks that also included conventional fighter planes, torpedo planes, and kamikazes. This would allow some of the mother planes to slip through a confused melee and launch their super weapon.

There was another plan for the Ohkas that could have been devastating if it had been ready in time. Japan had the two largest submarines in the world. They were just under 400 feet in length. And the I-400 super subs had an enclosed hanger deck capable of carrying three planes. Technicians were working on a way to mount and catapult the Ohkas from these subs. The submarine could have slipped under the radar of picket ships, surfaced within range of the fleet and launched their manned rockets in a matter of minutes.

The Japanese were desperate. Hundreds of suicide crash boats, manned torpedoes, and swimmer delivered mines had also been prepared and hidden on the islands around Okinawa. They planned to launch ten massive air attacks – called Kikusui - that would include kamikazes, Ohkas, bombers and fighter escorts. Kikusui translates to "Floating Chrysanthemum." This was the imperial symbol that stood for prolonged life. Kamikaze pilots believed in an honorable life after death.

> *Goro Nagamine, pathfinder pilot for a Special Attack unit: I would say to myself, "So are you ready now?" and there was a self that would answer "Yes sir! I'm ready to go," but there was still another self who never stopped yelling "I don't want to die."*

Japan's military planners decided to allow the Okinawa invasion forces to come ashore. Then they would destroy the supporting fleet and leave the soldiers stranded without means of resupply or support. If the battle could be prolonged and made too painful and costly for the "weak" Americans, they would beg for a conditional end of the war. It was a plan that might have worked, but the U.S. fleet was a 1400 plus ship armada. The combined American and British ships outnumbered the Jap planes that would eventually try to penetrate the defensive line of radar picket ships. No...the U.S. fleet couldn't be destroyed by kamikazes and Ohkas. Near the end of the battle for Okinawa, Japan's leaders no longer justified losses of student pilots in terms of military success. Their true value would be selfless sacrifice. A kamikaze pilot's death would be a positive example for future generations.

But there was an impact of the Special Attack units. It couldn't be measured like ships sunk. Troop morale has changed the outcome of many historic battles. From a military standpoint kamikazes at Okinawa inflicted untold TERROR. Destroyermen assigned to a radar picket line at Okinawa lived in constant fear. One picket ship sailor explained it like this "If you were down below and heard some-one running on the deck, you didn't wait for General Quarters to be sounded. You went right then. We'd hear over the loudspeaker that bogeys were 30 miles away, then 20 miles away, and then 10 miles. That's when your hair would stand up!"

Admiral Matome Ugaki, the commander of Japan's Fifth Air Fleet in 1945. He addresses kamikaze pilots preparing for attacks against American ships at Okinawa.

Chapter 3

The Destroyermen

Commander Mullaney, USS Hadley DD-774: No Captain of a man-of-war ever had a crew who fought more valiantly against such overwhelming odds. Destroyermen are good men and my officers and crew were good destroyermen.

THESE were two of the lines from Commander Mullaney's farewell letter to his crew. He had been transferred to new duty following the *Hadley's* heroic battle with kamikazes on 11 May 1945. His badly damaged ship would never sail under her own power again.

These thoughts were shared by many captains of radar picket ships at Okinawa. Destroyermen shared a bond. Crews of picket ships shared a terror greater than anything the Navy had previously experienced. There were 15 radar picket (RP) stations set up around Okinawa. Their purpose was to provide early warning of air attacks to the massive invasion fleet off the Hagushi landing beaches at Okinawa. The newer class of destroyers had been built with advanced radar capabilities for detecting both surface and air attacks. The Combat Information Center (CIC) that housed the radar had become the nerve center of these destroyers.

Doug Aitken, USS Hadley: Our ship was among the first destroyers that had a CIC constructed from start to finish. The other destroyers had modified a compartment that was located up close to the bridge. Normally, it was a division commander's stateroom. They just took that room away and made a CIC out of it on older destroyers.

The RP stations were positioned 35 to 50 miles from Okinawa. Picket ships patrolling these stations could provide the fleet with a 15 minute early warning of approaching aircraft. The ships, stationed at the landing beaches, would then go to General Quarters (GQ) and have all battle stations manned and ready. Aircraft carriers launched fighter planes to intercept the enemy aircraft. The destroyers protecting the front line defense of Okinawa, shot down many enemy planes that were trying to sneak past their ships. It was a plan with one flaw. There was no perfect defense against the thousands of kamikazes and conventional attack planes unleashed on the fleet at Okinawa. Japan committed ten times more the number of planes to kamikaze attacks than war planners had expected.

Okinawa is an elongated island that is part of the Ryukyu archipelago. It includes hundreds of islands that stretch out across 600 miles of the East China Sea. This was Japan's last defensive position before Americans would invade their homeland. Okinawa is less than 400 miles south of Japan and 300 miles east of Formosa. Well within range of their many airfields. Even Japan's run down and rickety planes could reach Okinawa. Military analysts thought they could only have about 500 planes left in 1945. But in fact they had over 5,000. Any or all of these could be designated as a kamikaze. The only requirement for a kamikaze plane was the ability to take off, fly 350 miles and have a pilot willing to crash dive into a ship. Japan would use trainers, float planes, patrol planes, WWI vintage bi-planes, damaged bombers or fighters, and the new Ohka rockets as kamikazes. The threat of kamikaze attacks was expected. But no one could have anticipated attacks by hundreds of kamikazes at the same time.

It was crucial to defend the U.S. fleet at all costs. There were over 180,000 ground troops on Okinawa. They required over 1,000 tons of supplies every day. The supply line was thousands of miles long. The loss of a single transport or supply ship was costly. Battleships and cruisers provided artillery support for ground offensives. It was a destroyer's mission to protect these high value ships. In naval terminology, "A destroyer is a fast, maneuverable, long-endurance warship intended to escort larger vessels in a fleet, convoy or battle group and defend them against smaller, powerful, short-range attackers." In fact the WWII destroyers became the go to ship for every assignment that required speed, fire power and adaptability. They defended capital ships by attacking below the water with depth charges, on the surface with torpedoes, or in the air with anti-aircraft shells. Destroyers were called upon for close-in shore bombardment from their accurate five-inch guns. They could also provide search and rescue, mine clearing and perform smaller commando type landings. The most dangerous duties were assigned to destroyers. They were expendable.

At first, destroyermen felt the radar picket duty would be a lonely, but safe assignment. It was the 1400 ship fleet at Okinawa that the Jap planes would be after. The RP destroyers only needed to slowly circle their patch of ocean and be the eyes and ears of the fleet. That assumption was dead wrong! On 6 April the USS *Bush* would be assigned to the northern most picket station - RP#1 - with one LCS support ship. This was the day Japan launched their first of ten Kikusui (Floating Chrysanthemum) attacks. There would be 700 planes – kamikaze and conventional – flying over the RP1 sector that *Bush* was patrolling. That day was anything but lonely for the USS *Bush*.

A destroyer on radar picket duty would circle their station at about 15 knots. This took away their speed and maneuverability. They were sitting ducks if a kamikaze slipped in under radar. While transports, carriers and battleships were the primary targets of the kamikaze - a lone destroyer, with no other ships for reference - looked very big to an 18 year old pilot on his first and last mission. Destroyers on the RP line became primary targets for many young kamikazes. And once the Japanese high command figured out that the destroyers had sophisticated early warning radar, they became the primary targets.

Despite the vulnerability of their mission, destroyermen were damn proud to be "tin can sailors." Many of them requested destroyer duty. Battleships and cruisers were more glamorous, more comfortable and a little safer with actual armor hulls. But to destroyermen, their ships were a thing of beauty. At full throttle of 36 knots, the ships would put up an impressive ten-foot rooster tail. They could make tight turns to avoid torpedoes or a diving kamikaze.

> **Jim Reeder, USS Bush:** *We could really travel. You're going forty-five miles an hour on a ship that size, you know you're bound to throw up a rooster tail. That's about the best we could do with both engines going. It was a good experience for me.*

> **Bob Bell, USS Hadley:** *At Pearl Harbor I was assigned to a sonar shore station at the entrance to the harbor. I watched all types of ships enter the harbor. The destroyer was my favorite. I thought it was the most beautiful ship in the Navy. I complained about my duty station and requested destroyer duty until I got transferred and assigned to the Hadley.*

Destroyers were designed for about 300 men but the war time compliment might be 360. Unlike a battleship with over 2700 sailors aboard – destroyer crews were a close knit family. Very close! Enlisted men slept on canvas bunks stacked three high and 20 inches apart. "Hot Bunking" was common with two sailors assigned to the same bunk. One slept while his bunkmate was on watch. Berthing areas were often in passageways that had 24 hour traffic. Sleeping compartments were hot, stuffy, noisy and very cramped. In the tropics many men slept up on the deck. Thin skinned destroyers were designed with slip joints in the deck. This was an important feature that kept the ship from splitting in two during high seas. When the midship slip joint decided to squeak, nobody slept.

Sailors relieved themselves in shared "heads" with commodes lined up side by side over a trough of running saltwater. No stalls, just four seats along one side of the head, facing more seats on the opposite bulkhead and sinks where men shaved. All waste and garbage was pumped right into the sea.

Harvey Fehling was a Chief Water Tender on the USS *Van Valkenburgh* (DD-656). He grew up on a farm in Lowell, Wisconsin, worked in the CCC camps and joined the Navy in 1939. His first ship assignment was on the cruiser *Milwaukee*. He served in European theater earlier in the war. Experienced crewmembers were needed for destroyers and Fehling was reassigned to the USS *Van Valkenburgh* in 1944. Transferring from a cruiser to a tin can was a rude awakening for Fehling.

> **Harvey Fehling, CWT, USS Van Valkenburgh:** *Destroyers were a lot smaller than a cruiser or battleship. The cruiser Milwaukee was 555 feet long and had a width of 55 feet. Destroyers are only 300 and something long with a 35-foot beam. Every spot on a destroyer is used for something. It's either to stack shells, or ammunition, or a gun, or food. Whatever the space, it is utilized for something. In fact I slept on a bunk under the number two turret up forward in the chief's quarters. I had shells all around my bunk. When I slept, my arm would hang over the shells. Life is a lot tougher on a destroyer.*

There were no portholes for ventilation. Fans pumped some air down below, but in the tropics the heat and smell of men working hard could be nauseating. The watertenders in the boiler room worked in 130 degree temperatures. They were covered in sweat constantly. Showers were shared with three or four other guys and could run only long enough to get wet, soap up and rinse. When fresh water was scarce the ship's boilers got it first. Then showers would be cold salt water. Baths were only for the very adventurous.

> **William King, Lt. USS Hadley:** *I once sat in a big bucket that was lowered over the side for a rare bath. When showering we'd only use*

enough water to wet the skin then "soap up" before turning on the shower for a final rinse.

In rough seas these narrow (35-40 foot beam), light weight ships could roll almost 60 degrees. Sleeping in a bunk or eating off a tray was impossible during heavy seas. The men swabbed, and scraped, and shined and painted by day. They worked four hours on and four hours off in the war zone. Sleep was wherever and whenever you could get it. There were no holidays and no days off. They went to battle stations at sunup and sundown and whenever a plane was spotted on radar. There might be no more hot food for the last sailors in the chow line. Everyone got a turn at scullery duty – cleaning up meal trays and garbage from 300 plus men.

Harvey Fehling, CWT, USS Van Valkenburgh: Destroyers ride rough you know. In storms you don't eat as good on a tin-can because you don't have all those amenities that you have on a cruiser. So a destroyerman's life is a lot different than being on a bigger ship – a carrier, or a battleship or something.

Meals were normally hot, nourishing and well-liked by most crews. But picky eaters complained that food was only good until the cooks got a hold of it. Foul weather or General Quarters meant cheese sandwiches for breakfast, lunch and dinner. On long cruises without resupply of their food stores, rice might become the mainstay of every meal. And yet most destroyermen speak fondly of their experiences aboard ship. It became a brotherhood of men who loved their ship and each other. They were close to the sea, close to their ship and close to one another. They thought of their ship as a living, breathing being, and referred to the ship as "she." A destroyer seemed almost human to the crew. When their ship was sunk it was like losing a member of their family.

Destroyer crews became very resourceful. With limited space and supplies they found ways to improve their living conditions. They'd find hidey holes where a few hours of undisturbed sleep could be had or extra food could be stored. Pilfering spam, snacks and bread from the ships storerooms was a regular game. Sailors on the hated mid-watch (midnight to 0400) would slip down to the bakery and slip out with a loaf of hot bread. It's often said that the navy runs on coffee. On some ships the non-regulation coffee pots outnumbered those included in the blueprints. The black gang down in the boiler rooms could make the best coffee. They had access to the hottest, cleanest, distilled water on the ship. They'd attach a coil of copper tubing to one of the boiler steam lines and run it into an enamel pot. By adding a couple handfuls of coffee and turning on the valve... presto, great coffee in seconds! They called it "a cup of joe" in honor of the infamous decree by former Secretary of the Navy Josephus Daniels. He banned alcohol on all naval vessels. This was a ban that was winked at by most destroyer Captains who maintained a well-supplied and well-secured beer locker aboard their ships.

A warship at sea is dangerous duty. But these young men went to sea feeling invincible. They were trained until they worked together like a well-oiled machine. They took pride in their ability. Gunnery crews would compete for bragging rights. Engineering departments squeezed pounds of power from the boilers when full speed was ordered.

Joe McMannus, GM2/c, USS Bush: I was Gun Captain on #3 5 inch 38 gun .... We picked our own gun crews more or less and trained them. Of the nine men, Pointer, Trainer, Fuse Setter, Sight Setter, Shellman, Powderman, Spademan, and Hot Shellman, I was most particular in choosing the right men for Pointer, Trainer and especially Powderman. The shellman had to be of good size to handle the 54 lb. shell but the powderman had to be strong enough to knock off the protective cap on the powder case as it came up from below. He then needed to be fast enough to seat it in the gun tray before the shellman could load the shell. This took coordination and he had to be fast and accurate. Believe me, we spent many hours in daylight and darkness practicing on the loading machine.

Destroyermen felt they could face and conquer anything the enemy or sea could throw at them. That is until they faced off with kamikazes.

Nothing can prepare a man for the terror of an approaching kamikaze plane. It's a nerve racking experience to watch the plane get bigger as it dives, 350 miles an hour through gun fire with pieces of fuselage and wings ripping off. The gunners have something they can do to stop the plane. Their concentration covers up fear. Men loading shells are too busy to look up. But those with nothing to do just clench their teeth and pray. The plane's engine screams over the thumping and rattling gunfire from 40s and 20s. Hearts pound, nerves tingle, the plane explodes. And then everyone's heart stops for an instant, muscles relax and legs turn to rubber...until the next kamikaze starts his dive and the cold chills return.

Phil Holywood, FC2/c, USS Melvin: I joined the Navy at age 17. My parents let me go to New York to enlist thinking I'd be turned down without their consent. I was accepted anyhow. I was trained to be a fire control technician. The day I set foot on the USS Melvin was the proudest day of my life. Patriotism was raging in my blood. Destroyers were the tip of the spear in battle. But kamikazes were a new experience to us. We were trying to kill an opponent who not only wanted to kill you but not survive himself. The kamikaze...that was scary to me. My fire control telescope would be on the plane watching it get bigger and bigger as my heart is pounding. Looks like he is coming down my throat. Anybody who says he wasn't scared isn't telling the truth. There were moments when I was so afraid, I didn't know if I would live or die.

Once a sailor had faced-off with a kamikaze, they knew they were not invincible. They saw the damage to other ships. They heard the horror stories of men blown to bits or burned beyond recognition. After being assigned to radar picket duty at Okinawa, there wasn't a question of if they'd get hit...but when and by how many.

And yet, every sailor at Okinawa knew his daily existence was a hundred times better than the conditions experienced by the GIs and Marines fighting from foxholes. The ground battle for Okinawa became a slugfest. It would only be won by the side who had more men and supplies. In stark contrast to the horrifying sight of a kamikaze, the soldiers on Okinawa were fighting ghosts. The 110,000 Japanese troops were burrowed into caves and holes all along three defensive lines. American soldiers had to fight their way up ridges and hillsides, foot by bloody foot. The Japanese defenses were so well concealed that attackers seldom saw who was shooting at them.

Destroyermen spent hour after hour at general quarters, just waiting and watching for the next attack. But the American ground troops endured around the clock bombardment by artillery and mortars. Sleep could be had only from total exhaustion. Their bed was a muddy foxhole. They hoped their foxhole buddy would stay awake during his watch to fight off any infiltrating Jap who was intent on cutting their throats. Food was cold K-rations gulped down during lulls in shooting. They lived in the same muddy uniform for a month at a time. Their clothes and bodies smelled of sweat, blood, urine and feces. The only thing worse than their own stench was the smell of death that was all around them. The battlefield carnage, torrential rains, dead and mutilated buddies brought more soldiers to the breaking point at Okinawa than any other Pacific War battle.

By contrast, the salt air was fresh and clean on the deck of a destroyer. Sailors aboard a no frills tin can knew they were better off than ground troops. They also knew that the RP stations were the very front line of defense. Their mission was crucial to the Okinawa campaign. Those who served and survived on radar picket duty had a swagger about them.

The Destroyermen – (last stanza)
They're a lusty crowd and they're vastly proud
Of the slim, swift craft they drive ;
Of the roaring flues and the humming screws
Which make her a thing alive.
They love the lunge of her surging plunge

And the murk of her smoke screen, too,
As they sail the seas in their dungarees,
A grimy destroyers crew!
By Berton Brakey – written during WWI

The invasion of Okinawa was launched just one week after final shots were fired on Iwo Jima. The landing beach at Iwo had been bloody chaos. The American forces suffered 26,000 casualties during the one month battle. The small island of Iwo Jima was just 11 square miles defended by 21,000 Japanese. Okinawa covered 560 square miles and was defended by over 100,000 Japanese. The Army, Marines and Navy all expected the worst. But, surprisingly the Okinawa invasion began like a parade in the park!

Deck gang on the USS Hugh W. Hadley (DD-774). Top row L-R: Johnson, Kuneman, Ebel, Jacobson, Frank, Calcom, Tice. Front row L-R: UK, UK, Gray, Keller, Jones, UK, Lt. Robbins. (UK are unknown)

*Best buddies from the USS Hadley. L-R: Vernon Frank,
Leo "Dutch" Helling, Bill Tindell and Ed Fryar.*

Chapter 4

Easter Parade

Action Report-USS LSM-57: 1 April 1945. Arrived at Okinawa Shima and at H+30 minutes, launched swimming tank at a point approximately 300 yards off Purple Beach #1.

ENSIGN Fred Lee arrived off the shore of Okinawa with five other LSMs at dawn, 1 April, Easter morning. These six amphibious ships were to launch pontoon-equipped swimming tanks in the seventh wave of the L-Day (Love Day) Okinawa invasion. The LSMs moved into position and waited for Hour Plus Thirty (30 minutes after first wave) to launch the DD Sherman tanks.

The "DD" designation on these tanks was for dual drive. They were powered in the water by two rear propellers. Each tank was equipped with an air-filled canvas float screen. A similar design had been used during the D-Day invasion of Normandy. Half of those tanks sank due to heavy seas. The floatation skirt had been improved, but was still very susceptible to puncture from bullets or shrapnel. Tank crews nicknamed their DDs the Donald Ducks.

The army guys hadn't missed the irony of launching swimming tanks on April Fool's Day. They asked if Ensign Lee would conduct a church service the night before the invasion. He agreed to conduct a Protestant service if one of them would follow up with a Catholic service. They sat on boxes between two Sherman tanks and performed readings and hymns that were very inspirational.

At first light the LSM crews could see they were not alone. Ships of every size and shape filled the horizon. There were over 1400 ships in Task Force 58 – the largest invasion force of the Pacific War. Ensign Lee wrote the following letter home describing the invasion of Okinawa. It was typed and mailed thirty days later, in accordance with censorship regulations.

Fred Lee, Ensign, LSM-57 – Letter Home: As dawn broke early on Easter morning (April 1), we were approaching the western coastline of Okinawa in the central part of the island where we were going to strike an amphibious landing. Just as the color of orange and blue in the sky erased the twilight, and the sun, a red ball of fire, began rising over the horizon, a line of our battleships opened-up with the most terrific barrage of anti-aircraft fire I have ever witnessed. Red tracers, millions of them, stabbing up into the sky following one lone Jap plane, that didn't have a chance in a million of ever getting through, burst into a red ball of flame and disintegrated in the sky. One more Jap plane attempted to get through that curtain of fire, and met with the same burning fate. Our guns did not open fire as we were out of range. It certainly was a beautiful sight to watch, just like in the newsreels, only in color. As we approached the beach, the battleships let go with their broadsides, and now I know what a sixteen-inch battery sounds like when it goes off beside you. We were right under their protecting guns now as we moved past them. The blast would shake our little ship. Ahead of us, LSM(R) s, (rocket ships), were blasting the shore line with rockets, and planes were dive-bombing the beach and hill positions. The noise was a din and smoke almost covered the island, and it made clear vision difficult.

The *LSM-57* moved into position for launching the tanks. Lee could see cultivated fields, green hills and buildings on fire. The first waves were on the beach and heading inland mostly unopposed. Everything was going as planned. The first tank was preparing to discharge into the water and then a whoosh went over the ship with a splash just beyond the port side. A Jap gun on one of the hillsides was zeroing in on the 57. Another whoosh came in and sent a gush of water over the starboard side. The shells had straddled the ship – an artillery-man's dream. Everyone was sweating the next round. Tanks were hurriedly plunging off the bow ramp. But the next shell never came. An army amtrack on the beach fired on the gun placement and silenced it just in time.

At Iwo Jima, a month earlier, the Japanese had waited until the beach was packed solid with men and machines; then they opened-up with artillery, mortars and machine guns. Casualties were horrific. The same tactic was never used at Okinawa. Troops were able to land in orderly fashion as though on parade. The two main airfields were captured. Men and supplies poured ashore. The expected kamikaze attacks were only harassing in nature. Japanese planes scored some hits but most were shot down before reaching their primary targets…the aircraft carriers. Optimism about the campaign was growing among the ground troops and the fleet.

Not everyone shared those feelings though. Two hundred destroyers were on hand. They included *Bush, Colhoun, Abele, Hadley, Aaron Ward* and *Laffey*. These were newer class destroyers with Combat Information Centers (CIC) housing advanced air search radar. Many of them had participated in previous campaigns. Some had witnessed the first kamikaze attacks at the Philippines. Their mission on L-Day was to screen for the fleet and provide close-in shore bombardment. They fired at the few Jap planes that made it through the combat air patrol (CAP) defenses. Destroyers also chased down wooden suicide boats that attempted to crash into ships with torpedoes strapped to their bows. They pinged deep with sonar for submarines. Compared to other Pacific beach invasions – day one resistance was very quiet and very light.

Donald Malcolm RT2/c, USS Hadley: *April first, Easter Sunday, we led a whole group of ships out to Okinawa for the invasion. It was a dark night. For some reason we had our surface search radar on short range. When someone flipped it to long range, suddenly we were* *surrounded by ships. It could have been the whole Jap Navy. Turned out to be Task Force 58.*

Jack Garska's diary, USS Hadley: *April 01, 1945 D-Day – GQ at 0300. Sporadic air attacks all night. Jap torpedo planes and bombers. One dropped a bomb off starboard quarter. During the night there were 3 planes shot down and Japs sunk one LST with a suicide plane.*

Kamikaze pilots were not supposed to be sacrificing themselves and their planes to sink an LST. Their targets were big ships…battleships, transports and the carriers. Japan's generals believed they could sink these ships with mass kamikaze attacks. This would take away the off-shore gun support, air support and supplies the invasion force need-ed. Ground troops would be stranded and defeated. What Japan's war planners never envisioned was an invasion fleet of over 1400 ships. The 40 plus carriers were spread out far from the shores of Okinawa. They could launch planes while cruising 50 miles away. They were harder to find than an LST heading into the landing beach.

The biggest carriers included the *Bunker Hill, Enterprise, Randolph* and *Bennington*. Parachute Rigger 1/c, Thomas P. Oswald from Chicago had joined the *Bennington* crew in 1944. Oswald knew this cruise would be historical. In defiance of Navy regulations, he began keeping a diary on April 1, 1944. Page two includes a poem he wrote with two buddies titled, "The Bitching Benny CV-20." They were proud of their ship and their division. The poem ends with, "And then there's Air Group 82 – The best damn air group that ever flew." Oswald was on the *Bennington* off the coast of Okinawa on Easter Morning.

T.P. Oswald, PR1/c, USS Bennington: *Easter Sunday, sent napalm hop to Okinawa at 0545 to help Marines and Army make landing. Hop went out two hours before invasion to soften them up for the "wrap leggens." Largest invasion to be pulled off in this war. "A*

*swell Easter Sunday for some." Air group is one-year-old today. Nice
Birthday Present.*

Commander Julian Becton, skipper of the *USS Laffey*, was less opti-
mistic. He found the unexpected quiet to be disturbing. His destroyer had been at the Philippines. That's where the kamikaze tactic was
first tested. Japs sank the air craft carrier *St Lo CVE-64*, by crashing
a single plane into the flight deck. Only then did kamikazes begin
attacking in earnest. Coordinated attacks from half a dozen or more
kamikazes proved to be nearly impossible to stop. Only one kamikaze
hit was needed to cripple or sink a ship. Becton had seen the damage kamikaze attacks could inflict. He kept his crew on high alert.
The sporadic air attacks and light resistance from Japanese troops on
Okinawa felt like the quiet before the storm.

Commander Becton's gut feeling was dead on. The Japanese 32nd
Army on Okinawa was commanded by General Ushijima. He was a
tough leader and brilliant military tactician. After the Marianas fell
to the island-hopping Americans, it was obvious that Okinawa would
be a last defensive stand for Japan. The island's northern two-thirds
was rugged, hilly and lightly populated. The southern tip had a series
of rocky ridges that extended the width of the island. Most of the
400,000 inhabitants lived in and around the cities in the south.

Ushijima had a well-armed, well trained army of 110,000 that included 20,000 conscript Okinawans. He realized that defending the
entire island was not feasible. Instead he spent nine months building elaborate defensive fortifications across the southern third of the
island. His conscripts dug a network of interconnecting caves and
tunnels through the rocky ridges and rugged hillsides. Inside the natural and man-made fortifications, the Japanese had electricity, supply rooms, barracks and everything they needed to stay underground
and invisible. Each defensive position could provide crossfire from
any approach. Artillery could be wheeled out to a gun port, fired and
wheeled back.

General Ushijima correctly guessed the American landings would take place on the west central beaches. He made no attempt to defend against the landings. As a thousand amphibious boats churned toward shore, Ushijima watched with binoculars. He and his commanders had balcony seats for the show. They stood on top of Mount Shuri on the southern tip of Okinawa. They watched the massive bombardment from the distant safety of their fortified command post. Japanese officers and staff joked and casually smoked cigarettes. The invasion was progressing exactly as planned.

The two military airfields located near the landing beaches would also be sacrificed. Okinawa was only 350 miles from the southern tip of Japan. Ushijima's air support would come from Japan's southernmost airfields and Formosa to the west. The Okinawa airfields of Yontan and Kadena wouldn't be needed. His concealed artillery and mortar positions were within range of the airfields. He would make the airfields one of his killing zones and keep them useless to the attackers.

Ushijima knew that once the Americans came ashore they would need daily resupply of food, water and ammunition. The second part of the plan was to destroy the support fleet with waves of conventional planes, kamikaze planes, manned rockets, suicide boats, and a naval attack by Japan's remaining warships. The U.S. ground troops would be cut off, under siege and eventually defeated. The thought of surrender or defeat was not part of Japan's military thinking. It was important for the morale of Ushijima's army that Plan A was for victory.

But, Ushijima had a Plan B. By 1945 the military strength of America appeared to be unstoppable. If he couldn't defeat the Americans, he would make them pay in lives and time. He would make Okinawa an American graveyard. He would delay the capture of Okinawa for as many months as possible. Japan needed time to build up the defense of the homeland. If Okinawa fell, Japan was next. Maybe, if the battle for Okinawa was so painful to America, they would agree to a peace treaty that was still favorable to Japan.

This was a do-or-die last stand for Japan. Ushijima's 32nd Army would fight to the last man. Surrender was not an option.

By the end of L-Day there were over 60,000 American troops on Okinawa. Over 100,000 shells had been fired at the beach area prior to the first wave landing. The sea wall that was to be the Marines first obstacle, was demolished. The ladders they brought for scaling the wall were not needed. Men just walked over the rubble. There were no defensive positions behind the wall. Most of the shells had fallen on empty landscape leaving huge craters behind. The only Japanese encountered were some conscript soldiers. They were either dead from being caught in the bombardment or ran away when shots were fired. The Okinawans had no fanatical desire to die for Emperor Hirohito. The island was quickly cut in two with the entire central zone in control of U.S. forces. The Marines moved north and the army began probing to the south. Soldiers picked fruit and vegetables along the way. They shot pigs and chickens for dinner. Easter Lilies were seen blooming. This was the best invasion of the war. One seasoned Marine Sargent warned his squad. "When an attack seems too easy, you're walking into an ambush."

Sargent R.V. Burgin, USMC: We were told we'd lose a hell of a lot of men on the beach. On the way in I said, "God I'm in your hands, take care of me." It was absolutely mind boggling that so close to Japan we had no opposition.

Navy brass had the same concerns. Where were all the kamikazes they had heard about? The invasion fleet was now within range of Japan's airfields. Naval Intelligence believed that Japan could still put over 500 planes in the air. Any type of plane could carry a bomb and be crashed into a ship. In anticipation of this threat, an early warning system with fifteen Radar Picket (RP) stations had been set up around Okinawa. The RP stations would be patrolled by destroyers equipped with advanced air search radar. Each station was placed close enough to neighboring stations so the radar would overlap. This would provide enough warning time for the Combat Air Patrol to intercept planes before they ever reached Okinawa.

> **Doug Aitken, Lt., USS Hadley:** *We were part of the largest invasion armada ever assembled. There were many squadrons of destroyers. The kamikaze was a known threat that came into being at the Philippines. The Navy had a plan laid out for the kamikaze attacks.*

The RP system was working well. Only a few attackers had reached the fleet. Some Jap planes sneaked in low on the water and under radar. Others may have followed navy squadrons returning from bombing raids on Japan's airfields. Plus wooden float planes made very effective kamikazes because they were invisible to radar. The few planes that made it to the fleet were shot down by the massive firepower of so many warships in a concentrated area. The USS *Hadley* was credited with their first kill the night of 31 March. Aitken was the junior CIC officer. His crew was eager to be assigned an RP station and the gunners wanted to add a few more kills to their scoreboard.

Day one casualties were very light. In fact, most were caused from friendly fire and accidents. A navy plane was shot down by a nervous LST gunner. Three swimming tanks sank with their five man crews. There were the usual accidental self-inflicted wounds.

> **Fred Lee, Ensign, LST-57:** *One time our guns were firing before I could get to the conn tower. Being gunnery officer it was my duty to give the orders to open fire. Our gunner was firing at a crippled navy fighter coming in low and wagging his wings. Other ships were firing too! I shouted "Cease fire." The poor guy veered left and crashed into a mountain.*

With resistance so light, many of the destroyers and amphibious ships had nothing more to do. No close-in shore bombardment was needed. The heavy equipment had been unloaded. Many of the smaller ships were sent out beyond the landing area for the night. This would reduce the chance of collision in the crowded anchorage; and less chance of being hit by friendly fire when every gun opened up on a single plane.

Rudy Minster, MM2/c, LSM-337: There was another scary part about the kamikazes. Not only do they come in and hit the ship, but they fly low between the ships. So what were we doing with our 50 caliber machine guns? Ships were firing at each other. That is terrible, but it is part of the game.

Everyone kept asking, "Where are all the Japs?"

The landing beach on day one of the Okinawa invasion was an orderly procession of men, machines and materials. Marines and GIs walked ashore wondering if the lack of Japanese resistance was an April Fool's Day joke.

The LSM-57 is a landing ship medium. The 203-foot amphibious craft had a crew of five officers and 54 enlisted men. On L-Day of the Okinawa invasion her crew launched five Sherman tanks equipped with floating pontoons. The tanks were propelled to shore from beyond the reefs with auxiliary power.

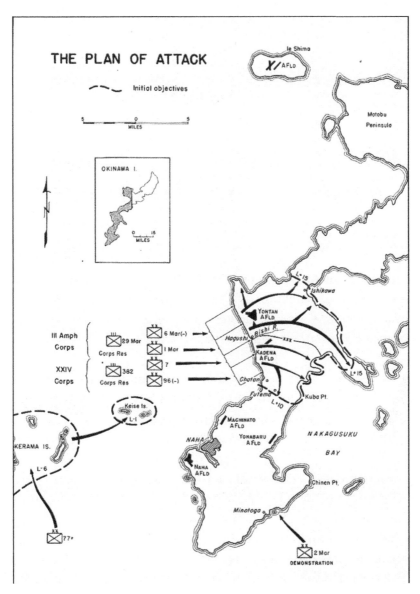

THE PLAN OF ATTACK

Two divisions of Marines and two divisions of the Army invaded Okinawa on Easter Sunday 1945. The central part of the island was in control by the end of the day. Marines moved north finding very little resistance. The Army probed south. They ran into the entire Japanese force and the most extensive defensive fortress ever encountered. It would take 12 bloody weeks to secure the southern third of Okinawa.

Chapter 5

Bush Going Down Fast

Message sent to U.S fleet - **CINCPAC:** *X Day for KIKUSUI #1,
operations now established as 6 April. Beginning around 0400 large
scale air attacks expected against Blue surface and land forces in
Okinawa general area by planes from Kyushu and Formosa.*

A message from Japan's High Command had been intercepted
by Commander In Chief Pacific Fleet (CINCPAC), decoded
and sent out to the Okinawa invasion fleet on 5 April 1945.
American intelligence had broken the Japanese code. Commanders
of Operation Iceberg were aware of Japan's plans throughout the
Okinawa campaign. This would be the first of ten Kikusui (Floating
Chrysanthemum) attacks involving hundreds of kamikaze and conventional attack aircraft. The chrysanthemum flower had been the
imperial family emblem since the 8th century. It represented longevity
and invoked powerful emotions of chivalry among pilots.

The decoded attack information was extremely valuable. Radar
picket ships were on high alert. Pre-emptive bombing strikes against
Japanese airfields could be launched. This hampered the effective-
ness of planned Jap attacks by destroying planes still on the ground
and intercepting those approaching Okinawa. A total of 699 planes

would still be able to participate in Kikusui #1. Over half of them were kamikazes. This represented many more planes than Naval Intelligence had thought were available. The USS *Bush* (DD-529) would be in their direct path of attack!

The veteran crewmembers of the *Bush* were proud to be selected for Radar Picket (RP) Station #1. They thought this to be one of the most important posts in the first line of defense. All hands were toughened from their previous experience in New Guinea, the Philippines and Iwo Jima. *Bush* gunners had shot down Jap planes and were anxious to add more to their scoreboard. These men relished their assignment regardless of the perils associated with the duty. But what they experienced in previous operations would never compare to the waves of planes attacking RP#1 on 6 April 1945.

The USS *Bush* relieved the damaged USS *Pritchett* on 3 April. The *Pritchett* had been hit by a 500 pound bomb that bounced off the fantail and exploded under the stern. For the next three days the *Bush* crew spent more time at general quarters than off. Jap planes continuously snooped, harassed and attacked in small groups. Men ate and slept at their battle stations.

Tom Owen, XO, USS Bush: We were sent to Radar Picket Station #1 some 60 miles north of Okinawa. On the way we saw several mines floating and took them under fire to explode them. One of our destroyers had been sunk by a mine the day before. We arrived on station and remained at either General Quarters or a modified version thereof continuously.

Bob Thompson, SC3/c When we were on G.Q. we made thousands of sandwiches. The food was brought to the men in tins at their battle stations.

Paul Pedersen, QM2/c: When we were in condition 1E, our usual meal was a sandwich consisting of two slices of bread with one slice of American cheese-no butter, no mustard, nothing.

Mac McKinnley, Bkr2/c My battle station was loading a 20mm on the port side. Between baking at night and that 20mm I never had to worry about sleep. I didn't get that much.

The *Bush* was a *Fletcher* Class destroyer. It was equipped with new radar equipment housed in the Combat Information Center (CIC). This advanced air-search radar capability allowed the radar men to identify enemy aircraft that were still 50 miles away. The ship was well armed with 22 multi-purpose guns that could be brought to bear against air attacks. She was named for Lieutenant William Sharp Bush, USMC who was killed on the USS *Constitution* – "Old Ironsides" - during the War of 1812. The men were proud of her history. They took pride in their gunnery and trained like their lives depended on it; and they did. Shells wouldn't be bouncing off the *Bush*. There were no ironsides on this thin shelled tin can. The men knew a single kamikaze could slice the *Bush* in half!

When enemy planes were identified on radar, the CIC officer notified the fleet anchorage at Okinawa. Land and carrier based fighter planes would be launched and directed to intercept the enemy planes. Picket ships provided early warning for the heavies (carriers, battleships, and transports) that were the primary targets of the kamikaze. Destroyers on picket duty were never expected to take the brunt of the air attacks. They might help thin the attacking force by shooting down a few passing planes. But the 15 RP stations circled around Okinawa were only intended to be forward lookout stations...not the first line of defense. Each station was being patrolled by a single destroyer on 6 April 1945. Some had one or two smaller support ships with them. *Bush* had only *LCS(L) 64* for support. That strategy would prove deadly for *Bush*.

Ed Cregut, S1/c, (& Radar Striker) USS Bush: I was on watch in the CIC room on the SC-2 Air Search. When I picked up an echo "blip" about 90 miles N.W. from our ship, I mean it was a very large "BLIP". Once in a while we pick up storm clouds, but this was so different. Lt. West took a look at the scope. He too was puzzled. And he said let's track it. We recorded the course and speed. My gosh, it had a speed of about 145 knots. Lt. West looked up and said, "There must be hundreds of planes."

The first Kikusui attacks began after midnight on 6 April. Planes took off from a dozen airfields throughout southern Japan. Their approach to Okinawa would bring them directly over Radar Picket stations #1, #2 and #3. At 0245 the *Bush* took four aircraft under fire and splashed one. The USS *Colhoun* on RP #2 was attacked by at least eleven planes in the pre-dawn hours. All of these planes dropped bombs and fortunately all of them missed *Colhoun*. Hitting a fast-moving ship with a bomb is difficult for an experienced pilot. This is why the kamikaze tactic was developed. Japan now had manned bombs that could be guided by even their most inexperienced pilots. At 0600 an Ohka rocket was launched from the belly of a Betty bomber. Luckily, that one ton, man guided rocket missed the *Colhoun* too!

At sunup the CAP fighter planes arrived on station. Their job was to intercept Japanese planes headed for the fleet. On this day, they needed to provide air support to the picket ships as well. At times, there would be 30 to 40 planes circling over *Bush and Colhoun*. Ten or twelve more were circling and harassing *Cassin Young* over RP #3. Jap pilots were looking for an opportunity to attack the destroyers. The destroyer crews wondered… did a single destroyer look like a battleship to these inexperienced kamikaze pilots? Were they attempting to crash into just any ship before being shot down by a Corsair? Or had the picket ships become primary targets? The sky over the RPs was filled with planes zig-zagging, looping and exploding in flames. One carrier squadron reported shooting down 46 Japanese planes. They described their mission as a "turkey shoot."

Earl Sechrist, LTJG: While the BUSH was on Radar Picket Station No. 1, waves of enemy planes filled the sky. They were buzzing around and over the BUSH like a flock of blackbirds.

By midday the attacks aimed at the picket ships had increased. The *Bush* fought off three more raids of planes within a half hour. Then at 1515 their luck ran out. A lone kamikaze came at them about 30 feet above the water. The Jill single engine bomber twisted and turned with roller coaster like moves while being hit constantly with shells. Still the pilot came on. The Captain ordered a hard-right rudder to swing the stern clear. The plane changed course too and hit at deck level between the number one and number two stacks.

Coit Butler, Ensign, USS Bush: He came in on our bow, low on the water and heading right for us. The five-inchers, 40s and 20s were all firing. There was so much metal in the sky you'd think he was bound to run into something. But this pilot knew what he was doing. He hit us at the most perfect spot possible – between the two stacks and right at the water line.

His bomb went through the hull and exploded in the forward engine room. Those men were killed instantly. The blast sent a six-foot section of the engine room blower – weighing over 3,500 pounds – into the sky, knocking off the radar antenna and landing on the port wing of the bridge. Water poured into the forward compartments, power went out and the ship listed 10 degrees. The effect of smothering steam from the ruptured boilers put out most of the fires. Damage control put out a few smaller fires. Most of the main battery guns were jammed or inoperative. The *Bush* was in dire need of help. The emergency generator kicked in long enough to radio the *Colhoun* and LCS support ships in the area.

Action Report – USS Colhoun (DD-801): 6 April 1945. Heard TBS transmission: "Any station this circuit, this is Helper" (USS Bush) no other transmission heard from Bush, assumed her in need of assistance.

Harry Stanley, Lt., USS Bush: *We caught the first one between the stacks, right at the waterline, which flooded the three forward engineering spaces and left us like a sitting duck with no power, lights, etc. We didn't see him till he was about 8,000 yards away as we'd just finished shooting to port and knocking down two...This one came in low and fast and how he ever got thru all the stuff we threw at him I'll never know, but he did.*

Al Blakely, SoM2/c, USS Bush: *I was gun 43 captain on the starboard amidships 40MM. As the first plane to hit us came in, we had shot off most of the wings and it looked more like a torpedo when it struck than a plane.*

James 'Okie" Reeder from Oklahoma was in his radio shack when the plane hit. Reeder was a Radioman Third Class. His little room was called "emergency radio." He had a transmitter/receiver, typewriter, a chair and a desk. After the first plane hit, something told him to get out of there. His power was out. He couldn't do anything anyway. That decision would save his life.

James Reeder, Radioman 3/c, USS Bush: *I was in between the smokestacks in my radio room when the plane hit. That knocked out the power. I was unable to run the transmitter/receiver, and so I thought there is no sense in me staying here. I walked out and was about 50 feet away when the next plane came straight down on top of the radio room.*

A flight of four CAP Corsairs were circling above. They were providing the nearly defenseless *Bush* with some air support. Work parties formed and top weight was jettisoned off the *Bush*. Five-inch ammunition was removed from handling rooms and thrown overboard. Wounded were cared for on the fantail. After a careful survey of the damage, it was determined the ship could be saved. Rescue ships were on the way. When the *Colhoun* was in sight, the CAP planes – who were "bingo" short on fuel – left for their base.

John Littleton, Ensign, XO, LCS(L)64: We first heard from the BUSH that it was in trouble at about 3 o'clock in the afternoon of the 6th. At that time, the Bush was out of sight to our northeast. As we proceeded in that direction, the sight of circling planes and the sounds of gunfire guided us to her. As we neared, we also saw the COLHOUN somewhat to the south of the BUSH, coming up from the east.

The *Colhoun* was speeding to the aid of *Bush* when she intercepted a flight of 11 kamikazes heading for the burning destroyer. *Colhoun* downed three of the planes but received more wrath in the effort. A fourth plane swooped in, dropped its bomb on the fantail and crashed into a 40mm mount. The bomb exploded in the after fireroom and the shattered plane spread flaming wreckage across the aft section of the ship. Then a trio of kamikazes attacked from the starboard side. The first two went down in flames but the third crashed into the starboard side. The plane's bomb broke the *Colhoun's* keel, knocked out the remaining boilers and blew a 20-foot hole in the hull below the waterline. Now both ships were dead in the water. Yet the kamikazes weren't done with them.

LCS-64 came alongside *Bush* and tossed lines. Two more planes began circling the two ships. The still working 40mm and 20mm guns on the *Bush* prepared for more action. All the five-inch guns were useless. Their crews were helping with damage control, caring for wounded men. Some were at secondary gun stations on the 20s and 40s. Two of the 40mm guns were still able to fire on manual. As the *LCS-64* began tying up to the *Bush* the two circling Vals resumed the attack. A Chief Petty Officer on the *Bush* began frantically waving off *LCS-64* so she could defend herself. Ropes were cut and guns from both ship blazed away. The first Val was fought off. But the second plane skimmed over the fantail of the *Bush*, rose up and began strafing as it dove into the ship's portside between the stacks. The explosion sprayed shrapnel all over the escaping *LCS-64*.

Robert Aguilar, SKD2/c, USS Bush: One of the Japanese planes flew across the fantail close enough that we could see the pilot. He waved, gained altitude, started his dive and crashed into the same place targeted by the first plane, evidently hoping to cut the BUSH in half.

The mid ship section was now severely damaged on both the starboard and port sides. Access from one end of the ship to the other was completely cut off. The captain ordered knotted ropes over the side. If the Japs strafed again, men could go overboard to escape bullets and climb back up after the attack. Combat Air Patrol planes never returned – they were needed to fight off hundreds of kamikazes at the fleet anchorage. *LCS-64* remained on station to fight off attackers and pick up *Bush* survivors who had been blown overboard. *Colhoun* could no longer be of any help. Her crew was battling to save their own ship now.

Despite taking two kamikaze hits and losing power the *Colhoun* gunners kept firing on manual. Fires burned all over the ship. The smoke obscured vision of attacking planes. They were still able to shoot down one more plane and damage another before it crashed into the fantail. This third kamikaze hit blew a three-foot hole in the hull and spread even more fires throughout the decks. As the crew fought fires, pumped water and tended to wounded, another kamikaze began his approach with the setting sun behind him. Lookouts spotted the plane, gunners loaded, aimed and fired by hand but couldn't stop him. The plane slammed into the *Colhoun's* bridge area starting another huge fire and causing more casualties.

As the sun began to set, the *Bush* crew fought fires and assessed damage. Captain Peterson still thought the ship could be saved. All hands were ordered topside. Wounded were lowered into rafts that were tied to the fantail. The men on the forward and aft decks created easy targets for Jap fighter planes who strafed the ship continuously. Each time a plane started its run everyone – except gunners - would dive overboard. Some men dove over and climbed back up five or six times.

Bob Shirey, EM3/c, USS Bush: After the second plane hit I went up to the bridge. There were no officers there at that time. I got a can of V-8 juice and a couple of the Captain's cigars. I returned to my gun, and had a big old time drinking V-8 juice, smokin' a cigar, and shootin' at Japs.

A group of planes were still circling above. A Zeke peeled away from the group and began his dive toward the starboard side. He strafed and weaved as he closed in. The 40s and 20s opened up as men dove over the side. Just when it was certain the plane would crash into the starboard beam, he pulled up, cleared the bridge by five feet, gained altitude and winged over toward the forward part of ship. The forward port 40mm was blasting away at the cockpit. The plane leveled out and came on very low. The pilot looked over to the men on the fantail…as if to say, "How'd you like my show – now for the finale." The plane smashed into the main deck on the port side below the #2 five-inch gun mount. This pilot was no novice. A fire ball erupted. Gas ignited on the entire forecastle of the ship. The plane's tanks were full which increased the incendiary damage. The ward room, where wounded were being treated, was demolished and consumed in flames. The captain ordered abandon ship. The time was 1745.

Coit Butler, Ensign, USS Bush: The third and final suicide attack was unforgettable. At the very last moment the pilot pulled up in wing-over out of his dive towards the midship area, clearing the stacks by maybe 10 feet, swung around in a tight turn to crash into the bridge area. From where I was on the fantail I couldn't see where he hit but I did actually see his face clearly as he was pulling out of his dive and off to the side. He seemed to be looking right at us standing on the fantail, turning his head to watch us as he pulled away.

Bob Thompson, SC3/c, USS Bush: *The ship was buckling up and down, up and down. We were strafed again. The wardroom was hit. I went over the fantail. Gerriets went over starboard, he was a ball of fire. That's when he died.*

Robert Aguilar, SKD2/c, USS Bush: *Albert Brody, PhM3/c was badly burned and we were trying to apply ointment on his back, but the flesh would come off on our hands. He said, "Thanks for trying to help me, fellows." and jumped into the ocean to drown.*

Al Blakely, SoM2/c, USS Bush: *I was forward on the foc'sle with Dick Day .... The 3rd Plane was loaded with gas, and it must have been an inch thick on the deck. I turned around and spotted Mr. Willis completely covered in flames .... Soon afterwards, I looked at Dick Day and said, "This looks like the time," and we abandoned ship. About 200 yards out, I looked back as the ship folded and sank. The sizzling sound as the flames were extinguished by the sea were spectacular and loud, something I won't forget.*

Jim Reeder, Radioman 3/c, USS Bush: *She went down bow up and stern up, and the American flag is still flying down there five hundred-forty feet below the surface of the water.*

Ralph Carver, BKR3/c, USS Bush: *At the order to abandon ship, people began to jump over the side and gather in groups on life rings and debris. The sea by this time was becoming quite rough and the groups would appear and disappear on large swells. Bob Thompson and I were still on the fantail with the Chief Torpedoman. We helped him disarm the depth* *charges by removing the primer and tossing them over the sides. This was done to keep them from exploding when the ship went down, thus saving many lives from the concussion of the explosion. We joined a group of about 15 men on a life ring. Shortly after joining up with the group, we looked back and watched the BUSH. The bow had risen out of the water and joined the fantail almost at the same time. She slipped below the waves. She was a great ship, led by a great skipper, with competent officers. It was a sad time for all of us and some men openly wept.*

The *Bush* went down 50 miles north of Okinawa. The waters were still cool in this part of the East China Sea. The sun was setting. Those who had survived the kamikazes, the strafing, the fires and sinking of the ship…would now have to survive the sea. The wind had picked up. There were whitecaps and 10 foot swells. Groups on rafts tried to maintain sight of each other. It was hard to do as daylight faded and waves obscured other groups of shipmates. Word was relayed to ships of Task Force 58 that the *Bush* was going down fast. A half dozen support ships raced to the scene of two destroyers in distress.

William Russell, Lt, LCS(L) 24: *A message was received that the USS Bush and USS Colhoun were under heavy attack in RP1. We were ordered to get there at flank speed along with the destroyer USS Bennett. We were 50 miles away. Needless to say, Bennett arrived before we did. We arrived at 2230 hours on 6 April. Bush had sunk, Colhoun was barely afloat. The sea was rough, there was a strong current and it was very dark.*

John Littleton, Ensign, XO, LCS(L)64: *About 1830 we established contact with Cassin Young and LCS-84 and 87. Searching north of Colhoun we saw no sign of the Bush. It was clear she had sunk.*

The *Colhoun* was still afloat…but just barely. Her skipper, Commander Wilson, ordered all men but a skeleton crew to abandon ship. He stayed aboard to direct the efforts of getting his badly damaged ship under tow. But the continuous flooding and severe damage made the ship impossible to tow. At 1900 hours she was abandoned and set adrift with fires still burning. After midnight the USS *Cassin Young* (DD-793) fired a volley of five-inch shells and sank the *Colhoun*. Final muster showed the human loss to be 35 killed and 21 wounded. USS *Colhoun* received a Battle Star for her action on 6 May 1945.

Over 200 crewmen from the *Bush* were in the water. Robert Aguilar described the scene. "The night was dark, the swells were high, and the water was cold. We were very hungry, very thirsty, tired, sleepy, and scared." The kapok life jackets most men wore would ride up over the mouth and nose with each swell. If not pulled back down the man's face would be in the water. Those who were too weak to pull it down would drown...in their life jacket. Many men clung to floating nets meant to hold about a dozen men.

Dan Tontz, LTJG, USS Bush: *After I hit the water I removed my shoes and dropped my .45, holster, and belt into the water. I left the ship about 6 pm and was able to stay afloat by clinging to a 4x4 piece of lumber. I was eyeball to eyeball with Ed Cregut. Four other men were hanging on with us. Only Ed and I survived.*

Harry Stanley, LT: *We had a hell of a time in the water – it was cold and fairly rough. We lost a lot of men who couldn't last. There were 35 of us on a floater net, which is a mean ride.*

Art Woolfolk, TM3/c: *A bunch of us were hanging onto a raft. One man found containers of K-rations tied underneath. There were malt tablets and Spam. I always hated malt tablets, but they sure tasted good then.*

Russell Youngren, TM3/c: *The water was cold and we were feeling numb. A couple of times I pee'd in my pants and the warmth felt really good.*

As the night wore on some men just gave up. They'd slip down out of their life vest and disappear. Others would let go of the raft and say they were swimming for shore, which was about 70 miles away. The ship's medical officer was Lt. George Johnson. He swam after several men and hauled them back to the rafts. His heroic efforts were stopped by his raft mates who feared he'd drown from exhaustion. Bob Wise realized mental and physical fatigue could overtake his sound thinking as well. He tied a line around his waist to make sure he'd stay with the raft. Life jackets had a one cell flashlight attached to them. Jap planes could be heard flying overhead. Survivors worried about shining their flashlights to get the attention of the search ships and end up getting strafed by a Jap pilot. Jim Reeder was on a floater net with a large group of men. They decided to take their chances by tying a flashlight to a paddle and waving it back and forth. They were finally spotted by an LCS and picked up after midnight.

> *Jim Reeder, Radioman, 3/c: There was one guy on our raft who had an American rifle slung over his shoulder. He pointed to the rifle and made the stupid statement that, "If there is anybody who survives this thing, it's gonna be me." I just reached over with my Bowie knife and cut the strap and let the rifle fall. Now he was in the same boat as all of us. We were on that raft until about 12:30 midnight. They saw that flashlight waving back and forth.*

> *J.C. McLendon, FC2/c, LCS(L)-64: After dark, we sailed back in to the area of the sinking, killed our engines, turned on our search lights and began to take on survivors. I think we rescued ninety men, some critically wounded.*

> *Russell Youngman, TM3/c: We saw search lights for us and when the lights went off, we feared they missed us. We found out later they shut off the search lights because there were enemy aircraft in the area.*

Bob Carney, Ensign: When helped aboard an LCS someone asked if I would like some coffee. I quietly quipped, "Yes, with cream please."

Harvey Miller, GM2/c, LCS(L)-37: We stayed in the area all night, and when daylight came we found three more sailors, but it was too late, they were all dead.

Of the nearly 320 men aboard the *Bush*, 94 died and 34 were wounded. Their experience on radar picket duty changed how RP stations would be patrolled from then on. The 200 plus destroyers assigned to the defense of the Okinawa invasion fleet was commanded by Captain Moosbrugger. It was now obvious to him that more firepower and support ships would be needed at each picket station. He increased the RP compliment to two destroyers and four support ships at most RP stations as the Okinawa campaign dragged on. With the invasion force already on land, there were many amphibious ships without a defined mission. The LSTs, LCSs, LSMs and LSM(R)s could be diverted to picket duty support. The mine layers and mine sweepers - which were converted destroyers - could accompany a radar equipped destroyer on RP patrol.

Defending the fleet from massive kamikaze attacks at Okinawa was on the job training for the invasion of Japan. Nothing of this magnitude had ever been experienced by the Navy. Tactics were being developed during the heat of battle. Destroyer captains recommended removing torpedo tubes and adding 40mm guns for more anti-aircraft defense. The LSM(R) skippers wanted to get the rocket ordnance off their ships. Their ammo magazines carried more firepower than two Iowa Class battleships. LSM(R)s were floating bombs. They were never built to withstand the crash landing of a 5,000-pound plane.

The 129 men who died on the *Bush* and *Colhoun* did not lose their lives in vain. Changes were being made to the radar picket stations that would save lives in the months ahead.

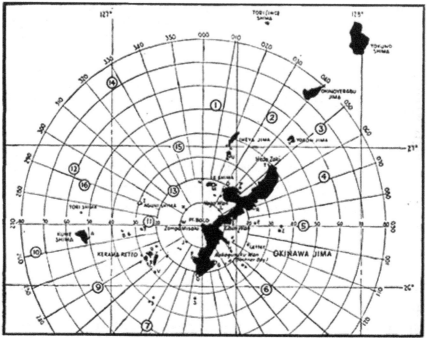

Map of Okinawa area showing locations of radar pickets

Fifteen radar picket stations were established to protect the invasion fleet at Okinawa. Each station was patrolled by a destroyer with advanced radar and an experienced Fire Director (FIDO) team. Their mission was to detect enemy aircraft and vector Combat Air Patrol (CAP) to intercept the attackers. RP stations 1, 2, and 15 were the most dangerous. These stations were in a direct line of attack from airfields in southern Japan.

Chapter 6

Baka Sinks *Abele*

KIKUSUI #1 had been a wake-up call. The Japanese military could still put hundreds of planes in the air and inflict terrifying damage. In addition to the sinking of *Bush* and *Colhoun* there were 24 other vessels hit during Kikusui #1. A destroyer, an LST and two ammo ships were sunk at the Hagushi landing beaches. Eight other destroyers were badly damaged, towed to the ship graveyard at Kerama Retto and never returned to the war.

On 6 April 1945, the casualties to navy personnel as well as losses to U.S. shipping were disastrous. This was not an exaggeration. Returning Japanese pilots painted an erroneous picture of destruction that gave their superiors hope for an Okinawa victory. Their battle report claimed the sinking of two battleships, three cruisers, eight destroyers, five transports and seven other warships. Japan's losses that day were much greater than the actual damage to the U.S. fleet. Of the 700 planes in the huge attack only a small percentage returned to base. Many were shot down by CAP before reaching Okinawa. And the kamikaze pilots – with only enough fuel for a one-way trip – were never heard from again.

The aircraft carriers – a kamikaze pilot's number one target - all survived. But the U.S carriers got a taste of being within range of

Japan's home based planes. Previous campaigns had kept highly valued carriers beyond the range of the homeland airfields. They were now vulnerable even when patrolling 100 miles from Okinawa. The USS *Bennington* CV20 was one of them. Parachute Rigger, Thomas Patrick Oswald from Chicago was assigned to the V-2 Division of Avenger torpedo bombers. His diary – which defied navy regulations – provides action report details of *Bennington* missions.

T.P. Oswald, PR1/c, USS Bennington: APR 6, 1945 – Today was a very lucky day for all of us and a turkey shoot for the air group. The air groups of Task Force 58.1 shot down 149 Jap planes...the San Jacinto and the Bennington were attacked by 4 planes. The San Jacinto shot down 3 and the Bennington shot down 1. It had gotten so close that when it blew up it scattered parts up and down the flight deck. I made a dog tag with a piece of exhaust pipe. I saw six Japs shot down. Very good day. Lost two DDs today (Bush and Colhoun).

Japan's biggest loss was from the biggest kamikaze of all – the 863-foot battleship *Yamato* - the biggest and most powerful battleship ever built. She was the pride of Japan's Navy. A suicide naval task force of 10 Japanese ships was also sent to Okinawa on 6 April. Its mission was to divert U.S. fighter planes from the defense of the U.S. carriers. This would give kamikaze and conventional attack pilots a better chance of successful missions. It was thought the *Yamato's* 100 anti-aircraft guns, plus additional protection from one cruiser and eight destroyers would be sufficient defense against U.S. air attack. Once the *Yamato* reached the northern shore of Okinawa it could begin pounding the carriers, battleships and transports at the fleet anchorage. *Yamato's* 18 inch guns could hurl 3,200 pound shells over 26 miles with devastating accuracy. The range of the 16 inch guns on U.S. battleships was 20 miles. Once U.S. warships were crippled the *Yamato* would be beached and fight on with her powerful batteries in support of the ground battle. Her sailors would go ashore and reinforce the defending Japanese army. The skipper, Captain Tameichi Hara had no thoughts of surviving the mission.

> **Lt. Fred Lee, LSM-57:** *Unknown to us at the time, the Japanese had dispatched the 69,000-ton battleship Yamato to repel the American invasion force on Okinawa. She had eighteen-inch guns that could fire a projectile nearly 30 miles.*

Part one of the *Yamato* suicide plan was successful. U.S. carriers launched 386 planes to intercept and attack the Japanese task force. This did reduce the available air support over Okinawa. But the attack began while the battleship, one cruiser and eight destroyers were still 200 miles from Okinawa. They had been spotted by a U.S. submarine while getting under way from Japan. Part two of the plan never had a chance. Three waves of U.S. bombers and torpedo planes overwhelmed the AA defense of the task force. The *Yamato* was hit by six bombs and at least eleven torpedoes. It took over an hour to sink the massive ship. The cruiser and four destroyers were also sunk. Out of a crew of 3,332, the *Yamato* lost over 3,000 men. This was the single biggest loss in maritime history. The attack cost Japan six ships sunk and more than 4,000 sailors killed. The four surviving destroyers were badly damaged. They limped back to Japan in disgrace.

> **T.P. Oswald, PR1/c, USS Bennington:** *APR 7, 45 – Caught part of the Jap fleet. Bombers sunk Battleship (Yamato)...air group sunk the rest of them. Air group shot down 7 planes, ship got one more. One bomber was lost. LTJG Fuller and Chuck Williams ARM3/c are missing. Also, lost one DD. This action took place west of Kyushu.*

Only ten American planes were shot down by the *Yamato* task force. The U.S. Naval force of eight battleships, seven cruisers, and 21 destroyers which was sent to intercept *Yamato*...was never needed. Air power and aircraft carriers had long ago changed naval warfare. Long range guns of battleships and cruisers were no threat against naval forces with aircraft carriers. The 18 inch guns of the *Yamato* were never even fired. The sinking of the mighty *Yamato* was bittersweet for many career naval officers. It marked the end of an era in naval history when battleships ruled the oceans.

While the Navy was fighting off hundreds of body crashers, army and Marine foot soldiers were having trouble finding anybody to fight with. It took the two army divisions four days before they found enemy resistance to the south. They probed and sent recon units to test the Jap's first line of defense along Kakazu Ridge. The Army underestimated the strength and will of these defenders. Initial assaults on the ridge line resulted in 50 percent casualties for some of the Army units. The sightseeing vacation was over in the southern sector of Okinawa.

In contrast to the bloodshed experienced by Navy and Army forces, the First Marine Division was wondering if they had landed on the wrong island. Their march up the northern two-thirds of Okinawa was more like a Boy Scout camping trip. No need to dig fox holes. They slept in pup tents at night. Marines picked tomatoes and fruit along the way. They commandeered pigs and chickens for their evening cookouts and sing-alongs. K-rations were gladly given to the local children. None of the local population ran away. There was no place to go. The civilians they encountered seemed glad to see them. Strict Japanese censorship had kept Okinawans completely in the dark about world news. Most knew nothing beyond their rice fields. The Okinawans were nothing like the Japanese encountered by Marines on previous island campaigns. The Marines had no idea of the pure hell that would be facing them when they joined the Army divisions in the south.

Despite Japan's terrible losses of planes, ships and men, preparations were underway to launch Kikusui #2. It had been scheduled to begin on 10 April 1945. Poor weather delayed it until the 12th. There would be a total of 185 kamikaze aircraft plus 195 planes for escort and conventional attack. Once again, the U.S. Military Intelligence Service knew Kikusui #2 was coming. They had intercepted and decoded messages providing details of the attack. One message mentioned Betty bombers equipped for Cherry Blossom attacks. The captured Ohka at Yontan Airfield had cherry blossoms painted on the fuselage nose. It was decided that these manned rockets would be part of the attacks. A Jap pilot who had been shot down on 6 April was picked up by the destroyer *Taussig*. The young pilot was talkative. He boasted that the next major attack would destroy the American fleet. A message sent to all American units warned of the imminent attack.

Rear Adm. J.J. Clark, 11 April 1945: Be prepared for very heavy air attacks tomorrow commencing before dawn. Indications are that the Japs will make another major effort tomorrow using all types of planes including obsolescent types and trainers. Some of these look like our planes.

Mannert L. Abele (DD-773) was assigned to RP #14 about 70 miles northwest of Okinawa. She had been there for three very quiet days without any action. Most of the RPs had been beefed up to include two or more ships. *Abele* was supported by two LSM(R)s. The *189* and *190* patrolled about 2,000 yards away on either side of *Abele*. The sky was clear and the sea was calm with only light wind. Commander Alton Parker was on the bridge.

At 1320 the air search radar operator in CIC identified bogeys approaching at 60 miles out. All three ships went to General Quarters. The first planes were sighted by Commander Parker. They were Val dive bombers. They split up and dove on *Abele* from two sides as Parker maneuvered the ship to bring all guns to bear. Two were driven off with 5-inch shells. The third Val made a run on the starboard side. The plane was hit, altered its dive toward *LSM(R)-189* and crashed after taking another hit from a 40mm shell. Two more Vals and a couple of Kates were shot down by gunners on the LSM(R)s. The "small boy" support ships were proving they could provide expert gunnery in addition to their less glamorous but much appreciated "pallbearer" duties.

By now the sky overhead was filled with circling planes. The skipper of *Abele*, Commander Parker, requested CAP support. At 1415 four Lilly bombers approached *Abele* at 9,000 yards. They were taken under fire by the five-inch guns and driven off. Then three Zeke fighters came at her from the northeast. One was shot down. Another made a run and crashed into the destroyer's starboard side. Its bomb exploded in the after-engine room, killing ten men and causing the ship to lose headway and power.

High above was a squadron of nine Betty bombers. They had taken off from a southern Kyushu airfield at noon that day. Each of them had an Ohka (Cherry Blossom) Rocket mounted under their fuselage. Several of the mother planes had already been shot down by CAP patrols. The Thunder Gods had already lost so many bombers and Ohkas to CAP fighters that they were attacking the first ship seen. As one of the remaining Bettys approached RP #14, the three ships were spotted. An air crewmember went to alert Ohka pilot, Lt. Saburo Doi...who was sound asleep. He was awakened and told his time for glory had come. Doi climbed down into his tiny cockpit, released his aircraft, fired the three rockets, then shot down from an altitude of 19,000 feet towards his target at 500 miles an hour. *Abele's* gunners tried desperately to score a hit. Lt. Saburo Doi hit the *Mannert L. Abele* amidships at the waterline with a tremendous explosion from one ton of TNT.

Herb Lewis, GM2/c, USS Abele: We were supposed to be on one of the safest RPs in the area. We had bogeys coming from all directions. I was the gun captain on a quad 40. We shot down one before we got hit by a Baka bomb – that was a man controlled bomb – someone actually rode the bomb. We were the first ship to be sunk by one.

Leonard Hartley, S1/c, USS Abele: I had put in for duty below deck on 11 April but it was denied. I would have been dead. I could hear the people who were trapped below deck banging on the walls and yelling as it sank.

The rocket bomb - nick named Baka for idiot by sailors - exploded in the forward fire room and broke the ship's back. The stern and the bow began to rise up in a V-shape. Lt. George Way was blown overboard by the blast. He grabbed a line and climbed back up within a minute. He gathered all able men to the forward part of the ship to cut loose and launch life rafts. Lieutenant Way opened a hatch to the plotting room to let those men out. Then he worked on the hatch to the port forward engine room. The dog – locking the hatch - was jammed. He grabbed a crowbar and broke off the dog to release the hatch, allowing those 10 men to escape as waves rose up over the deck. Just three minutes had passed when the ship went down.

Earl LaFountain, Machinist Mate, USS Abele: I was in the ammo room below deck when the explosion shook the ship. I got buried to my waist in powder cans. Lost my shoes trying to get free. I was the last one to climb the ladder out of the hole. Somebody slipped, kicked me in the head and I fell back down. I climbed again, but now the hatch had been closed. It was pitch black in there. I could feel the ship sinking. I worked with the hatch and finally got it open. When I got on deck everyone was gone. I wondered if I was the only survivor. Then I saw a guy on top of a wave. He hollered, "Hey, 30-day leave."

The automatic 30-day leave for surviving a sinking was the last thing on LaFountain's mind. Now he had to survive the ocean and he was a lousy swimmer. The ship was folding and his position on the bow was now 50 feet above the oil covered water. He jumped in and swallowed enough saltwater and fuel to make him sick. Suction from the sinking ship was pulling him down. He had to remove his life vest to swim away. He found a float net to hang on to, but now the Japs began strafing the survivors. They dropped bombs in the water which killed a dozen sailors from blast concussions. Sharks circled the life rafts. It was three hours before one of the LSM(R)s could pick him up. LaFountain was greeted by two of the ship's crew. One gave him a shot of liquor. The other handed him a lit cigarette. "That was the best tasting stuff I ever had," he remembered.

In Commander Parker's Action Report, he praised the support *Abele* received from *LSM(R)-189* and *190*. "They were worth their weight in gold as support vessels, splashed two of the remaining attackers, repulsed further attacks, and rescued the survivors." The *189* took a kamikaze hit that damaged its rocket launchers and injured four men. Their damage control team fought fires while shipmates continued their search for *Abele* survivors. The casualties were high. The *Abele* had 79 killed and 35 wounded. It would have been worse if not for the LSM(R)s. The *Abele* was the first and only ship ever sunk by a Baka (idiot) bomb. The crew of the Betty bomber that launched their Ohka saw the explosion when the *Abele* was hit. They were jubilant with their success and reported that they had sunk a battleship. Three other Bakas made hits that day too! They caused damage but there would be no other ships sunk from these "idiot" bombs. But the terror they delivered was undeniable.

James Stewart, Captain, LSM(R) 189: – Action Report 12 April 1945 - It is difficult to say what it was that hit the DD-733. This officer personally saw what appeared to be two (2) planes orbiting in a northerly direction from the DD-733, and then suddenly, what appeared to be, one plane, accelerated at a terrific rate, too fast for us to fire at. This plane dove at an angle of approximately 30 degrees, starting at four miles away.

Captain Moosbrugger took heed of the warnings for Kikusui #2. He had increased the number of ships patrolling Radar Picket Station

#1 on 12 April. He didn't want to see a repeat of the *Bush* and *Colhoun* disaster. This station was closest to Japan's southern Kyushu airfields. It would be in the direct line of their attack. He upped the patrol to six ships. There would be two destroyers, the *Cassin Young* and the *Purdy* plus four LCS(L) support ships. They could have used six more.

RP #1 came under heavy and continuous attack from over 40 Vals, Kates, Zekes, Oscars and Bettys at 1337 that afternoon. A Val was taken under fire by *Purdy* while dive bombing the *Cassin Young*. The Val's bomb missed. The plane circled back with both ships blasting away with their 40s and 20s and crashed into *Cassin Young's* starboard quarter. From then on there were many planes attacking. Only one of the six ships didn't get hit. *Cassin Young* headed to port for repairs and to transfer 59 wounded. She was replaced by *Stanley* (DD-478) ordered over from neighboring RP #2. She was also hit and suffered several wounded. *Purdy* was hit in the side by a kamikaze. A bomb was released prior to impact. It exploded inside the ship. She had to limp back to Okinawa with damaged steering, 13 dead, and 27 wounded. The *LCS(L)-57* was hit by a kamikaze on their forward 40mm mount that opened the starboard bow to the sea. They were listing and had to return to port. Another ship was taken out of the war.

At 1500 the *LCS(L)-33* was attacked by two Vals while assisting the damaged ships. The first was shot down but the second one hit amidship, exploded in a ball of flames and broke the fire main. They couldn't fight fire. The ship was engulfed in flames with magazines exploding. The order to abandon ship was given at 1505. She continued to burn but wouldn't sink. The USS *Purdy* had to sink the *LCS(L)-33* with two 5-inch rounds 90 minutes later. It was estimated that 25-30 Japanese planes were shot down during the 86-minute battle at RP #1. Casualties for all seven ships involved in the action totaled 20 killed and 120 wounded. The captain of the *Purdy* included some personal observations in his action report for that day.

Commander Frank L. Johnson, USS Purdy: The prospects of a long and illustrious career for a destroyer assigned to Radar Picket Station duty is below average expectancy. That duty is extremely hazardous, very tiring, and entirely unenjoyable.

Being ordered to Radar Picket Station #1 was becoming a suicide assignment. Every tin can sailor dreaded RP #1. Later that day word was received that President Roosevelt had died. One picket ship sailor lamented, "While we were on picket duty we heard of President Roosevelt's death. Everyone was pretty shook up – because here you are in the middle of a war and the **President dies!"**

A captured Ohka plane (code named Baka Bomb) sits on supports in Japan. These rockets had no landing gear or wheels. Once released from the belly of a "mother" Betty Bomber they could only crash into a ship or the ocean. A cherry blossom (ohka in Japanese) is painted near the nose.

Chapter 7

Laffey Lives On

WHEN word of President Roosevelt's death reached Japan on 13 April 1945 the Japanese high command began organizing another major attack. They wanted to take advantage of any possible distraction among the U.S. naval personnel. The news of Roosevelt's death was a shock to all Americans. He was loved by military men. He was their "Commander in Chief" and the only President some of them had ever known. There was no time for sorrow. They were fighting for their own lives. Their bigger concern was for the guy next to them along with their own skin. That's all that would matter when kamikazes filled the sky again. With the death of Roosevelt, Japan's propaganda branch saw an opportunity to demoralize the American troops. Instead, most who saw it got a good chuckle.

Japanese Military's Condolence Message: To American Officers and Men. We must express our deep regret over the death of President Roosevelt. The "American Tragedy" is now raised here at Okinawa with his death. You must have seen 70% of your CV's (carriers) and 735 of your B's (battleships) sink or be damaged causing 150,000 casualties. Not only the late President but anyone else would die in the excess worry to hear such annihilative damage. The dreadful loss that led your late leader to death will make you orphans on this island. The Japanese Special Attack Corps (Kamikazes) will sink your vessels to the last destroyer. You will witness it realized in the near future.

Propaganda must be believable to be effective. Even the officers in General Ushijima's 32nd Army had to be questioning the inflated numbers of American ships being sunk. They could watch the sea battles taking place from their hilltop defenses. They hadn't witnessed a single aircraft carrier or battleship being sunk. And everyone knew there weren't 735 battleships in the entire U.S. Fleet let alone the East China Sea.

The next several days provided some quiet time on the RPs and along the landing beaches. Air attacks were sporadic and mostly just harassment from single planes. The amphibious ships assigned to the anchorage were back to their regular job of delivering and unloading supplies for the ground troops. Fred Lee on the *LSM-57* wrote home about their Sunday dinner of roast chicken and real mashed potatoes while listening to the radio. "Damn Jap music playing on the radio, boy what corn. Sounds like my childhood attempts at playing the piano," he wrote.

> ***Lt. Fred Lee, LSM-57, Letter home 15 April 1945:*** *We were alongside a larger ship yesterday, and they usually have everything we need so we were bumming stuff off them all day. We stocked up on frozen meat, dry stores, spare parts, saw their doctor, dentist and stole their old magazines. Had a little church service today, thought about you as the crew read the scriptures. All the ships are flying their flag at half-mast in memory and respect for President Roosevelt.*

Despite the ridiculous propaganda from Japan's high command, the first two weeks of radar picket duty actually had been terrible. Three destroyers and one LCS(L) had been sunk. A dozen other ships had been damaged. RP crews suffered 235 men killed and 304 wounded. Kamikazes made it past the outer defenses of the picket line and combat air patrol and attacked the fleet anchorage. Attacks on the invasion fleet sank five ships, damaged 39 and inflicted over 2400 casualties. And the battle for Okinawa was just getting started.

On the morning of 13 April 1945 the USS *Laffey's* communication officer decoded a message that left him shaken. He took it directly to Commander Becton with wide eyed concern. Becton read the order and tried not to show his own concern. They had been ordered to Kerama Retto, the destroyer graveyard, to rendezvous with the damaged *Cassin Young*. There they would take aboard the *Cassin Young's* specialized radar team called Fighter Director (FIDO) and proceed to Radar Picket Station #1. Every ship that had been assigned to RP #1 had been attacked. Twelve of them had been hit and three of them sunk. This wasn't an order the men of the *Laffey* wanted to receive on Friday the 13th!

The *Laffey* steamed into the Kerama Retto lagoon at dusk on the 13th. This is where all the damaged ships were sent for repairs. It's what Pearl Harbor must have looked like after the Japanese surprise attack. Dozens of ships – mostly destroyers – were so badly damaged they no longer resembled warships. The destroyer, *Stanley*, had a huge hole in the bow that allowed an unobstructed view right out the other side. A Baka bomb had passed through the thin hull. Mercifully, the manned bomb hadn't exploded until it hit the water on the other side of the ship. The *Purdy* had a hole under the remains of her superstructure big enough to park a truck. As *Laffey* pulled alongside the beat-up *Cassin Young* her crew shouted dire warnings to the new men headed out for RP duty. As much combat as the *Laffey* crew had seen, some of the younger men were still shaken. One veteran quartermaster turned away from the horrifying sight of broken ships and announced that he was going below to change his underwear. Most got the joke, but some younger guys wondered if it was true. Humor is a way of coping that helps sailors face danger. When they stop cracking jokes a captain knows his ship is in trouble.

Charles Weygandt, QM3/c, USS Laffey: On the starboard deck, I chatted with a sailor from this destroyer who pointed out the loss of their huge main radar antenna to a kamikaze. The loss resulted in their being relieved from a radar picket station about 50 miles northwest of Okinawa. Their job was to report incoming Japanese planes to Okinawa. My first thoughts after learning the Laffey was their replacement was that this did not sound like a pleasant naval duty assignment. I was right.

The *Laffey* crew loaded up on ammunition and fuel from supply ships. Commander Becton realized many of these ships were new arrivals from the states. They had mail. Nothing could boost a man's morale better than letters from home. But it would take days for all the mail to be sorted and delivered to ships. He needed it now. And he had just the motivation to make it happen. When the *Laffey* was being fitted out in Boston Harbor, Becton had instructed his supply officer to secure an ice cream machine. Destroyers never had space in their galley for such a luxury. But they made space and got one installed. So a message was sent to all ships in the lagoon that said, "Five gallons of ice cream for immediate delivery of any mail for the *Laffey*." The first reply that came back just said, "Send boat!" They had seven sacks of mail within the hour and a crew that could stop thinking about kamikazes for a while.

Ari Phoutrides, QM1/c, USS Laffey: Early on the 14th, our skipper went out of his way to get mail for us. We had been underway for about seven weeks without getting any mail and the crew was pretty much in the dumps about it. We knew we were going to get hit. A measly letter would sure help out.

After all the harrowing stories the crew had heard while in anchorage, they were almost relieved when *Laffey* steamed north toward her assigned area, Radar Picket #1. Now every man had a job to do. A warship at sea required manned stations from bow to stern. They were either at work, on watch, eating chow or catching some sleep. Some found a few moments to prepare for the worst. Letters home were written - just in case it was the last. Valuables were removed from foot lockers to prevent losing them if the ship sank. These items would be stowed in the sailor's button down shirt pocket. Rings, photos and money could be sealed in a waterproof rubber safety device; one most every sailor carried in his wallet.

Lonnie Eastman, S1/c: As we were heading out to picket duty, I was thinking about the destroyers that were coming back from their picket duty. I knew it was our turn now and we were going to die.

The ship arrived on station Saturday 14 April and relieved the destroyer minelayer *J. William Ditter.* At this point in the war the Japanese fleet was no longer a threat, so a destroyer minelayer was no longer needed. The *Ditter* was one of many ships without a primary mission which was sent out on the RPs. Amphibious ships were no longer needed for beach landings. The *LCS-51* and *LCS-116* were assigned to support and rescue on RP #1 as well. *Ditter* and the two "small boys" had been lucky. No kamikazes and no bogeys on radar while they were on patrol. This was ominous news for the *Laffey*. It was unlikely the Japs would remain quiet for much longer. The destroyer took up patrol flanked by the two amphibs. Within an hour enemy activity started again. Three bogeys were spotted on air search radar. The FIDO officer in CIC directed a squadron of CAP fighters to intercept them. "Tallyho" was heard over the *Laffey's* radio. The first, the second and then the third plane were all shot down. American pilots had adopted the ancient "Tallyho" term from the British. It was derived from fox hunters on horseback who chased their prey with hounds. When the sly fox was finally spotted, fox hunters would yell "tallyho" to urge on the hounds. Now allied fighter pilots announced spotting their prey in the same way fox hunters had at

England's Keswick Hunt Club. It was a reassuring phrase whatever the origin.

CAP fighters kept the few Jap intruders at bay. The *Laffey* guns remained silent throughout the day. To keep the gunners alert, they never stopped targeting planes...even friendly ones. Commander Becton had instructed the gunnery division to target every plane that was within range. As night fell the ship slowed to reduce the visible phosphorescent wake a ship left behind. No smoking topside. No lights of any kind were allowed on decks or in hatchways. Guns remained silent if the snooper plane they had nicknamed "Washing Machine Charlie" was spotted. No point in giving away their position to a heckler plane. These old twin engine Betty bombers sounded just like mom's ringer washing machine to the sailors. "Charlie's" purpose was to harass the enemy and deprive them of sleep. On this night, some men were able to nap at their gun station. Others caught several hours sleep in their bunk. Everyone listened for the hum of the loudspeaker which would precede an announcement of General Quarters. But there were no bogeys that night.

> *Jerry Liebertz, PMM1/c: There was the inevitable "Washing Machine Charlie." The lone Japanese plane of questionable vintage and fire-power but nevertheless an unfriendly bogey on our radar screen. And then it was GQ for all hands. It was all about harassing.*

Mornings at sea are a true delight. The waves glisten as the early twilight begins to shine in the east. Navy coffee was brewing throughout the *Laffey*. They had more non-regulation coffee pots than the regulation ones installed as per the blueprints. The smell of breakfast cooking floated up from the galley. During happier times the Executive Officer (XO) would already be up on the bridge shooting morning stars with a sextant. Lieutenant Commander Charlie Holovak still practiced the ancient art of mariner's navigation whenever weather permitted. It was a needed skill if the ships navigation system should fail. Nautical twilight is when the horizon can be defined. It provides the perfect light for using a sextant. Degree readings would be taken on navigator stars…Canopus, Capella, Vega, Sirius and maybe Jupiter or Venus; but not this morning. The *Laffey* crew went to General Quarters at 0450. A lone snooper plane had been picked up on radar about 20 miles out. The XOs battle station was in CIC. There was no time for morning stars on 16 April 1945.

The Jap pilot stayed out of range. Probably a scout. When he left, the *Laffey* crew remained at battle stations. Sunrise would be at 0607 and the normal routine on RP was to go to battle stations an hour before sunrise. When breakfast was ready, a few men from each battle station were released for chow. The men rotated until all were fed. When the first Val dive bomber appeared at 0744 most everyone had a full tummy to help quell the nerves.

Laffey gunners were ready to fight. The five-inch guns opened up with a crescendo of double blams. The variable time (VT) fragmentation shells exploded all around the plane. They had the Val in their cross-hair sights. The Jap pilot dropped his bomb into the sea and turned tail for home. He knew Marine Corsairs would be chasing him down. With less weight, he'd have a better chance to escape. The *Laffey* crew knew he'd be back with reinforcements. Sure enough, at 0829 a large swarm of reinforcing bogeys appeared on the radar screen approaching from the north. Within minutes lookouts were identifying Vals, Judys, Kates, and Oscars.

Merle Johnson, S2/c: *After general quarters was sounded, the bridge kept announcing, "Twenty miles, Fifteen miles, Ten miles." Then you could see little dots in the sky.*

Commander Becton ordered full speed and began giving the helmsman steering orders over the voice tube. He wanted to keep the ship moving fast to make it harder to hit. And by maneuvering broad to beam against attackers, all guns could be brought to bear. As the crew watched the sky above fill with circling planes they could only shake their heads and pray. Then four Vals with fixed landing gear peeled off from the group and attacked. Before any gun could fire they split up, two on the starboard bow and two astern. A pincer tactic forcing guns to target in two directions. A crewmember yelled, "Here they come, here they come. Here. They. Come!"

All six five-inch guns opened-up when the planes were 9,000 yards out. The ship shook, light bulbs broke, unsecured items flew onto the deck. When the Vals swerved to avoid the full broadside of guns, Becton ordered "Hard left rudder." The first two bow planes were splashed by the forward guns. One of the stern Vals came in too low, caught his landing gear on a wave and cartwheeled into the ocean. The fourth plane was destroyed by relentless converging fire from the 20s and 40s of the *Laffey* and the *LCS-51*. Both support ships were trying to keep up but were falling behind. They were at their 15-knot maximum speed and would soon be out of gun range to help the *Laffey*.

The next attackers were two Judy dive bombers. The first was downed by the starboard 40s. Becton swung the ship sharply to take on the second plane as it came in low on the port side while strafing the ship. The forward guns knocked it down just as the pilot released his bomb. The 500-pound bomb was now a projectile skipping across the water until it exploded close aboard midship. Shrapnel sprayed a 20mm gun crew wounding 19 year-old Bob Robertson and critically wounding gun captain Fred Burgess. Robertson had been saved when quick thinking Burgess shoved him to the deck. Burgess lost a leg and later bled to death. The explosion also took out the surface radar antenna. Detecting Japanese ships was no longer a critical need; but a low flying plane was. *Laffey* had lost one of her defensive eyes.

Attackers number seven and eight came from a Val on the port side and a Judy off to starboard. The Judy was splashed. But the Val kept coming low at the stern. The kamikaze appeared to be aiming for the 53 mount (five-inch #3) which was now firing at it in a battle to survive. Inside the mount, 54 pound shells were desperately loaded and fired...until one barrel jammed. A misfire in a red-hot barrel loaded with powder can be deadly. Gun captain Larry Delewski had faced gun jams before. He'd always come up with his own way to fix them. He grabbed a rawhide maul and swung it hard at the breach. The gun fired. The blast at point blank range caused the Jap pilot to lose his aim. One wing dropped and the other grazed the mount and clipped the after-deck house before crashing into the sea. Delewski's cool won the gunfight. There were 12 other men in the mount who were shaking. Burning gasoline drenched the rear deck area but damage control teams quickly put out the fires.

Larry Delewski, GM2/c: I don't know what possessed me but I grabbed this leather maul and hit the breach.

The officer of the deck was maintaining the bridge log. He looked at his watch and recorded 0842, eight attackers and eight kills. Only 12 minutes had passed since the fight had begun. It felt like hours. The sky was still filled with planes. The screaming of another plane engine could be heard approaching from the port bow. It was a Val racing just above the waves and headed for the *Laffey*. The 20mm guns sent slugs and tracers into the wings and fuselage. Gasoline and pieces of wing spewed away. The plane pulled up slightly missing the port side gunners, dipped one wing, missed the forward stack and crashed into the 20mm guns on the starboard side. It killed three gunners and spread burning fuel everywhere. Several men jumped overboard to escape the fires. This ninth kamikaze knocked out two 20mm mounts and disabled two 40mm guns at mounts 43 and 44 with flaming gas. Racks filled with 40mm brass shells became hot and began to explode. These opened holes in the deck for gas and flames to go down into below deck spaces. Men frantically grabbed hot shells and tossed them overboard. Others fought fires with hand billies (extinguishers) and hoses.

Robert Kerr GM2/c: The fires set off the 40mm ammunition stored around Mount 44. The gun covers on Mount 43 were burning. It was time to get out of there. As I crawled on my stomach around the gun tub and toward Number 2 stack, exploding ammo kept whistling by. I headed down to the main deck and heard a voice say, "Please help me." There stood Fred Burgess with only one leg. I tied a tourniquet on his leg and carried him to the ward room.

Some of the communication lines had been cut. The engine rooms had no phones to the bridge. Engineering officer Lt. Al Hanke instructed his men to keep up steam and full power. They would steam to the sound of guns. Smoke and fumes were being sucked down ventilator shafts to the aft engine room. The smoke was so thick they couldn't see. They managed to get the ventilator shaft closed but then the temperature quickly soared to over 130 degrees. Machinist Mate John Michel knew his work station blindfolded. He found the exhaust fans, got them operational and soon cleared much of the smoke and heat.

E.A. "Al" Henke, Lt.: As another kamikaze approached, we would hear the bang, bang, bang of the 5-inch guns, then as it got closer, the pow, pow, pow of the 40mm guns, followed shortly by the rapid ta, ta, ta of the 20mms, ending with either all quiet or a sudden shudder of the ship as it took another hit.

Joseph Stuer, BTG2/c: My GQ station was midship repair. I was the oil king and my job was the fuel oil tanks. After each hit I'd check the tanks for leaks. I was about to go back and check on my service tanks. Lt. Sheets told me he was going aft, he'd check for me. That was the last time I saw him. When he got aft another plane hit and he was killed.

The Japs weren't done with *Laffey* yet. Another Val was attacking from the stern, so low to the water that the propeller of the plane was creating prop wash. The three 20mm guns in the fantail tub were tearing the Val apart but momentum kept it coming. It crashed through the 20s killing six of the gunners and slamming into Delewski's five-inch mount behind them. He had been hanging out a side hatch to direct his guns which were now on local firing control. The impact of the plane shot him out of the turret and into the depth charge thrower, 15 feet behind the gun. He ran back to his mount to find six of his men dead and all of the others badly wounded. Fires were raging and threatened to blow the ammunition magazine below the 53 mount. Valves were opened to flood the ammo rooms below.

At 0847 kamikaze plane number eleven crashed into starboard side of mount 53. Since nearly all of the guns were disabled on the rear of the ship, this was where they were targeting. Two minutes later, plane number 12 dropped his bomb on the torn up and fire ravaged fantail. He chose not to join his buddies in the afterlife and headed back to Japan. His 550-pound bomb hit just above the rudders and jammed one of them to port. The *Laffey* was now locked in at a 26 degree turn to port. She was steaming in circles, belching enough fire and smoke to attract every kamikaze north of Okinawa.

E.A. "Al" Henke, Lt.: *When we took the bomb that cut communications between the bridge and the engine room, we decided that when the guns were not firing we would slow down to permit fighting fires. As the five-inch units starting firing again, we would accelerate as rapidly as possible, knowing that with the sea calm and the rudder jammed at 26-degrees port, this would be the most appropriate action we could promote.*

James Spriggs, MM3/c: *After the rudder jammed hard left, the only way we could maneuver and get diving planes to miss was to change speeds or reverse direction to throw the pilot's aim off. We also tried to make smoke from the boilers so the ship could hide under it. I wasn't as concerned for my safety as I was for my shipmates up on deck.*

Fortunately, the *LCS-51* had managed to stay within sight of the *Laffey*. It had been able to provide support from its 40mm by shooting down several planes while trying to avoid being hit. One kamikaze crashed so close to *LCS-51,* its engine hit the ship, causing damage but no casualties. With the *Laffey* steaming in a continuous circle, it was no longer a problem for the "small boy" to keep up to a faster destroyer. The *LCS-116* had fallen far behind. She had her hands full fighting off kamikazes until a CAP squadron of Corsairs came on the scene. The Marine pilots shot down or drove off the kamikazes that had threatened *LCS-116*. Then they went searching for the stricken *Laffey*. The FIDO officer on the *Laffey* had been pleading with the naval task group for CAP support. Finally, four Wildcats from the *Shamrock Bay (CVE-84)* arrived on RP #1. They shot down a half dozen of the *Laffey's* tormentors before running out of ammunition. As their fuel also ran out the pilots returned to *Shamrock Bay,* totally convinced that the *Laffey* was going to sink.

> ***Glenn Radder, GM3/c:*** *It sure wasn't a pretty sight when I finally got a chance to look around. The amazing thing was that our whaleboat, which was right next to a 40mm mount that had exploding ammunition and fires, wasn't damaged at all. The Jap that crashed into our rear head, was sitting on his motor, fried to a crisp. It was a real gory sight.*

Two more Jap planes were heading for the ship's port quarter, one behind another. It was a straight-line formation. Becton ordered "Flank Speed" through the voice tube. This was the only maneuver left for a ship with a jammed rudder. Every gun that remained poured out lead. The 13th kamikaze covered his face with his hands as he plowed into the after-deck house. The 14th followed right behind and exploded in a ball of flames in the after berthing compartments. Damage control men inside were killed instantly. The berthing spaces became an inferno. Two men escaped to a small generator room at the back of the ship but they were trapped with no way out. The heat, smoke and lack of oxygen could soon kill them. They called for help on a communication phone. One shipmate chiseled a hole through a bulkhead for ventilation. Others took torches to the deck above and cut a two-foot hole to haul them out. For one short moment – standing amidst horrible death and destruction - there were smiles and laughter at their successful rescue. Elsewhere on the deck sailors were tossing bodies and body parts over the side. A couple of bodies were Jap pilots but a few others were shipmates that were mutilated beyond identification.

Steve Waite, MM1/c: I don't know how many of the crew were buried without ceremony, but some were.

The 15th attacker was an Oscar fighter/bomber with a Corsair on his tail. The Marines had arrived. The Jap was headed right for the pilot house. He came in a few feet too high and clipped the yardarm of the mast. The *Laffey's* flags went down and so did the wounded plane. The daredevil Marine had followed so closely he caught a wing on the search air radar - called the bed spring - sending it crashing to the deck. The pilot gained altitude and bailed out before his Corsair crashed.

The Corsairs were now hunting 30 or so enemy planes still in the area. The Jap pilots must have realized they needed to attack or get shot down. No time for pincer or straight line formation tactics. A Judy attacked from the port side with a Corsair on its tail. The 20s and 40s put it into the water about 50 yards from the ship. Its bomb exploded sending shrapnel through the door of the five-inch 52 mount located below and forward of the bridge. It took out electrical power to the mount and wounded several men. Mount 52 was without electrical control. They had wounded men and could only aim and fire with manual controls. Yet the 52-mount gun crew put on a gunnery show by taking out two more attackers with direct hits. It was an impressive display since their communication lines to the bridge had also been cut. Ordinary men were now making extraordinary decisions. Ensign Townsly hooked up a microphone to the ship's loudspeaker system and climbed on top of the pilot house. He directed the 20s towards the next attacker and they put another plane in the water.

It was then that an assistant communications officer came up to Commander Becton and said, "Captain, we are in pretty bad shape aft. Do you think we'll have to abandon ship?" Becton's reply would become famous. He turned to the young Lieutenant and calmly said, "Hell no, we still have guns that can shoot. I'll never abandon ship as long as a gun will fire!" Mount 51 on the bow underlined that thought by shooting down the 19th attacker at 500 yards. Number 20 came in directly over the stern where no guns were left. The dive bomber dropped his bomb dead center tearing an eight by ten-foot hole in the mangled deck. A Corsair made him pay the price of victory just 300 yards into his escape.

The 21st attacker came in strafing the *Laffey's* bridge. Everyone hit the deck as lead pierced the bulkhead and shattered everything inside. The 20mm gunners below the bridge stood their ground, shooting continuously as a bomb was released. It landed directly on the four-man gun crew. Two men were killed and everyone nearby was wounded. They had managed to hit the plane with their 20mm shells though. As the plane struggled for control a Corsair finished it off. Finally, a Judy began strafing the port side as he made his kamikaze run. Slugs ripped through a 40mm forward mount as the plane aimed directly for the pilot house. The gun crew and everyone on the bridge hit the deck. A Corsair dropped plane number 22 before it could do further strafing damage. But the plane dropped a bomb that went off when it hit the water. Crewmembers were peppered with another dose of shrapnel. One man caught 37 pieces and lost a front tooth, yet never felt a thing until his legs gave out and he hit the deck. He earned his Purple Heart. Gunner Francis Gebhart felt warm liquid dripping down his face. He felt no pain but was sure it was blood. His buddy smiled and said, "Gebby your blood is green." A shell had punctured the holding tank filled with antifreeze coolant for the gun mount. It had dripped on Gebhart's head. During a lull, Ari Phoutrides was checking on damage aft, and saw John Schneider. He asked, "What are you doing John?" The torpedoman gave a dazed reply, "Looking for a small piece of rust to crawl under." Gallows humor helped to keep men sane during the insanity of battle.

Up on the bridge somebody shouted, "Look at all those planes up there." Heads jerked skyward to see how much more terror was coming their way. Relief was felt when they saw two dozen Marine Corsairs and Navy Hellcats circling above. It was a good thing. The *Laffey* was down to four 20mm guns, some rifles and their sheath knives. The battle against kamikazes was over. The battle to save the *Laffey* from the sea and to save sailors from their wounds would continue through to the next morning. Luckily no one aboard the *Laffey* was aware of another threat to their existence. This time it came from one of the Thunder Gods. Several Corsair pilots spotted a Betty bomber with a Baka bomb under its belly. It was headed for RP#1. The Corsairs gave chase in hopes of preventing the launch of the rocket. Once launched, stopping the 550-mile per hour manned rocket was nearly impossible. Planes couldn't catch it and naval gunners would never be able to target it. As the Marine pilots closed in on the Betty the Baka dropped. They watched in horror waiting for the rockets to fire. But the Baka just continued to drop. Either the rockets failed or the bomber crew saw the Corsairs and dumped their load. Dropping 4700 pounds of dead weight would give them a chance of evading the feared "whistling death" dished out by Corsairs. But 20mm cannons were already ripping huge holes in the Betty. She plummeted to the ocean managing a relatively smooth water landing. Several crewmembers survived the crash. One was seen standing on a wing while shaking his fist at the Marines...as his plane sank beneath him.

The day had been a disaster all along the RP line. *LCS-116* came under attack again after CAP had driven off earlier attackers. A kamikaze drove his plane into their 40mm gun mount killing 12 men and wounding 12 others. As the *Bryant* rushed over from RP #2 to help the *Laffey*, it was attacked by six kamikazes. *Bryant* managed to shoot down several of them. But they took a hit at the base of their superstructure. That plane took out their CIC and all communications. Casualties were high with 34 killed and 33 wounded.

On RP#14 the minesweepers *Hobson* and *Harding* were both hit and had 44 casualties between them. Then *Pringle* (DD-477) with the FIDO team aboard was attacked by three low flying Vals. The first went down from shell wave splashes, the second veered off, but the third crashed into the base of the smokestack on the forward deck. A huge explosion rocked the ship and split the keel. The ship sank in five minutes taking 65 sailors down with it. There were 110 wounded among the survivors.

LCS-51 pulled alongside the crippled *Laffey* to help with fires and wounded. That's all she could provide. The *Laffey* really needed heavy pumps to stay afloat and a ship powerful enough to tow her in a straight course to the Destroyer Graveyard at Kerama Retto. They were losing the battle of pumping out the flooded aft compartments. Waves were lapping at the deck of the fantail. If any watertight doors on the flooded spaces were to give way, the ship would be in real peril of sinking. Also, there were wounded who needed fast transport to hospital ships.

At 1430 hours, the minesweeper *Macomb* was the first rescue ship to arrive. She supplied more help with damage control and took *Laffey* under tow. *Macomb* was built for speed not power. Progress was painfully slow. When two tugs arrived, they took over towing and helped raise the stern with their powerful pumps. This finally gave the *Laffey* crew the relief they needed. Badly wounded men were transferred to faster ships and sent ahead to Okinawa.

Lawrence "Larry" Delewski GM2/c: *I was advised in gunnery school to have a cook on your gun crew. That way if they got to serving coffee, soup or snacks you'll get fed first. I remember I was sitting* *on the portside rail during the tow when a cook brought me a cheese sandwich. I looked down to take a bite and there was a finger laying on the deck.*

Frank Manson, LTJG: *The kamikazes made it clear that they had the Laffey targeted for what Tokyo Rose called the "graveyard." Twenty-two kamikazes attacked. Eight were shot down. Seven missed the ship. Seven hit us killing 32 and wounding about 60 – nearly one third of our complement.*

Ari Phoutrides QM1/c: *There is nothing more terrifying than to see a kamikaze strike a ship. We had seen at least 100 individual attacks while in the Pacific. Most would invariably aim for the superstructure. This tactic saved a good portion of the U.S. Destroyer Fleet. Had they hit at the water line, I feel certain one plane could sink one destroyer. This is not the way you're supposed to fight a war.*

Over the next five days the *Laffey* received temporary patching. Her rudder was fixed, holes were sealed and communication lines were repaired. She was going home where major repairs could be performed. There were stops at Saipan and Pearl Harbor. Structural re-inforcement was added to the stern for the final leg to Seattle. The degree of damage sustained required a shipyard with major facilities. Also, the Navy war department had bigger plans for the *Laffey* and her crew. They were famous, coast to coast. Their story had appeared in all the newspapers. Now the Navy wanted to put the ship on display. With VE Day and the war nearing an end in the Pacific, shipyard production and War Bond sales had slacked off. Navy brass wanted to show the nation that the war was not over yet and their support was still needed. The twisted hulk that was once the proud *Laffey* was the perfect way to drive their message home. Thirty-nine days after its kamikaze ordeal the *Laffey* was berthed at Pier 48 in the Seattle ship-yards. Thousands of people toured the riddled decks of "The Ship

That Would Not Die," as she was aptly tagged by the media. They saw first-hand what sailors were up against at Okinawa.

The official Action Report would show that during the 80-minute engagement the *Laffey* shot down 9 planes, was hit by 7 kamikazes and 4 bombs, and suffered 32 killed and 71 wounded. The ship would receive the Presidential Unit Citation. The crew was awarded 18 Bronze Stars, 6 Silver Stars, 2 Navy Crosses and 1 Navy Commendation. The fighting war had ended for the men of the *Laffey*. For the men still patrolling on the Okinawa Radar Picket Line the worst fighting was yet to come.

USS Laffey (DD-724) lives on at Patriots Point Naval & Maritime Museum - Charleston Harbor, SC. The museum ship is the most decorated World War II era US Destroyer still afloat. DD-724 was named in honor of LAFFEY (DD-459), sunk during the Naval Battle for Guadalcanal. Both ships are named for Seaman Bartlett Laffey, a Civil War Medal of Honor recipient.

Chapter 8

Gators Join the Fray

O N December 7, 1941 there wasn't a single amphibious ship in the U.S. Navy. Thousands of these shallow draft ships had to be built during the next four years. Dozens of configurations were developed. The specialized needs for beach landings required very specific designs. Amphibious ships were designed to land men, equipment and supplies on a beach while under enemy fire. Although they were given armament for attacking the beach and defending against air attack; patrolling the open seas against kamikazes had never been a consideration. Now it was.

The big warships referred to amphibious ships as the "small boys." Compared to a 45,000-ton battleship or even a 2,200-ton destroyer, these ships were very small. The 158 foot LCS (Landing Craft Support) displaced just 250 tons. A 203 foot LSM (Landing Ship Medium) displaced 900 tons. The amphib sailors referred to themselves as "gators," for their ability to land right up on a beach. Destroyer sailors who patrolled the RP line with several amphibs in support, called them the "pall bearers." After a destroyer was pummeled by kamikazes, these support ships would pick up dead, wounded and surviving destroyermen.

Captain Moosbrugger commanded the ships assigned to the picket line. He decided the amphibs could perform on RP as gunships to help support the radar picket destroyers. A dozen LSMs had been converted to rocket launching ships. They could fire a barrage of aircraft rockets for short range beach bombardments. These new LSM(R)s carried more firepower per square foot than a battleship. That fact also made them more vulnerable. Their ammunition magazines were packed with rockets, powder cases for their five-inch guns plus 40mm and 20mm shells. A single hit near one of those magazines or a rack of armed rockets was a very hazardous event.

Life Magazine Photo Caption for a LSM(R), 16 April 1945: Each of these tiny ships has amazing firepower, greater at short range than the combined firepower of two mammoth Iowa class battleships.

The LSM(R)s had performed well during their first assignments. They provided pre-landing bombardment of the Kerama Retto Islands on 26 March 1945. These islands were located 15 miles southwest of Okinawa. They were needed by the Navy for supply and repair bases. This island chain encircles a huge deep water lagoon. The Japanese hoped these islands would be overlooked. They maintained only small garrisons, maybe to avoid notice. Within the backwaters and seaside caves the Japs had hidden hundreds of small wooden motorized boats. Each was designed to carry an explosive charge in the bow. These were suicide crash boats. They were sent out at night to crash into warships and transports of the U.S. fleet anchored at Okinawa. The Japs were totally surprised by the early morning barrage on 26 March.

The LSM(R)s could launch 480 five-inch rockets within 30 seconds. For a beach invasion this provided a devastating saturation bombardment. When the LSM(R)s unleashed their rockets on the Kerama Retto beaches, the surviving Japs headed for the hills. Some surrendered. Resistance was very light for the army landing force. The hidden crash boats were all left behind and soon found by U.S. troops. They were blown up and machine gunned into useless wood pulp.

Lt. Lyle Tennis, LSM(R)-190: The island of Kerama Retto is where we started with our rockets in full force. It became a training ground for all twelve LSM(R)s to see if the new rockets were functional. These were the first ships to have rockets on them of that size. Five inch – big rockets. We found they were pretty effective.

Twenty-four-year-old Machinist Mate John Stavola – an Italian New Yorker - was on the *LSM(R) 191* that morning. He was one of the experienced petty officers needed to man the new LSM(R) rocket ships. He'd been sent to Little Creek, Virginia to help get these ships ready for the Pacific invasions. Now all 12 rocket ships formed a line and headed for the Kerama Retto landing beach. They unleashed over 5,000 rockets, clearing the way for the troop landing crafts following closely behind.

John Stavola, Motor Mac 2/c, LSM(R)-191: So, all 12 ships are in line. In we go. We took them by surprise with our rockets. We just about made our turn when they began opening up on us. Naturally we were firing back with our 5-incher. Our XO ordered full speed to get the heck out of there. When they start opening up, you move. We passed the lead flag ship which was still going standard speed.

On 1 April, the LSM(R)s also led the charge onto the Okinawa beachhead. Each ship fired over 4,000 rockets during the first three days. They flattened an area six miles long and almost 5,000 yards inland for the Marines and Army. Next the LSM(R)s pulverized the Ie Shima beachhead for landings on this small island. It's located just north of Okinawa and had an airfield that needed to be secured. Now their primary mission was done.

John Stavola, LSM(R)-191: When we hit the beach at Okinawa there were no landing casualties. The Japanese had pulled back. I guess they feared our "baby battleships." Tokyo Rose talked about our ships on the radio. She said, "The U.S. Navy has a new weapon – baby battle-ships – she called them". That's a fact. She called us "baby battleships."

The LSM(R) rockets had no guidance system. They provided massive quantity but lacked precision targeting. A moving target was never part of their design. Yet, Moosbrugger was looking for solutions on the picket line. The kamikazes were attacking in waves of 30 to 40 planes. Maybe a wall of rockets would decimate or at lease disrupt a massive kamikaze attack. In late April 1945 Moosbrugger began assigning the 12 LSM(R)s to the RP line. The most active RP stations would now have one or two destroyers, an LSM(R), and several LCS gun boats. In addition, one LSM(R) would be stationed about 10 miles behind the RP. Its mission was to intercept planes that got past the RP and provide timely search and rescue if a picket ship was sunk.

As a landing support ship the LSM(R)s performed well. But they had a limited ability to defend themselves against air attacks. They had no air search radar. The five-inch main battery and 40mm guns had no fire director control. Their considerable size and a top speed of only 13.2 knots made them a large slow-moving target. The side placement of their conning tower and flat deck gave them the appearance of a small air craft carrier. This could fool an inexperienced Jap pilot into thinking it was an escort carrier. The LSM Flotilla Commander recommended that LSM(R)s not be used as picket ships.

Action Report - Dennis Francis, LSM Commander, Flotilla Nine:
LSM(R) ships are not particularly suited for picket duty. Since their primary function is to deliver rockets during invasion operation, it seems feasible that subjecting them to continual enemy air attack will allow this secondary duty to seriously affect their ability to perform their primary function due to damage.

These recommendations would become prophetic in the days ahead. During the last two weeks of April 1945 the picket ships caught somewhat of a break. Weather was lousy for flying. The Japanese Special Attack force was beaten up. Kikusui #4 was delayed until 28 April and only 115 kamikaze planes took part. Their primary targets were the U.S. carriers. The carrier *Intrepid* was the only one that took a hit, killing ten and wounding eighty-seven. There were seven picket ship destroyers damaged during this time period, but the only ship sunk was the *LCS(L) 15*. Some Navy commanders thought the worst was over. They were wrong. The Japanese had other plans.

On the night of 28 April 1945 one of the worst atrocities of the war occurred. The hospital ship, USS *Comfort,* was heading for Saipan with 700 wounded soldiers and sailors from Okinawa. Also on board were the Army doctors, nurses and crew of the *Comfort.* The ship was painted white with a broad green stripe around the hull. Huge red crosses were painted on the sides and superstructure decks. Lights were turned on at night to clearly identify the vessel as an unarmed hospital ship with wounded. By the rules of International Law outlined in the Geneva Convention, this ship was not to be attacked.

Seaman 1st Class Elmer Brandhorst was on the bridge of the *Comfort* that night. "I saw the plane when it made its first dive, but it was too dark to identify it as an enemy or ours." The kamikaze pilot had no trouble identifying the well illuminated ship. He circled around and came in dead ahead in a steep dive. The plane hit the ship's superstructure and exploded. The impact sent the plane's motor crashing through three decks and into the operating room below. Surgery room oxygen tanks exploded killing surgeons, nurses and the patients they were trying to save. Six doctors, six nurses, nine corpsmen and seven patients were among 28 killed in the attack. Another 48 crew and patients were wounded. The pilot carried documents confirming that this attack was intentional and other hospital ships were targets. Americans at Okinawa were infuriated.

One amphibious crew took matters into their own hands. Their badly damaged LST had been grounded on a reef for several weeks. They filled the hull with empty and sealed ammo cans, to give it extra buoyancy. It was towed and anchored at the location of the *Comfort* attack. They strung lights on their decoy hospital ship and hoped the kamikazes would return. Scuttlebutt indicates that it took five kamikazes to sink her. No other hospital ships were attacked after this unofficial incident.

Japan was resorting to desperate tactics. Their Navy had ceased to exist. Hundreds of suicide crash boats had been destroyed. They were running out of attack planes. They began transferring all types of aircraft from Korea, China and northern Japan to their southern airfields. Non-military and any relic aircraft that would fly were added to the special attack units. Kikusui #5 was scheduled to begin on 3 May and continue through 4 May 1945. This was to be an all-out assault to help support a counter ground offensive by General Ushijima's 32nd Army on Okinawa. His staff was tired of the defensive battle being waged. They wanted to strike a decisive blow against the invaders. Ushijima reluctantly agreed to the plan. It would include a massive artillery barrage; a frontal attack by three regiments supported by tanks; and two amphibious landings behind the U.S. front lines. This aggressive plan would be coordinated with massive kamikaze attacks on shipping. In addition, Japan's air force would bomb U.S. supply depots on Okinawa. The artillery barrage on the U.S. front lines began just after dusk on 3 May.

At 1830 hours the first wave of kamikazes approached RP stations #9 and #10 from the southwest. This was typically a quiet sector. These planes were likely coming from Formosa or mainland China. RP #10 was being patrolled by the destroyers *Aaron Ward* and *Little*. They had four support ships *LCS(L)s 14, 25, 83*, and *LSM(R)-195*. The *Aaron Ward* was first to come under attack by two Vals. Both were shot down but one crashed so close that the engine and wing catapulted onto *Ward's* deck. A third plane came in from the port side dropping a bomb and crashing into the ship. The engine spaces were flooding and power was lost. *Ward* was in trouble as more kamikazes kept up the attack. The *Little* and support ships sped to her aid.

The *LCS(L)-14* knocked down another attacker that was diving on *Ward* and began assisting with fires. The *Little's* approach was cut off by a new swarm of over 20 kamikazes. She took two hits on the port side, then a Zeke crashed her starboard side and another made a vertical dive into her deck. Fire, explosions and flooding took over the mortally wounded ship. She sank four minutes after the abandon ship order was given.

The *LSM(R)-195* was having engine trouble. This large slow target fell far behind the *LCS* ships headed for the *Ward*. Now she was a sitting duck for a new wave of attackers. A Nick twin engine fighter came from starboard while a Dinah recon plane dove from port. The five-inch gun and 40mm were busy downing the Nick, leaving only 20mm guns to defend against the Dinah. These guns weren't powerful enough to stop the twin engine reconnaissance plane. It crashed into the port side damaging two rocket magazines. When the rockets went off they sprayed shrapnel from one end of the ship to the other. This set off fires, more rockets and more explosions. The fire mains and auxiliary pumps went out. Flooding and fires couldn't be stopped. The ship was abandoned at 1920 and sank 15 minutes later.

W.E. Woodson, CO, LSM(R)-195: *The second plane started an attack run on our port side coming in at a very low altitude and maneuvering violently to confuse our two port 20mm gunners who had taken him under fire. This plane was strafing on its way in and hit the port side ripping the main deck all the way into midship. The rockets that were loaded in the launchers topside, began exploding in every direction. These rockets were propelled only short distances with numerous hits about the deck causing fires. The plane penetrated the forward rocket assembly room causing those rockets to be propelled throughout the ship and the areas surrounding it.*

The LCS crews watched in horror as the *195's* rockets lit up the sky. They were glad to be well out of range. These three amphibs now had their hands full. They crisscrossed through the carnage of the *Little, LSM(R)-195* and the smoldering *Ward,* picking up survivors while fighting off kamikazes. The *Little* suffered 30 men killed and 79 wounded. The damaged hulk of USS *Aaron Ward* was no longer recognizable as a *Sumner* Class Mine Layer. But she was still afloat and under tow by the USS *Shannon.* Her losses would be 45 dead and 49 wounded. Her story of survival would be told again and again. *LSM(R)-195* lost eight men killed and 16 wounded. The USS *Bache* came to her rescue.

> ***Action Report – USS Bache (DD-470):*** *3 May 1945. A large group of survivors was sighted by the flashlights they held and all were re-covered by our boats. All survivors picked up by this vessel had been attached to LSM(R)-195 and by 2145, five officers and 69 enlisted men and one dog were on board. Medical assistance was administered to the wounded.*

RP #10 was relieved by five fresh ships the next day. The destroyers *Cowell* and *Gwinn* scanned the sky with radar while *LSM(R)-192,* accompanied by three LCS(L)s, provided support. Bogeys started appearing on radar just after morning chow. CAP Corsairs were directed to intercept them. Throughout the day small raids threatened RP #10 and were taken under fire by CAP and picket ships. Planes went down and three ships took hits causing 21 casualties. The *LSM(R)-192* narrowly escaped disaster when an Oscar attacked from the bow and attempted to crash the aft rockets and five-incher. Gunners on the 40mm and 20s tore into the plane. His wing clipped the rocket launchers spinning the plane off course and into the sea. Only minor damage was received in an attack that could have launched a fireworks show that nobody wanted to see.

The picket ships on RP #12 weren't as lucky. At 0805 two Vals made a pincer attack on the destroyer *Luce*. One was downed close to starboard but the bomb holed the hull. The other crashed into the number 53 gun. Power was lost. Several more planes were seen diving at the port side of the *Luce*. Explosions and confusion made it impossible to know how many hit. The ship was listing from the hole in the starboard side and communications were knocked out. The abandon ship order was passed along by word of mouth. Many men below deck never got the order. The men who made it into the water were now covered in oil, dodging bullets from strafing planes and fighting off sharks. There had only been time to launch a few life rafts. Many men hung on to floating ammo cans and debris.

The *LSM(R)-190* had witnessed the sinking and was heading to the rescue of *Luce*. A Dinah flew over, dropped a bomb and missed. Then a Val made a run on the *190's* fantail with a Corsair on its tail. The kamikaze was set on fire by the Corsair. But it still crashed into the five-inch gun on the stern of the LSM(R). Communications officer Lyle Tennis from Racine, Wisconsin was in the radio room. He came out to help fight fires. Another explosion on deck sent shrapnel everywhere. Tennis was hit with fragments in his back and neck. His ship had been on RP duty for 30 days. Tennis and his crew had seen it all. Now they were also feeling the pain.

Lyle Tennis, Ensign, LSM(R)-190: That first kamikaze that hit us bounced on the deck and bounded up and hit the five-inch gun mount on the stern of the ship. That mount just spun around, there were nine people in the mount, and all nine of them were killed. Just a flash fire, and nine killed instantly. The next one hit just along the port side. It just grazed the side of the ship, so we got the fire hose out and tried to wash down the deck while it was on fire. No water pressure, so we were out of luck. Before we could recover from that, another one came in and this one hit us at the water line, in the engine room. The engineers said there is no way we can plug this hole.

When the first kamikaze hit the *190*, the gunnery officer and coxswain were killed. The skipper, Lt. Saunders, was knocked down and badly injured. No one was left in the conning tower. Next in command was the XO. But none of the crew liked him, including the skipper. Saunders sent word for Ensign Tennis to take command of the ship.

Lyle Tennis, Ensign, LSM(R)-190: When it came time for somebody to go up to the conn and take over the ship, the skipper could have called the XO, but he didn't. He called me. So I had to go up and take command of the ship. I put us on a zig zag course trying my darndest to get away from getting bombed or strafed, or anything else.

The engine room was flooding. The stern was sinking low in the water. Fires were burning uncontrollably which threatened the rockets and ammunition magazines. Tennis told the skipper they were going to have to abandon ship. "Oh no," moaned the skipper, "we can't do that." Tennis called down to the engineering department for an update on the situation. The engineering officer came running up to the conn-tower to make sure his message was understood. "Yes, we have to abandon ship. We have no hope. We are sinking by the stern now. We are going down and we better get people off if we are going to save anybody," said the engineer. Tennis gave the order to abandon ship. Life rafts went over the side. He helped carry the commanding officer down and got him over the side. They didn't know what to do with the Gunnery Officer. He was dead, laying up there in the conn. Tennis said, "Lets at least save his body. Make sure he gets a decent burial." They went back up, put a life preserver on him and lowered him into the water. Tennis told the radioman to call the beach and let them know there were survivors from the *Luce* and *LSM(R)-190* in the water.

Now only the radioman, a quartermaster, the engineering officer and Ensign Tennis were still on the ship. Water was lapping over the fantail. "Are we sure everybody is off that is alive," said Tennis. He decided they'd check the smoke-filled ship one last time looking for survivors. They ran through the passageways as the bow rose and stern dipped lower. Nobody responded, so the last four crewmembers abandoned ship. Tennis was last to go into the water. They swam to a life raft and paddled to get far enough away from the suction of their sinking ship. The *190* was going down bow up. Of the 50-man crew, 37 men were clinging to life rafts.

The badly wounded were placed inside the rafts. Two more men would die later. Sharks circled the men in the water. They took turns riding in the rafts while others hung on, kicked their legs and kept a look out for sharks. A rescue ship arrived an hour and half later and picked up survivors and the dead.

Tennis filed the Action Report. His crew was awarded four Silver Stars, four Bronze Stars, many Purple Hearts and he received the Navy's top honor...the Navy Cross.

Navy Cross – Awarded for actions during WWII: The President of the United States of America takes pleasure in presenting the Navy Cross to Ensign Lyle S. Tennis U.S. Naval Reserve, for extraordinary heroism and distinguished service in the line of his profession while serving as Communications Officer on board the USS LSM(R)-190, a close-in fire support ship, in action against the enemy on 4 May 1945 off Okinawa in the Ryukyu Islands.

Luce had lost 149 killed and 94 wounded...over 70% of the crew were casualties. But this deadly day was not over. The infamous RP #1 was being patrolled by two destroyers *Ingraham* and *Morrison* with four gators *LCS(L)s 21, 23, 31* and *LSM(R)-194*. Enemy activity over this sector had been continuous.

Morrison's radar began picking up large raids of approaching Japanese planes. They requested more CAP support and soon 48 Corsairs and Hellcats were flying overhead. This action would develop into one of biggest air/sea battles of the Okinawa campaign. The sky was filled with bursts of AA shells, flaming planes, zig zagging dogfights and geysers of water from bombs, planes and spent shells. Twenty-six Jap planes were shot down. The confusion above was so intense that the FIDO team on *Morrison* stopped trying to direct planes to enemy targets on the radar screen. The radio airwaves were completely jammed with pilot to pilot talk. A Val dive bomber made a dive at *Morrison* with four Corsairs tearing up its tail. The plane strafed and grazed the bridge as it crashed 25 yards off the starboard beam. The *Morrison* had been unable to take the Val under fire for fear of hitting the Corsairs. The *Morrison* was now the main target for more strafing. Then two Zekes winged over and came at the destroyer from out of the sun. Guns from the *Morrison* and CAP couldn't stop them. One hit at the base of the forward stack and the other hit the aft deck. One boiler exploded. The bridge was heavily damaged. All power went out forward of the stack and fire erupted everywhere. She was in serious trouble. The Japs were hungry for the kill. A half dozen twin float bi-planes made a run at the starboard side. Proximity shells being fired from *Morrison's* five-inch guns were useless. They would not burst because these planes were made from fabric and wood. The radar detonator in the shells only detect metal. Still several planes went down from 40mm and 20mm shells, but two crashed the *Morrison* with devastating effect. The first plane hit below the stacks and a second crashed into the aft ammo room for the 53 gun. This ignited the powder. The massive explosion opened the hull to the sea. The *Morrison* rolled over and sank with 152 men.

While Morrison was under attack the column of four support ships – three LCS(L)s and the *LSM(R)-194* closed in on the battle.

LCS(L)-21 came under attack from three Vals. Gator gunners downed all three but took several minor hits as plane wreckage grazed her deck and hull. Another Val was hit by gunners on *21* and *194*. The kamikaze burst into flames, dipped a wing and plunged down into the stern of the rocket ship. A bomb from the plane went off in the aft engine room, blowing up the boiler, rupturing sprinkler systems and flooding the rear compartments. *LSM(R)-194* began sinking, stern first, as sailors abandoned ship. *LCS(L)-21* splashed a Pete float plane and turned back to help survivors. Many men were still in the water when the *194* magazines blew up under water. The concussion damaged the steel hull of *LCS(L)-21*. It was also deadly to men in the water.

Once *Morrison* and *LSM(R)-194* were sunk, the remaining Jap planes turned their attention to *Ingraham*. Five planes attacked her, four were shot down, but the fifth hit at the portside waterline taking out the forward engineering spaces and half of the ships power. *LCS(L)-31* shot down two planes but their wings clipped the ship, causing some damage and casualties. A third plane came through a hail of shells and crashed into the main deck starting fires and silencing several of *31's* guns. Her other guns continued to fire and knocked down another plane headed for *Ingraham*. It was estimated that 40 to 50 planes had been shot down by CAP or picket ships during the RP #1 battle. *Ingraham* was towed to Kerama Retto. The losses this day on RP #1 totaled 197 dead 164 wounded and three more ships out of the war.

The surviving LCS ships were loaded down with wounded and survivors from all the sunken ships. Heavy black oil covered the water. Men were covered with it. They would wave their arms but none were crying out. They were too exhausted. Gators pulled men out of the sea who were cut up, bloody, and burned. Some were naked or their clothes hung in oily shreds. The LSMs hurried back to the hospital ships with men who were horribly burned, missing limbs and in shock.

Throughout the 3rd and 4th of May all ships on RP were listening to TBS (talk between ships) radio communications. What they heard was terrifying. Ships were requesting CAP support. They were directing pilots to intercept kamikazes and reporting disabled or sinking ships. The USS *Hadley* was patrolling an RP station for the first time. She was accompanied by the minelayer USS *Shea* (DM-34), three LCS(L)s and the *LSM(R)-189* on Radar Picket #14. They had intruders both days and shot down several planes but were not attacked in force. Signalman, Jack Garska, spent watches on the bridge of the *Hadley*. He heard much of the TBS chatter. It was nerve racking wondering when the attacks would reach RP #14.

> *Jack Garska's diary, SK3/c, USS Hadley:* We have just secured from GQ after spending a complete night at our battle stations. We were called to GQ just before sunset to repel an air attack. No planes came over us but 50 attacked the very next picket post. The Aaron Ward DM-34 took six suicide plane hits. One time we received word that they were abandoning ship but later found out that she was in tow by some other destroyer. We would have had no chance against such odds. How I'd like to lie down for few minutes. All that sinking, hits and action was just 30 miles away.

The *Shea* had the FIDO (fighter director team) aboard to direct CAP pilots throughout the day. Dozens of enemy planes were detected on *Shea's* radar. Marine Corsairs were sent to intercept them. The Marine pilots attacked a raid of Dinah recon planes that included a Dinah carrying an Ohka rocket. These smaller twin engine planes had been considered too light to carry the Ohka. This meant Betty bombers were becoming too scarce and an alternative mother plane was needed. The Marine pilots reported seeing the Baka bomb released. The Dinah was immediately shot down but all they could do was watch the Baka race toward *Shea*.

Donald Malcolm RT2/c, USS Hadley: I didn't get much sleep on picket duty. I was up about 48 hours and pretty tired. I was sitting on deck when we spotted what we thought was a Betty bomber way up in the sky – almost out of sight. It looked like the wing fell off. It was actually a Baka bomb dropping. There was a flash of light coming down at our picket ships. It went in between our two destroyers and hit the Shea.

Gunners on the *Shea* had just shot down a Dinah on the port side. The Baka was approaching her starboard coming in out of the sun. When the high-speed rocket plane was spotted by a lookout, only seconds remained for one 50 caliber machine gun, a 20mm and a 40mm to fire a few bursts. The rocket struck *Shea's* superstructure on the starboard side, penetrating the bridge without exploding. Its flimsy wood and fabric wings were sheared off. It emerged on the port side - exploding 15 feet away - on the water and perforating the ship's portside with shrapnel. The bomb's concussion blew a hole in the ship's hull at the waterline. This was one time when the thin skin of a destroyer was a good thing. The detonator on the nose of the rocket was designed to explode a few seconds after impact of a steel hulled battleship or carrier. This detonator didn't become armed until it felt impact from both sides of the tin can and then the ocean.

The Baka smashed through the sonar room, traversed the chart house, a passageway, and hatch before exploding in the water. Fire broke out in the mess hall, CIC, chart house, division commander's stateroom and several other compartments. Shrapnel, burns and shock killed 34 men. Eleven officers and eighty crewmembers were wounded. *Shea* had lost all communications, two of her five-inch gun mounts, and several 20mm guns were damaged. The impact jammed much of their equipment and fires threatened to blow magazines. Repair parties and survivors did a miraculous job of controlling fire, managing flooding and bringing power back up. The *Shea* retuned to Okinawa under her own power. *Shea* received the Navy Unit Commendation Ribbon for the gallant fight to survive on RP #14.

Jack Garska's diary, SK3/c, USS Hadley: The kamikazes are bothering us 24 hours a day now. There were 14 raids of aircraft trying to get in today. Our CAP fighters shot down 60 planes during those raids. But one plane got through and suicided into our sister ship (the Shea) just a few hundred yards off our port beam. Tonight, we moved in closer to Okinawa. How I dread sunset. That is the time all the "cans" have been sunk until the Shea was hit this morning. If we get by sunset there's a long period til dawn that the moon is out. A three-quarter moon, clear sky, easy to see us and our wake. Yes, I'm really one worried guy. Everyone is though for that matter.

Kikusui #5 was finally over. The damage was awful. This was the worst two days for the radar picket ships. Fifteen picket ships had been hit. Six were sunk. Three destroyers and three LSM(R) rocket ships had gone to the bottom with many crewmembers. There were 475 men killed and 484 wounded while defending the picket line on 3 and 4 May. The picket ships and CAP pilots had done their job though. None of the capital ships – battlewagons or carriers – had been hit. Japanese sorties were estimated at 350. There were 249 Japanese planes confirmed as destroyed.

The Japanese ground offensive that was to be supported by kamikazes was a dismal failure. The Jap amphibious troops attempting to flank U.S. lines, were discovered and wiped out before their landings. Most of the tanks and artillery participating in the offensive were destroyed. Five thousand troops were lost. The fate of Ushijima's 32nd Army was now accepted by his staff. The battle for Okinawa would be lost. But the beaten Japanese would prolong the inevitable by defending to the death.

To the destroyermen and gator sailors patrolling the radar picket line…the end couldn't come soon enough. For destroyers damaged as severely as the *Aaron Ward*, their ability to fight was over but their terror continued at Kerama Retto.

The rocket ship LSM(R)-190 fires a salvo of five-inch Fin-stabilized Aircraft Rockets. When fully loaded, 480 rockets could be fired up to 4,000 yards with devastating effect on a target.

Chapter 9

Admiration for Aaron Ward

A signal light flashed in the night on 4 May. The *Aaron Ward* (DM-34) was being towed past Okinawa by the destroyer USS *Shannon*. A Morse code message of dots and dashes was decoded by the *Ward's* signalman.

> **USS McKinnley, signal light message 4 May 1945:** *We all admire a ship that can't be licked. CincPac Advance HQ shouts action to Aaron Ward. Congratulations on your magnificent performance.*

The message was from Fleet Admiral Nimitz. He was head honcho of the Pacific Fleet. Messages of *Aaron Ward's* heroic fight had already flashed back to Okinawa and the Kerama Retto anchorages. The men on board *Aaron Ward* paid little heed to the congratulatory messages on this night. They were dazed, dirty, tired and hungry. Crates of oranges were brought up from below. The ice cream machine was raided. Men sat on oil soaked, bloody wreckage peeling their oranges with shaking hands. Soupy ice cream was devoured.

The *Aaron Ward* limped along at the end of a towline toward the destroyer graveyard at Kerama Retto. She was without engine power. Her radar was out. Her main deck was perilously low to the water.

The smell of battle and death hung in the air. Gunners manned the few remaining 20mm guns that were operational. *Ward* was mostly defenseless should another kamikaze plane attack. Those who were able continued to help keep the ship afloat and care for the wounded. Officers began the task of remembering details of the battle. Action Reports would need to be prepared the next day.

About eight hours earlier, during *Ward's* "second dog watch" 25 bogies were reported. They were bearing 090 degrees, 27 miles away and closing. The first enemy plane was spotted low on the water at 1830 hours. Guns opened up and the battle raged continuously for the next 51 minutes.

The *Ward* was a destroyer minelayer. She had been built as a *Sumner* class destroyer (DD-773) and converted to a minelayer as part of the planning for the invasion of Japan. She was laid down at San Pedro, California alongside sister ship USS *Hugh W. Hadley* (DD-774). *Ward* was commissioned 29 October 1944 just one month before the *Hadley*. *Ward* was the third ship to be named after Rear Admiral Aaron Ward. The first was a four stacker commissioned in 1919 and sold to Britain at the start of WWII. The second (DD-483) - was sunk at Guadalcanal. Commander Bill Sanders knew the legacy of his ship's name. He instilled a fighting spirit in his crew that had already been tested at Okinawa. During one quiet stretch on picket duty, Sanders sent a message to the Force Commander, Admiral Halsey. "Request Permission to go to Guam and engage in AA practice." Halsey came back with a terse message. "Permission denied; plenty of live targets on picket station for you to shoot at." He was right. The spirit and will to fight on was about to be thoroughly tested on Picket Station #10.

On the afternoon of 3 May, the weather cleared for the first time in several days. Commander Sanders expected to start picking up bogeys on radar. At 1822 it started. Enemy planes were approaching from the west. General Quarters was sounded and word was passed throughout the ship. Down in the after engine room Pete Peterson passed along the news that about 25 enemy planes were headed their way. He told his men to light all fires. The *Ward* would need full power and speed. Then Peterson made a fresh pot of strong coffee. Up on deck the gunnery department was ready too. Lt. Lefteris "Lefty" Lavrakas was at his station in the gun director behind gunnery officer Lt. Rubel.

Lefty Lavrakas, LTJG: On the Aaron Ward, I was positioned behind the gunnery officer who controlled the five-inch guns and directed communications with CIC. I controlled the 20mm's and the 40mm's. We had two quad 40mm's port side aft and on the starboard side, so that was eight guns. The 20's were single barreled and we had four of those. The range for my guns was 3,000 and 4,000 yards. The five-inchers could reach out 12,000 yards.

Ward's CIC officer directed CAP to intercept the approaching planes. Four Hellcats caught up to the Jap planes just as they came within range of *Ward's* five-inch guns. The navy pilots were warned to turn away so the ships guns could open up. By this time two Vals were 4,000 yards away. Lt. Lavrakas directed his 40mm's and then 20mm's to begin firing. Pete Peterson could hear the 40mm's WHOOMP and the 20mm's RAT-A-TAT way up above the engine room. The planes were close. More speed. More coffee.

The first plane was torn up by 40mm shells and a direct hit by the aft five-incher. His suicide dive came up 100 yards short. But the impact on the water hurtled the plane's engine and propeller onto the deck of the *Ward.* The mangled pilot – strapped into an unopened parachute - continued his crash landing over the ship's deck and into the water on the other side. The plane's engine became wedged under the turret of the stern five-inch mount. The mount crew had to pull the hot, smoking mass of metal free before the gun mount could turn. Their power was damaged forcing them to switch over to manual.

The second plane was destroyed at 1200 yards. All guns went silent as CEASE FIRE orders were given. A sigh of relief was almost audible throughout the ship, but there was no time for cheering. Green dots were streaking all across the radar screen in CIC. Lookouts scanned the sky with binoculars. Spent shell casings were cleared from the deck. More ammunition was passed up from the magazines below. Peterson took a quick gulp of navy coffee.

At 1831 the number two 40mm (42 mount) began blasting rapidly off the port side. The shocked crew sucked in another collective breath. There had been no order to fire. This third plane had slipped in under radar. The 42 gun mount captain had spotted the plane and opened up. It was a Zeke with a big bomb mounted underneath. The kamikaze pilot was now making his run on the stern from port side. Every gun that could aim on target swung out and followed 40mm tracers with their own barrage. The five-inch number three gun on the fantail fired repeatedly with barrels aimed low. Only a direct hit was going to stop the Zeke now. But maybe a shell splash would alter the pilots aim. Despite repeated hits from 40s and 20s the plane came on, released a bomb, and crashed into the superstructure. The bomb hit the hull below mount 44 and exploded in the after-engine room.

Lefty Lavrakas in the gun director tub felt the ship shudder and saw flames envelop the superstructure. Two men were blown clear of the 44 mount. The rest were killed. Gunners manning four portside 20mms took the plane's impact head on and were blown to bits.

The bomb ripped a 50-foot hole in the hull of the after-engine room. Engineering spaces flooded, fuel tanks ruptured and the rudder jammed. The ship slowed to 15 knots and turned in a tight circle to port. Peterson and his surviving crew went up the escape ladder in the dark. Their clothes and skin were in shreds: ears were ringing from the blast, but they made it out before the compartment was completely flooded.

The plane's crash caused fires, explosions and many casualties around the afterdeck house. *Ward* was in serious trouble. The danger to nearby USS *Little* was even greater. Through the smoke, fire and explosions on *Ward's* deck, men could see one plane after another crashing into *Little*. Dave Ruble ordered ALL GUNS, AIR ACTION PORT. Another plane was lining up to crash into *Little*.

Lefty Lavrakas, LTJG: *I recall looking over at the Little. The Little was a brand new, beautiful 2100 ton destroyer. Her number was 803. I saw three kamikazes go in. The third one evidently hit her amidships and there was a tremendous explosion. The Little broke in two and she sank. It was amazing that she only lost about 40 to 50 people. I thought everybody had gone down with her.*

Ward's damage control teams rigged hoses, fought fires, strung emergency phones and tended to their wounded. With most communication lines down, instructions were passed to gun crews with whistles and hand signals. The bomb that wrecked the engine room also knocked out the gas ejection system for the five-inch mounts. Each time the breech blocks flew open, hot, unburned gases filled the mounts. Men retched, choked and passed out. If any powder spilled from a charge during loading, a flashback could turn the mount into an inferno. Gunners kept loading and firing and managed to keep the vultures at bay for another 20 minutes. By 1855 the sun was going down. In CIC they could see bogeys circling on their radar screens… just out of gun range. They seemed to be waiting for the CAP pilots to run low on fuel and head for home.

When the amphibs came to the rescue of the *Little*, they were also attacked. The *LSM(R)- 195* was next to get hit. Her boat load of rockets lit up the early night sky. *Ward's* sailors watched as the *195* joined the *Little* at the bottom and then continued their own efforts to survive. With the *Little* and *195* now gone the kamikazes turned their attention back to the circling and smoking *Ward*. A Val attacked from 8,000 yards out and flew into a wall of defiance from the *Ward's* gunners. It crashed with 2,000 yards to go. Next came a twin engine Betty. The five-inchers began pounding away when the plane closed at 10,000 yards. Staying on target was difficult with the ship making constant left turns. A fiery explosion was seen at 5,000 yards. It was a thing of beauty.

Only 38 minutes had passed since the first shots were fired. It seemed like an eternity for men fighting to stay alive. At 1908 two Vals tangled with a pair of Marine fighter planes. One Val was shot down. The other escaped the "whistling death" of a Corsair and chose to die for the emperor. The kamikaze went into a screaming, deep dive toward the *Ward's* bridge. Every gun barrel rose up and banged with a furious barrage. Shells burst and tracers ripped into the fuselage but the plane kept coming. Every man on the bridge and deck was thinking the same thing. "He's coming right at me." Somebody yelled, "Hit the deck." People on deck dove under anything they could find. When the plane was just 300 feet above the men on the bridge, they said their prayers. All of them knew their time had come. One man grabbed a piece of metal debris and threw it at the pilot. Others tightened up and waited for the crash. Some just closed their eyes. Men inside the windowless CIC couldn't see the plane but the scream of the engine drowned out the roar of the guns – they knew what was next.

But then, a sailor's prayer was answered. The right wing dipped. The plane banked over the bridge with the left wing clipping halyards, antennas, and the forward smokestack. It careened over the starboard side and hit the water like a skipping stone. Nobody moved. Nobody spoke. They stared at one another. The guns had gone silent. As the shock of what they had just experienced began to wear off, a shrill, ear splitting noise could be heard. It was the sound of the ship's whistle and siren. The impact of the plane had opened a steam line that was connected to both.

There was no time for conversation. And nobody could be heard over the wail of the siren. Another Val dive bomber was streaking in, aimed right at the bridge. The aft five-incher took him under fire. At 2,000 yards, and 75 feet above the water, the Jap pilot began strafing with his 7.7mm forward gun. Whacks and pings tore into the ship and anyone in the way. The pilot pulled up a little and aimed at the upper portion of the bridge and gun director tub. Rubel and Lavrakas could see the pilot's goggled head. Lefty heard Rubel shout, "This is it boy!"

The 40mm 42 mount was just below their position. With a steady flow of shells flowing from his gun, Larson calmly rose the barrel up and then down in an attempt to cut the plane in two. He almost did. One wing was sliced off, the plane dipped, swerved and crashed into the portside deck below the bridge sending flames high into the air. Seconds before impact the pilot released his bomb. It blew a hole in the portside hull, spraying the decks with shrapnel and flooding the forward engine room. The boiler drowned out, the engine stopped and the *Aaron Ward* was without any power.

Seconds later, as men gathered their wits and checked to see if they were still alive, another plane came out of the smoke and haze. It crashed on the main deck. Nobody saw it. No guns were fired. The people under this plane never knew what hit them. The destruction and chaos topside had reached unimaginable levels. Those below deck wondered how anyone up top could still be alive. Many expected they'd be trapped when the ship sank. With damage this severe, hatches can become jammed, passageways could flood, and fire might block escape routes.

In the wardroom, Doc Kennedy was trying to save the lives of mutilated men. His only light was provided by portable battle lanterns. Blood, guts and gore filled the room to overflowing. Walking wounded were sent to the mess hall for treatment. Stabilized patients were moved to officers' quarters...to make room for more wounded. When the wardroom began filling with smoke they radioed the bridge to see if they were going to abandon ship. The Captain's response was, "Hell no!" But some men had already gone over the side. Life rafts were launched. They filled the rafts with wounded to give these men a chance if the ship went down.

It was now 1916 and the decks were in total darkness except where lit by fire. A Zeke was coming in low from the stern. Too low for the five-inchers. The 40mm guns on mount 42 and 43 opened up but to no avail. The plane crashed near mount 43 and incinerated the gun crew with burning fuel. The inferno and exploding ammunition made survival on deck near impossible. Many more men went over the side. They were the lucky ones. Another plane was spotted at 1921. Gunners on the few remaining mounts couldn't see it until it was too close to stop. Tracers tore at the kamikaze until it crashed into the base of the after stack. Now men were going over the side with their clothes on fire. The decks were so littered with bodies and debris it was difficult to move from one end of the ship to the other. Fire hoses became useless and bucket brigades took over. The main deck was only inches above the water. Ammunition and twisted metal was tossed overboard. Depth charges were defused and jettisoned. The Captain needed to know if the ship could still be saved. He sent Lt. Lavrakas back aft to give him a damage report.

Lefty Lavrakas, LTJG.: The most important decision a captain must make in war time is whether to abandon ship or not. He decided not to abandon ship. He has to know enough about the ship and her condition. He sent me back aft. I checked the after part of the ship. I went below and I could report to him that everything from the bulkhead in the after engine room was tight. The after section had not been damaged in any way and water had not leaked in and it was all dry. He had spaces up forward that were dry so there was enough stability and buoyancy in the ship for him to decide not to abandon ship. When you abandon ship, you could lose more men that way.

The battle was over. The "pall bearers" approached *Ward* gingerly. *LCS-83* and *LCS(L)-14* pulled men from the water, provided fire hoses, pumps and medical aid. Word was passed that the lucky USS *Shannon* (DM-25) was on the way. *Ward* could have used some of her Irish luck earlier. She had withstood a carefully coordinated attack that killed 45 and wounded 49 of her crew. Her decks were totally devastated. Tow lines were attached to *Ward's* bow. A long, slow trip to the destroyer graveyard went on through the night.

Shannon and *Ward* entered the Kerama Retto harbor early the next morning. They passed anchored ships at funeral procession speed. Sailors who were watching her being towed, doubted there could be many survivors on the battered *Ward*. No sooner had they begun feeling a degree of safety in the anchorage than GQ was sounded from every ship in sight. *Shannon* dropped her tow line and sped off. A tug came alongside to take up the tow. They delivered hot coffee and chow. *Ward's* men could only hope that their charred and twisted hulk would look too pitiful to the kamikazes to sink. They ate, drank and let other ships battle the attacking planes. Their ability to fight back was too limited to be of much help.

The next day *Ward* was tied alongside the repair ship *Zaniah*. It was decided that *Ward* was beyond repairs that could be made at Okinawa. She would need to go home to be refitted with guns and superstructure. With this morale boost the *Aaron Ward's* crew worked to get their ship sea worthy enough to make the trip home. It would take six terror filled weeks. Every night the kamikazes and bombers would attack the 60 plus ships anchored in the harbor. Suicide swimmers would sneak under an empty food crate to attach bombs to ship's hulls. Suicide crash boats would make torpedo runs at a ship under the cover of darkness. Jap snipers on unsecured islands were taking pot shots at anything that moved on deck. The *Ward* crew who had faced fifty minutes of pure terror, now faced it 24 hours a day. Their only respite was in the form of another injured destroyer.

Eight days later another *Sumner* Class destroyer was towed into Kerama Retto and tied alongside the *Ward*. It was the USS *Hugh W. Hadley* – her sister ship. They had been built side by side in San Francisco. Now they were tied side by side to be repaired. The *Ward* became famous for surviving more hits than was thought possible for a destroyer. The *Hadley* would be famous for shooting down an all-time record number of 23 planes in a single engagement. The *Hadley* crew thought they had taken a beating on 11 May. After seeing the *Ward*, they felt real admiration for their counterpart. The *Ward* sailors felt a bit of relief. They were now sandwiched in between the *Zaniah* and the *Hadley*. They were a little safer from suicide boats, swimmers and snipers.

SHIP AARON WARD (DM34)

2200 Tons Standard

Damaged in Action off Okinawa 3 May 1945

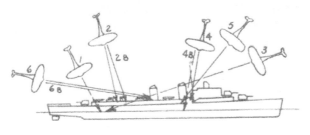

Line drawing of ship showing areas of damage.

The Aaron Ward survived hits from six kamikazes and three bombs. Her decks were devastated and damage below deck knocked out all power. She was towed to Kerama Retto for temporary repairs and then sent back to the states. Aaron Ward was still being repaired in New York Harbor when the war ended.

Photo # NH 62571 USS Aaron Ward after she had been damaged by suicide planes, May 1945

The Aaron Ward's twisted decks sit barely above water in Kerama Retto Harbor on 5 May 1945. The twin five-inch gun mount is the only identifiable structure on the aft-half of the ship.

Chapter 10

Aircraft Carrier Found

TED Davis looked out over the vast East China Sea from the signal bridge of the USS *Hadley* (DD-774). This was his watch station. The morning sun reflected off the water. It was 11 May 1945...the 41st day of the invasion of Okinawa. The crew had secured from morning General Quarters. All ships in war zones would go to GQ 15 minutes before sunrise and 15 minutes before sunset. Those were prime times for kamikaze attacks. Planes were harder to see at dusk, but ships were still easily spotted from above.

While some men not on watch headed for their bunks, others lined up for breakfast. *Hadley* was patrolling Radar Picket (RP) Station #15 northwest of Okinawa. This was one of the most dangerous RPs. It was on a direct route between Japan's southern airfields and Okinawa's landing beaches. *Hadley* had been assigned an expert Fire Director (FIDO) team to help man the Combat Information Center (CIC). The FIDO Team had brought along their own sophisticated radar equipment. This enabled the FIDO officer to give the fleet a 15-minute early warning of approaching aircraft. Then he'd send combat air patrol (CAP) to intercept the enemy planes. Twelve Marine Corsairs were circling above RP#15 to provide additional support.

Up on the signal bridge, Davis was alone with his thoughts. It was a peaceful morning. The sea was calm. A few clouds were scattered overhead. There was mist to the north that could hide an approaching plane. Davis was a signalman. He used semaphore flags to send ship-to-ship messages in daylight. He could send 20 words a minute by waving his flags. Shipmates called him the "skivvy waver". At night, a Nano Light was used with Morse Code. This enabled ships within sight of each other to communicate and maintain radio silence. There were five other ships patrolling RP#15 with the *Hadley*. Destroyer USS *Evans* (DD-552) followed in *Hadley's* wake. Both destroyers circled a formation of smaller amphibious gun boats *LCS-82, 83, 84* and *LSM(R)-193*. Every half hour the ships would do an about face and return to their starting point. Davis would signal the change of direction, which maintained radio silence and kept their position hidden from anyone who might be listening in.

Davis grew up in Sugartown, Pennsylvania on a 155-acre farm. His family milked 28 cows and raised corn, wheat and potatoes. He had five sisters and no brothers. Ted learned a strong work ethic early. At age 11 he went to work for a neighbor, milking cows for 10 cents a day.

Ted Davis – USS Hadley: *When war broke out I was a senior in high school. I came home from school one day and heard about Pearl Harbor on the radio. I asked my parents if I could enlist. Mom said no, finish school. Dad said, "You've been on your own since age 11 – you can make your own decision." I had enough credits to graduate, so I joined the navy.*

Gong, gong, gong interrupted thoughts of home, family and whatever for Davis and the entire crew. "General Quarters, General Quarters" came over the loud speaker. And then, "Commence Firing." All three double-barrel five-inch guns opened up with a womp, womp, womp, then the 40s and 20s joined in which meant a plane was very close.

Everyone topside scanned the sky for the intruder wondering how the plane had slipped in under their radar.

Davis could hear orders from the bridge to "Light all four." The Captain wanted steam from all four boilers and engines at full speed. An officer yelled to Davis, "Go down below the 40mm and help carry clips up to the 44-mount." There was no need for a signalman now. The Japs already knew *Hadley's* location. Plus, each of the other ships would be maneuvering for their own best defense. When Davis reached the main deck he looked up and saw a float plane heading straight for the bridge.

Ted Davis: Holy smoke I thought, a Jap plane. My brain said run, but my feet said whoa! I didn't know which way to go and my legs wouldn't move. I could see a big bomb, five-inch shell puffs, and 40mm tracers. Pings were hitting around me from strafing. Pieces of plane and the pontoons fell off. The plane kept coming. I stared into the pilot's goggled eyeballs. That plane was aiming right for the bridge. I was right below the bridge – the plane got bigger and then a direct hit blew the plane up into a huge fireball.

The pontoons separated from the float plane. They hit the water about 300 yards off the *Hadley's* starboard bow. They were filled with flammable explosives. The explosions sent shrapnel and debris so high that it was still raining down when the USS *Evans* passed through the crash site. A float plane is constructed with light weight material to increase buoyancy. Fabric and wood can't be detected by radar. The low hanging mist and wave top approach of the plane had made it difficult for lookouts to spot. The crew - relieved of their fear - gave loud cheers. Only then did Ted's legs stopped shaking. He went into a passageway that led below. He passed a man who had been shot. Strafing bullets had gone through the thin bulkhead and hit him in the chest. *Hadley* had her first casualty.

In CIC the relief was short lived. The radar screen had not detected the low flying float plane, but now it was filled with little green dots. Radarmen plotted dozens of bogeys heading straight for the *Hadley* on RP#15. The CIC officer radioed the information to Captain Mullaney on the bridge. Then he contacted fleet commanders at Okinawa and all available CAP planes. He estimated 156 planes were heading their way. It was unlikely two destroyers, four amphibs and the dozen Corsairs flying overhead were going to stop them all. The fleet – especially aircraft carriers – needed to be ready for this attack.

Doug Aitken, CIC Officer, USS Hadley: *Navy intelligence knew large kamikaze raids were due to strike the invasion forces. Radar picket stations operated by destroyers were the first line of defense. We required very specialized air controllers to direct CAPs (combat air patrol) of both Marine and Navy pilots. Lt. John Stevenson and Lt. Fred Hattman, and their assistants had reported aboard the Hadley on 8 May. We recognized them as experts and let them take charge.*

Despite the early warning and air cover from 12 Marine fighter planes, the crews of *Hadley* and *Evans* were in for the fight of their lives. For 95-minutes they battled wave after wave of kamikazes. Both ships were hit by kamikazes, strafing and bombs. Fires and flooding threatened to sink both ships. They fought until there were no more kamikazes to shoot at. Then they fought to save their ships and wounded shipmates. The powerless hulks remained afloat and were towed into the destroyer graveyard at Kerama Retto for repairs. Neither ship would fight again.

It was estimated that CAP pilots had shot down nearly 80 planes. *Evans* was credited with downing 19 planes. And *Hadley* made history. The USS *Hugh W. Hadley* (DD-774) holds the Navy's all-time gunnery record for having shot down 23 planes in a single engagement. Gunnery Officer Lt. Patrick McGann was awarded the Navy Cross for skillfully directing his men and maintaining effective gunfire against overwhelming odds.

There were many unsung heroes on the *Hadley* gun crews. One of them was Third Class Gunner's Mate A.W. Hodde Jr. He had been a 40mm gun instructor at the naval gun range in La Jolla, California. Hodde knew more about the 40mm guns than anyone on the *Hadley*. The other 40mm crews would come to Hodde for technical advice. His gunnery tips gave them the edge they needed. Captain Mullaney credited the four 40mm mounts as the most effective guns during the *Hadley's* 95-minute battle. Only a few Japanese pilots got through the first line of defense at RP#15 that day.

To turn the tide of their battle at Okinawa, Kikusui #6 called for massive kamikaze attacks. Japan committed every available aircraft. Knocking out the radar picket stations was the first phase of their plan. This would allow many more of their kamikaze pilots – all of which were inexperienced - to reach the fleet undetected. Mass attacks on aircraft carriers was phase two. Without air support the entire fleet and ground troops would be more vulnerable.

Navy intelligence knew the attack was imminent. U.S. bombers had attacked Japan's airfields on 10 May and destroyed many planes on the ground. These planes were being readied for Kikusui 6. Marine Corsairs and navy picket ships splashed more than a hundred airborne attackers the morning of 11 May. Most were stopped while still 50 miles from Okinawa. Mass kamikaze attacks on the carriers was no longer possible. Only a few of the attacking planes had penetrated picket line defenses. Then one group of surviving kamikazes spotted U.S. planes returning from a mission. They slipped in behind the planes. This would camouflage them on radar and maybe lead them to a carrier.

The USS *Bunker Hill* (CV-17) was one of 40 aircraft carriers supporting the invasion of Okinawa. This was the flagship of Vice Admiral Marc A. Mitscher's Task Force 58. On the morning of 11 May she was positioned 76 miles to the east of Okinawa. The sea was calm and the misty sky had partial cloud cover. Flying weather was good. In support of the ground troops there were 25 of her planes flying sorties over Okinawa. Thirty more planes stood ready on the flight deck fully fueled and loaded with bombs and munitions. Another 48 planes were being fueled and armed on the hanger deck below.

For several weeks, the operations on the *Bunker Hill* had settled into a routine. The ship would launch air strikes on Okinawa and surrounding islands over four consecutive days. On day five they would refuel, rearm and prepare for four more days of action. She had been resupplied at sea on 10 May. Her tanks were filled with aviation fuel and 1.8 million gallons of fuel oil.

On the morning of 11 May the business of running the ship went on as usual. Morning GQ had been held followed by launching a dawn strike on Okinawa. At breakfast the crew enjoyed the first fresh fruit they had seen in four weeks. Sailors got mail, wrote letters, and maybe visited the ship's store for candy bars or magazines. Thirty fighter pilots sat in a briefing room getting instructions on their morning mission. The ship's crew was getting on with the day to day routine of the war. They were at 1 Easy GQ – the lowest level.

Phillip Wilmot was a young Marine Corsair pilot assigned to the *Bunker Hill*. He was from California and had completed his civilian pilot's license before joining the Navy. They sent him to naval cadet school. When he graduated a couple of Marines came to speak to his class. They convinced him to transfer to the Marine Corps. Wilmot didn't want to land on aircraft carriers so he made the switch. But the larger *Essex* class carriers could launch and recover Corsairs. Wilmot had to learn to fly and land with the Navy anyway.

Phillip "Pots" Wilmot, 1Lt., USS Bunker Hill: Landing on a carrier was terrifying at first. It took a month or so. After a while we were as good as the navy guys. On 11 May we were doing a Tiger Cat, which is orbiting destroyers over the picket stations. They had launched us just before daybreak. Our first in command was Archie Donohue – he had 14 victories – we landed about 0900. We were all tired and gathered for debriefing. Archie was a sweet guy. He said: I think we oughta all go down to our bunks.

The *Bunker Hill* was one of 24 *Essex*-class aircraft carriers built during the war. At 27 tons, a length of 870 feet and top speed of 33 knots, these were the biggest and fastest carriers in the U.S. fleet. They had a formidable armament that included a dozen five-inch guns, eight quad 40mm mounts and 46 single 20s. They had a wartime crew of 3,000 and could carry up to 100 planes. *Bunker Hill* had seen extensive action during the past two years of war. Marine and navy gunners had successfully defended the ship from all attackers.

Dick Lillie was hanging out near a 40mm gun located aft of the #3 hanger deck on the starboard side. When he joined the Navy in 1942, the 17-year-old enlistee asked for Gunners Mate School. Lillie was told he'd be a torpedoman (TM). Torpedoes on an aircraft carrier were only used for the torpedo planes. So, during General Quarters his station was an ammo loader on a quad 40mm gun mount. Lillie was proud of his specialized TM "right arm" rating. He wore his stripes with pride on the right sleeve. This signified an older Navy rating versus the new Navy Air ratings for carriers. He also liked being part of a 40mm gun crew.

> **Dick Lillie TM/2, USS Bunker Hill:** *The 40 was a wonderful gun. It had a 4,000-yard range, fired 150 rounds per barrel and 600 rounds for mounts with quad. Bunker Hill gunners were very good. We only had one plane get near us at the "turkey shoot." A bomb landed nearby, exploded in the water and wounded 70. No other planes ever got close.*

The great "Marianas Turkey Shoot" took place in June of 1944. A Japanese fleet of nine carriers attacked Admiral Marc Mitscher's Task Force 58 that was supporting the Saipan invasion. At this point in the war, Japanese Zero pilots were greatly outclassed by navy Hellcats. Out of 471 planes launched against the U.S fleet, 426 were shot down. Only 29 U.S. planes were lost. Returning American pilots called the action a "turkey shoot." At Okinawa the following year, inexperienced Japanese pilots did not attempt to dogfight the well-trained Americans. The mission of a kamikaze pilot was to evade detection until they spotted a ship. On this morning, several kamikaze pilots would accomplish the hide-and-seek tactic.

> *Phillip Wilmot, 1Lt.: Somebody told us the Japs got smart and would tag us while returning to our carriers. We weren't smart enough at the time to leave a plane back from our division to cover our rear. We didn't figure this out until near the end of the war.*

At 1005 hours, a Jap Zeke fighter plane came out of the thin cloud cover above *Bunker Hill.* The Jap pilot sent a Morse Code message to his base, "Aircraft carrier found." The pilot attacked low on the starboard beam and crashed among the parked planes on the aft flight deck. The 30 planes, parked side by side, wing tips still folded up, began igniting like a string of firecrackers. The Zeke's bomb went through the side of the ship and exploded out of the port quarter.

> *Phillip Wilmot, 1Lt.: Just as I was getting ready to get into my bunk, I heard the 20mm guns. When the 20mm guns start, you know the enemy is very close. Right after that the ship shook and we got hit by the first plane. He went into a whole bunch of navy guys getting ready to launch. Right after that the second one hit at the base of the island and the bomb came off and went through the flight deck. It exploded down in the navy ready room, about 50 feet from where we had been for debriefing.*

Before the shock of what had just happened or the general alarm could be sounded, a second Jap "Judy" came streaking in at a vertical dive. A 500 pound bomb went through the flight deck and exploded below on the hanger deck. The kamikaze crashed into the base of the ship's island structure. The hanger deck and gallery deck below it became infernos from exploding planes and burning fuel. Oxygen was being sucked out of passageways and rooms on these levels. Blinding and choking smoke trapped sailors and pilots. The thirty pilots that had been in the briefing room made it into a passageway. But smoke, heat and lack of oxygen left them piled up against the bulkheads in an agonizing death.

> *Dick Lillie* – *A guy named Swen who was a Medal of Honor winner at Guadalcanal, was in a Bunker Hill fighter squadron airborne over us. We had 24 planes positioned 5-5-5, layered every 5,000 feet. Swen was in the lower group and saw the plane dive. He hollered on his radio, "Plane diving on Bunker Hill." We weren't in GQ. We were all hanging around the gun. Nobody fired at it. I think maybe one 20 did. There was a battery of 20s over my head. Out of 10 guns nearby only one was elevated like somebody fired it. The others were still locked down. So, he got a free ride. The second plane didn't get a free ride. He came in 30 seconds later. Our 20s were manned by a Marine battery. They were real pros on the 20s. They got on the second one but he still came through.*

The first plane flew right over Lillie's gun mount and crashed onto the flight deck above. When he saw it coming he ran up, cocked the gun, put it in fire mode…but there was nobody else at the gun. The rest of gun crew was hanging around the hanger deck. Only two more guys ever made it to the gun and all three of them ended up in the water when the gun caught fire.

> *Dick Lillie:* *The old man had us at 1 Easy GQ. This was the lowest level, so hatches were open. There was no watertight integrity. I was first loader on the 40mm #2 barrel. I put the shells in the clip. We had*

been under attack 63 times and never been hit. We would never have been hit if we had been at general quarters. We were too good.

Three of *Bunker Hill's* upper decks were now consumed in raging fire from amidships to the fantail. The 500-pound bomb had blown a 40-foot hole in the flight deck and peeled back one and a half inch of its armor plating. The aft plane elevator was warped by the heat into the shape of a peaked roof. Within three minutes, damage-control teams had broken out hoses and begun fighting the fires. The entire 3,000-man crew had trained for shipboard disasters, but nothing like this could ever have been envisioned. Even with this extreme disaster there was no confusion. All hands who were able joined the frantic struggle to save the ship, their shipmates and themselves. Burning planes were pushed over the side. Ammunition and bombs were jettisoned. Rafts were tossed over to those who had been blown overboard or forced to jump. Sprinklers were turned on to keep fires from spreading. Hatches and vents were closed to reduce drafts.

Phillip Wilmot, 1Lt.: A bunk mate and I went out on the flight deck and everything was on fire. I tripped and looked down. It was a cooked sailor. There were sailors all over the deck and they smelled like they'd been cooked. I was shocked; there was fire everywhere. We looked over the side and there was a kid hanging on from a knotted rope. He looked up at us and his eyes were as big as silver dollars. So, we pulled him up.

A squadron of 16 Corsairs code named Viceroy 11-1 was returning to *Bunker Hill.* They had completed their ground support mission over Okinawa. The squadron leader radioed *Bunker Hill,* and asked "Viceroy Base what time pancake." This was all code to get a time they were cleared to land. Marine fighter pilot Wesley Todd looked over at his wingman when they didn't get an answer.

Wesley Todd, Lt., Bunker Hill: On the way home to our base Bunker Hill, code name Viceroy Base, we radioed for a time to land. They would come back and tell you in code what time you're gonna land, because they don't want the Japs to know when we're taking on planes... that's a good time to attack. Well we didn't get any answer. We're all looking back and forth and wondering – and then we saw the stream of smoke. We figured it was Bunker Hill. When we reached the ship we could see guys going overboard. Destroyers were following the carrier.

The ship's engineering spaces had not been damaged. But the "snipes" who were keeping the engines manned and running were battling smoke and heat. Ventilation ducts had to be closed to keep more smoke out. Without fresh circulating air the heat in the engine and boiler rooms went up to 130 degrees. These men were all trained to find their way around these spaces blindfolded. One sailor groped his way through the smoke until he found and distributed an armload of breathing masks. Full power was maintained which was necessary for keeping fire hoses, guns and engines operational.

Captain George A. Seitz made full use of power with two critical maneuvers. First, he swung the ship broadside to the wind. This kept smoke and flames from running the length of the ship. When water and fuel flooded the hanger deck, Captain Seitz ordered a sharp 70 degree turn. This lowered one side of the ship and allowed tons of fuel and water to slosh over the deck's siding. At 1025 a third kamikaze made a low attack at the smoke engulfed ship. The black plumes could be seen for miles and may have guided the Jap plane to the stricken ship. A starboard 40mm battery shot the attacker down while still a half mile away. These would be the last shots ever fired from *Bunker Hill*.

On the hanger deck, molten metal dripped from above, caused by the intense heat. Firefighting crews battled to extinguish burning planes and keep ammunition from exploding. Below the hanger deck there were dozens of electrical fires. Burning fuel dripped down into passageways and smoke filled these enclosed spaces. Over 100 men died of smoke inhalation on the gallery deck.

Phillip Wilmot, 1Lt.: Our XO was Commander "Beno" Dyson. We called him Beno because every morning he would come on the horn and announce, "There will BE NO this or BE NO that on this ship... so we called him "Beno." He saw us and told us to grab a hose. We grabbed a hose and he grabbed a hose and he said to follow him. He went right into that damn fire. We followed until the heat got unbearable, then we turned back and got out of there. Commander Dyson was in there fighting the fire, I thought, my God that guy is fearless. He survived too.

The USS *Wilkes-Barre* (CL-103) pulled alongside to provide help fighting the flight deck fires. The parked planes on the aft deck were all filled with aviation fuel. As each plane exploded the burning fuel spread. The fire and heat was so intense that damage control teams couldn't reach all the planes with water. Also, there were men on the fantail who were trapped.

At 1115 Captain Porter nosed the bow of his light cruiser *Wilkes-Barre* against the starboard quarter of *Bunker Hill*. Forty men who had been trapped on the stern of the carrier were able to escape onto the forward deck of the cruiser. Ten more fire hoses from the cruiser helped douse fires on the carrier's flight deck. Additional firefighting equipment was transferred over to *Bunker Hill*. The destroyers *Stembel*, *Charles S. Sperry*, and *English* joined the fight with more fire hoses.

Captain George M. Seitz, Bunker Hill: "The Wilkes-Barre, the Sperry, Stembel and English did a magnificent job. They came alongside not knowing whether we were likely to have explosions aboard. The Wilkes-Barre evacuated our seriously wounded, and with their able assistance, we got through."

The ship began listing 11 degrees from the weight of water and burning fuel. Rumors spread that the ship was sinking. The Chief Engineer, Joseph Carmichael, calmed the crew's fears. He made an announcement over the loud speaker that the boilers and engines were secure and operating. He didn't tell them that the men in all four engineering spaces were dying of asphyxiation. Smoke was sucking down the ventilation system and turning the sealed off engineering spaces into a black hole. They couldn't see. They couldn't breathe. Breathing masks could only filter smoke for an hour. Ninety-nine men died at their station.

The Sullivans (DD-537) was one of the ships that came to the rescue of *Bunker Hill*. She was responsible for saving 166 men who had been forced over the side by fires. Dick Lillie was one of those survivors.

Dick Lillie: *The hanger deck behind me was on fire. It melted and drooped down 40 to 50 degrees, just like butter. The hanger deck was red hot. I retreated aft by swinging out over the water and hanging on to the girders that held up the flight deck. I'm 6 foot 2 and I have long arms and legs. I couldn't get into the hanger deck. I'd have been burned to death. The cruiser Wilkes-Barre was coming along side when I went into the water. She hit my gun mount and really butchered it.*

There was no time for proper abandon ship protocol. Men went over the side to survive. Some were on fire. Most were forced overboard by intense heat and smoke. They had to jump from 50 feet down into the sea. Sailors are taught to cross their ankles to protect their crotch, cross their arms to protect their face and step off so they drop straight down feet first. Hitting the water sideways could break a man's arms, legs or ribs. Hitting all the debris coming down from the flight deck might kill you. One sailor was seen jumping from his lookout station on the ships highest mast - the Vista – it was 137 feet above the water. Dick Lillie put on a life jacket, swung out and dropped into the water.

Dick Lillie: I had a kapok life jacket I got out of a whale boat. I went into the water and saw lots of people. There were four near me and none of them had life jackets. I took my kapok off and we held on to it. We were in the water 3-4 hours. The kapok got waterlogged. We never would have made it through the night. The tragedy was that if we had an abandon ship order, we would have had rafts and everything, but there was no time for that. It all happened so quick, 300 guys were spread out over 30 miles of ocean. Radio silence was in effect, so none of the destroyers knew where anyone was. The ship changed course eight times so guys were spread out over eight separate courses. Finding people was a real problem. And most were without life jackets.

Wesley Todd, Bunker Hill pilot: When we saw somebody in the water we would zoom over them so the destroyers would see where to go pick them up. When we finally started to get low on fuel the Enterprise called and said we could come aboard. We landed there. Later that day Admiral Marc Mitscher was transferred to Enterprise. They brought him over on a boatswain's chair – you know that chair that goes over water – ship to ship - on a couple of wires.

Many carrier pilots joined in the rescue efforts. They dropped marker dye, life vests and rafts to men in the water. A pilot's life vest is attached to his parachute. They would cut their own survival vest away from the parachute and drop it to men treading water. This left the pilot in danger if he had to ditch.

Dick Lillie: I saw one plane three hours later and he came over us low. He had his canopy open and tossed his Mae West out. It drifted off a couple hundred yards, then he made another pass and popped something behind us. We thought it was a life raft. Another guy and I agreed to swim for it. The weather was good. It was fairly calm and there was a cloud we could see. We used it as a bearing. It was 200 yards away. I was a good swimmer. We'd get separated and we'd hold up a hand every once in while so we could tell where each other was. We found a blue and yellow marker blanket. But it was down five or 6 feet. We were bushed. Diving for it was out. We could have bundled air in it so we should have got it. Had we needed to spend the night we never would have made it without some sort of buoyancy. Then we swam back.

The same pilot had stayed in sight. He saw what happened. He zoomed right over the men's heads and then pulled straight up. There was a destroyer on the horizon. It was *The Sullivans* (DD-537). The pilot did this twice to give the *"Sully"* a bearing to follow. This was the ship named after the five Sullivan brothers who were all killed on the cruiser *Juneau* which was sunk at Guadalcanal. Over 650 sailors went down with the *Juneau*. A 4-leaf clover was painted on *The Sullivans* bridge. Her captain was on a mission to save as many of the *Bunker Hill* sailors as possible. Dick Lillie was in luck. *The Lucky Sully* was headed for his group.

Dick Lillie: *The skipper of the Sully knew what he was doing. When he came to us, he didn't stop, he fired at us with line throw guns – 12 gauge shotguns shooting a self-line out the barrel. Then we pulled a heavier rope with belts on it out to us. Somebody on the bridge had a bullhorn and he is hollering at us, telling us what to do. We grabbed the belts, they slowed so there wasn't a jerk, pulled us until we were in the wake and hauled us in to the bumper guards on the stern of the ship. Two guys just reached down and grabbed us.*

The crew of the *The Sullivans*, grabbed 166 sailors out of the water that day. The first thing Dick Lillie did when he came aboard the *"Sully"* was ask for directions to the torpedo shop. He was a Torpedoman. Torpedoes were propelled on alcohol. He knew he'd find a supply of torpedo juice and a sailor who'd share his concoction. Torpedomen were skilled at filtering the alcohol and mixing it with pineapple juice to create a rather potent cocktail. Lillie needed a drink.

Dick Lillie: I have no idea the names of those four guys I was with. One died aboard the Sully. He was badly burned. He had no nose. His head was all swollen and hair was all burned off. He was a beautiful swimmer. He stayed 8-10 yards from us and wouldn't get closer. If we swam away he followed. If we swam to him he swam away...a beautiful swimmer. We never talked. We were living for preparation to die. There was no conversation other than for morale purposes. I don't know the names of any of them.

George Mendonsa QM2/c was the helmsman on the bridge of *The Sullivans* when *Bunker Hill* got hit. He could see the plumes of smoke even after the carrier zig zagged out of sight. The crew of the *Sully* was experienced at search and rescue for stricken sailors. Normally the search was for a ship that had sunk with sailors grouped in an area. The *Bunker Hill* search was unique. This ship still had power. It continued to steam on evasive courses that put it further away from enemy airfields. When men were forced to abandon ship, they became spread out and left far behind the *Bunker Hill*.

George Mendonsa QM2/c, USS The Sullivans: I could hear all the communications coming in from pilots who were locating men in the water. My battle station was on the bridge. I was the helmsman. The Bunker Hill was all in flames. We picked up a couple hundred men that day. Later we met with the hospital ship Solace and we put the wounded men on the hospital ship. A lot of them guys were in tough shape. Dick Lillie was one of them. I met him the first time on The Sullivans. We've gotten together several times over the years. He's been to my house.

Everything from the ship's island to the fantail had been engulfed in fire. It took over six hours to bring most fires under control on the *Bunker Hill*. Even then small burns continued through the night.

Wilmot and others who had been up since before dawn tried to get some sleep. All night there were announcements directing damage control teams to fire locations. Then began the grisly task of finding, identifying, and burying all the dead at sea. There were 396 crewmen dead or missing. Another 264 were injured. Many suffered horrible burns. *Bunker Hill* had lost nearly a quarter of its crew. Her war was over. The casualties of the *Bunker Hill* were the single worst loss of any kamikaze attack at Okinawa.

> ***Phillip Wilmot 1Lt.:*** *When I got out on deck the next morning I saw all these white blankets, nearly 400 blankets and under each blanket was a dead sailor with a 5-inch shell wrapped inside. They had a board on the edge of the flight deck with a couple of Marine guards with rifles. They'd put a body on the board, the Marine guards would present arms, they'd tip the plank and the sailor would slide off. They did this all day...about 400 times.*

Alfred Perdeck survived the fire and smoke on the *Bunker Hill*. The memories of dead sailors still haunt him. He kept a charred piece of wood from the flight deck. It's a grim reminder of all the men who died that day.

> ***Alfred Perdeck:*** *I was scared to death. I thought I was going to die. When I finally made my way up the ladder toward the fantail, I stepped on someone. I said, "What the hell are you doing? Get up!" I couldn't think that he was dead. This is a memory that is still in my head.*

Two days later the USS *Enterprise* got hit by a kamikaze. Vice Admiral Marc Mitscher had to transfer his flag staff again. This time they went to the USS *Randolph*. Mitscher was bad luck. If the *Randolph* were to get hit, crews in Task Force 58 joked about not allowing Admiral Mitscher on their ship.

USS The Sullivans (DD-537) came to the aide of the burning USS Bunker Hill after she was hit by two kamikazes. The "Sully" crew plucked 166 Bunker Hill sailors out of the sea after they were forced to abandon ship.

The hospital ship USS Bountiful is flanked by Bunker Hill on the portside and The Sullivans on her starboard side. On 12 May, both ships transferred burned and injured Bunker Hill crewmembers to waiting nurses and doctors on Bountiful.

An F4U Corsair fires rockets at enemy ground defenses on Okinawa. Once the powerful Corsair was adapted for carrier take off and landings, it became the most versatile attack plane in the fleet. It's speed, firepower and maneuverability gave it the highest dogfight kill ratio (11 to 1) of any aircraft in the Pacific.

Chapter 11

Elephant Burial Ground

WHEN the USS *Laffey* first entered the massive lagoon of Kerama Retto the crew was taken aback by what they saw. The anchorage was littered with charred and twisted hulks of ships. There were destroyers, transports, mine layers, gun boats, landing craft, support ships and vessels that could no longer be identified. The scene reminded one officer of the fictional elephant burial grounds he'd read about in books. The *Laffey* was lucky. They were only there for resupply on 12 April 1945. *Laffey's* orders were for radar picket duty the next day. The crew was worried. They feared their ship would soon be back as part of the carnage.

> *"The attraction of the elephant graveyard is manifold. Greedy hunters and marketers dream of the piles of ivory that must lie amongst the huge skeletons in this graveyard. They fantasize about the size of the tusks of thousands and thousands of majestic beasts who have found their final resting place in these mythical grounds."* Elepahntsforever. co.za

To the surviving sailors entering Kerama Retto aboard mangled ships – this was a haven from picket duty. They had survived and thought their terror was over. To the greedy kamikaze pilots Kerama Retto was a dream target. They would turn the anchorage into a huge ship graveyard.

Ward McDonald, Chief Signalman, USS Goodhue (APA-107): *When we came into Kerama Retto we began 82 days of consecutive kamikaze raids. They'd attack supply ships and warships and anything. Because I don't believe they had enough fuel to get the plane back home; they had to hit something.*

The USS *Goodhue* was an Attack Transport ship. Once its primary mission of delivering troops and supplies to Okinawa was done it was sent to Kerama Retto. Ward McDonald was from Seattle. He enlisted at age 18 in 1944. He volunteered for submarine duty but they trained him as a signalman instead. The *Goodhue* was designed to transport up to 500 troops and their supplies. When not needed for landings, she became a support gun boat.

Ward McDonald, USS Goodhue: *Kerama Retto is a group of islands south and west of Okinawa itself. And Kerama Retto is where we got our first real taste of the enemy. Because we were no more than 450 miles from Japan they could throw a lot of planes at us. We ran into a broad screen of kamikazes. They came every day. Just continuous day and night. You didn't get much sleep.*

The Kerama Retto island group is located only 15 miles from Okinawa. The circle of 22 small islands forms a huge protected lagoon. Strategic thinking identified this as an ideal anchorage for a forward resupply depot of the U.S. invasion fleet. The ability to replenish ships with fuel and ammunition so close to their objective was the primary goal of capturing the site. Maintaining a ship repair facility was of secondary consideration. The emphasis at Kerama Retto soon shifted to salvage and repair. "At one time, I counted 65 damaged man-of-wars in Kerama Retto, mostly destroyers," reported Nate Cook on the USS *Newcomb*.

The small Japanese garrison defending Kerama Retto was completely surprised by the American attacking force on 27 March 1945. A massive rocket barrage from the LSM(R)s was followed by landings from the Army's 77th infantry division. Most of the overwhelmed defenders fled into the rugged hills. The strategic importance of the island chain became greater when hundreds of suicide torpedo boats were found hidden in caves. These small kamikaze boats would have been used to attack ships at night. Radar was not able to detect these small wooden boats. Seeing them in the dark would have been difficult. Fortunately, most were captured and sunk by ground troops.

Harvey Fehling, USS Van Valkenburgh DD-656: They had these small wooden suicide boats with a bomb mounted on the front. They would use them like a torpedo boat and drive them into the side of a ship. We had rifles hanging all over the ship and we had orders, whenever we see something in the water to shoot at it.

Gunner's Mate, USS YMS-331: I was aboard Minesweeper YMS-331 and thwarted a suicide boat attack at about midnight on April 15th in the Kerama Retto anchorage. I saw a shadow and expended a round from the 3-inch deck gun into the suicide boat. There was a large explosion and some damage to one of our tillers.

The *Hadley* and *Evans* were towed into Kerama Retto on 14 May. Both ships had taken multiple hits from kamikazes and bombs during their 95 minute battle on RP #15. The painful experience showed on the crew's faces. Part of their battle story was evident by seeing the damage to their ships. The rest of the story had preceded them throughout the fleet. Many ships came to their aid and witnessed the horrible results of their battle.

Ray Bofardi's diary, USS Barber DE-161: I saw a Jap plane this morning. This one wasn't flying. It was lying on the stern of one of our destroyers. The Hadley was another victim of the kamikaze (the Divine Wind). We took off the casualties. It was a pitiful sight. Young boys, 17 and 18 years of age, with their faces and bodies burnt black. There were others with their arms and legs shot up, plus others whose bodies were distorted beyond recognition. My only wish is that some of the people back home were here to witness this horrible sight, then maybe they would realize that we are at war. We carried the casualties to the hospital ship USS Hope. Addenda: This was one of two destroyers (USS Hadley & USS Evans). In this engagement, together they knocked down 42 suicide planes in an hour and one half battle. This bag was the largest ever reported during a single engagement.

Waymond Dean from Granite, Oklahoma was a gun captain on *Hadley's* portside 20mm gun during the battle. His crew spotted the attacking planes first and immediately shot down two. They were so focused on the battle they lost track of how many they saw smoking or being splashed.

Waymond Dean, GM3/c, USS Hadley: I was on the number-one gun position, a twin 20mm forward of the bridge. After we shot down two planes all the other guns began firing. Although the official score was 23, we probably shot down at least 30 planes.

The *Evans* was moored in a nest of damaged destroyers alongside a repair ship, the tender USS *Vestal*. Some of these ships looked unsalvageable. At least *Evans* would be patched, pumped and towed to the states. There were dead crewmembers still trapped in the flooded spaces below. Pumping was the top priority. Those bodies needed to be recovered to help the crew recover from the loss of shipmates.

The *Hadley* was anchored alongside sister ship, USS *Aaron Ward*. The top side damage of *Aaron Ward* left her unrecognizable as a twin sister to the *Hadley*. But the damage to *Hadley's* hull and engineering spaces was a greater threat to survival. She had a stow-away kamikaze plane lodged in her engine room. A hole at the waterline was big enough for a bus to drive through. The five men who died in the flooded engine room were still down there. It would be 14 days before the huge hole could be sealed and the compartment pumped out enough to recover their bodies.

The crew of the *Hadley* felt an initial sense of relief to be at anchor. Work parties came aboard to help with cleanup and to take over with major repairs. Some crewmembers no longer had a job. Torpedoes and depth charges were of little use on a destroyer with no engines. Many compartments and work stations were too damaged to be useful. Undamaged guns, radar and sonar equipment were being stripped off to be used on ships that could be quickly repaired. Those ships and crews were being sent right back into the battle line. Some men on the *Hadley* were trained for jobs that were no longer needed. These sailors were experiencing a relaxed shipboard life. During the day, they watched the constant repair activity. At night, they'd find a poker game below deck to pass the hours. One hundred *Hadley* crewmembers would soon be shipped back to the states to be reassigned.

> ***Jack Garska's diary, USS Hadley:*** *Life on the Hadley has been rather like a vacation since we came to Kerama Retto. We've been eating like kings, plenty of rest, and not too much work to do. No watches, with the exception of one every 5th day. Movies are twice a day in the mess hall and usually different pictures. One is in the afternoon and one at night.*

Defenseless destroyers were tied up alongside repair ships in this floating graveyard. They relied on defense from shore batteries, gun boats and war ships positioned throughout the anchorage. Daylight kamikaze attacks were rare due to the massive anti-aircraft barrage that would go up. Nights, however, were very scary. The entire anchorage would be covered by a protective cloud that was spread by smoke boats. Attacks came nightly from individual kamikaze planes, suicide swimmers, suicide boats and snipers. All night, every night, there was a constant rat-tat-tat from machine guns and rifles.

Massive kamikaze raids were always aimed at Okinawa where the carriers, battleships and large transports were huddled. The nightly raids on Kerama Retto were more for harassment. Anchored ships provided known locations that were easy to find and attack at night. The Japanese troops hiding out on surrounding islands created a new kind of terror for sailors. Jap swimmers would come out from the islands at night. They'd be discovered sneaking up under orange crates or concealed in brush. There were several reports of Japs climbing up an anchor chain to slit the throat of a sailor on deck-watch. This kept most crew members off the decks at night unless they were on watch…and well-armed. Sailors on deck-watch shot at everything and anything in the water. Nothing was accomplished militarily by Jap swimmers and kamikaze attackers. But they certainly created fear and sleep deprivation.

Nate Cook, USS Newcomb (DD-586): I can't say that the ten weeks in Kerama Retto were pleasant. There were 75 of us – all volunteers – who stayed with the ship until substantial hull repairs were made so we could be towed home. Every night, ships were being hit by kamikazes. During the day it was fairly quiet, but at night it was different. The Navy used smoke making machines to create cover for defenseless ships. It was eerie; we could hear the planes but not see them. We were all in a state of shock and fear.

Ward McDonald, USS Goodhue: A Jap would come down from the hillside and get an orange crate or something to put over his head. He'd swim out and throw a hand grenade on deck. I stood a lot of night watches with a Thompson machine gun. I'd shoot anything in the water. I don't care if it was a grapefruit.

Allen Haas, Signalman, LSM-500: We were in Kerama Retto Harbor. There were a lot of suicide swimmers around. They would take a float-ing mine, and push it into the side of a ship. We'd take our boat and run it around the anchored ships with our smokers and completely smoke the ship. That would take care of the kamikaze coming in. But we still had to account for the guys who were suicide swimmers. So we'd circle the ship all night with a couple of guys on the fantail with Thompson sub-machine guns. They'd play shotgun and shoot at any-thing in the water. They'd do that all night long. Just sit there and rattle off blasts of machine gun fire.

The crew of the *Goodhue* got welcome news early in April. They'd be leaving Kerama Retto Harbor. No more snipers, swimmers and kami-kazes to deal with every night. *Goodhue* was needed to deliver equip-ment and supplies to the ground troops on Okinawa. They loaded up and pulled out of Kerama Retto on the evening of 2 April. But their convoy of transports and escort ships came under heavy attack before they escaped to open sea. Ward McDonald grabbed his helmet and went topside when GQ sounded. He came out of the number two hatch and heard a horrible noise.

Ward McDonald, USS Goodhue: I turned around and saw a Jap kamikaze. I could see his eyes. And he looked right at me. I figured my number is up. He wasn't shooting, but there was a Navy Hellcat behind him that was trying to shoot him down. Chunks of his plane are falling off. I turned to fall to the deck...and a roar went over the top and they missed us. It went over the top rigging. I don't know how he missed us. The Hellcat pulled away and the kamikaze plowed into the Henrico, another AP that was just ahead of us. It blew a hole right into her. Took out the bridge killing all in command. I'll never forget the expression on the pilot's face and my feeling of... this is what they call gettin' your numbers called.

McDonald, got up on trembling legs and continued aft to his GQ station on the fantail. There were 20mms, two 40mm AA guns and a 5-inch mount protecting the rear of the ship. The five-man crew of the five-incher had just fired at another plane 800 yards away. One shot and they all threw up their arms and cheered as the plane exploded.

Ward McDonald, USS Goodhue: The five-inch gun went "bam" and they all yelled, "We got a Jap. We hit a bogey coming in on our ships." God, we all cheered and it was a wonderful example of beautiful marksmanship. I was standing there watching them and cheering with them when their gun swung around as far forward as it could off the forward bow. It won't go all the way back so you don't shoot your own ship. I looked at the gunner and his eyes – just horror filled his face, absolute horror. And then there was one hell of an explosion. A Betty had come in over our bow. It hit our rigging. The plane along with two bombs came down on the after deck. I remember seeing a huge ball of flame and a plane engine coming at me.

The impact of the explosion blew McDonald inside a passageway. The plane's engines, bombs and burning fuel continued aft into the gun tubs on the fantail. McDonald was knocked out. When he woke up he was afraid to move. He knew it was going to hurt. Then he realized he was on fire and had to get out of there. His Chief's coat protected him from serious burns. He went back out to check on the gunners at his GQ station.

Ward McDonald: They were everywhere. There was hardly an identifiable part. I climbed the vertical ladder to the first deck where the 40 millimeters were. There was nobody. Gone. So I climbed the next one to an upper deck where the plane exploded and I found a finger with a wedding ring on it. That's the only part I could identify. There were about 10 men up there. A lieutenant spotted me and asked if I knew how to fire a 40mm. I said, "No sir, but I can learn."

The *Henrico* was dead in the water. *Dickerson* had been hit too. *Goodhue* had 27 men dead and 117 wounded. It did not suffer severe structural damage; but the damage was sincere enough that they needed repairs and had to return to the nightmarish graveyard at Kerama Retto.

Ships needing resupply and refueling at Kerama Retto timed their arrival for sunup. This enabled them to get what they needed and get the heck out before the evening fireworks began. About every 10 days one of the carriers would break off from its group off Okinawa and head in to the anchorage.

Edward Cafferty's Diary, USS Dennis (DE-405): Took a carrier to Kerama Retto today. Ended up leaving around sundown. A Jap plane was spotted. The carrier planes were off bombing Okinawa. The Jap circled our position on the horizon. It was a torpedo bomber. The man on our phones said we got orders from the carrier to stay between the carrier and the Jap's fish (torpedoes). At the moment, we were expendable. As I stood cuddling my greasy 40mm clip and cursing that Jap, my life flashed before me. A returning carrier pilot circled his ship once and then went after the Jap. The torpedo bomber was making his run on us and we were running along-side our carrier protecting her. I was scared. If the Jap drops his torpedo before our plane gets him, we'll have to take the hit if there is any danger of it hitting the carrier. Frank Dibella said to me, "Cafferty, I'm scared." The big Indian on the other side of Frank said, "Shut up – we're all scared". We watched and cursed as the drama unfolded before us. The Jap was about 2 ½ miles from us flying about 10 feet off the water, over a fairly calm sea. Our carrier pilot made his strafing run. He got him. We let out a holler as the Jap hit the water burning. He burned for about 20 minutes before he blew up. We neared the wreckage in time to see it sink and a lot of us were still cursing it.

On the morning of 4 May, the USS *Sangamon* (CV-26) came into Kerama Retto. The *Sangamon* was an escort carrier converted from an oil tanker. It carried 32 planes and about 1,100 men. Quartermaster Donald Schroeder from Wisconsin spent his watches on the bridge maintaining the log book and he'd take over the helm during fueling. The *Sangamon* was accompanied by the destroyers *Fullman* and *Dennis*. This was a bad day to be confined in an anchorage. Kikusui #5 was in full attack mode. The harbor was covered with a smoke screen and every ship was at General Quarters throughout the day. This put refueling behind schedule. It was dusk before *Sangamon* and her escort destroyers were able to leave.

> ***Donald Schroeder, QM 3/c, USS Sangamon (CV-26):*** *We got out of the harbor late. There was a channel you had to take out of there through the coral. We had a destroyer ahead of us and a DE behind us. We couldn't launch our own planes because we needed to get into the wind. The channel was too narrow there. Radar reported bogeys coming in. There was something like ten or twelve planes. One was a bomber, the rest were fighters. One kamikaze came in too high, clipped our antennas and crashed 25 yards off the starboard side. The explosion shook the ship. Nobody was hurt, but two guys jumped overboard at that time.*

Schroeder thought they had gotten lucky. Thirty minutes later they were nearly out of the channel. And then at 1733 hours a plane was spotted coming out of the clouds with the setting sun behind him. The guns on all three ships began firing at him, then he disappeared into another cloud bank.

> ***Donald Schroeder, USS Sangamon:*** *And all of a sudden he came out astern of us. The guns on the fantail were firing at him. I remember looking back, and I remember seeing that pilot in the cockpit, with flames around his face, but he kept coming. And when he got about*

50 feet from the bridge – right at the midships – he dove down into the ship with a 500-pound bomb and with himself. He went through the flight deck, through the hanger deck…he went through three decks. Two elevators got torn out of their sockets. They weighed about 25 or 30 tons apiece. I don't remember much of that day. They tell me that is not too unusual. When you go through trauma your mind wipes stuff out.

The mid-section of the *Sangamon* was an inferno of exploding planes, ammunition and fuel. The men on the bow were completely cut off from those on the stern. They were jettisoning planes over the side. The destroyer *Hudson* pulled alongside to help fight fires. A burning plane was jettisoned off the flight deck onto the depth charges on *Hudson's* deck. Fortunately the fire was quickly put out and depth charges were secured. But now the *Hudson* was wrecked too. The mast of the destroyer got tangled in debris of the carrier. Before it could pull away from the entanglement and unload the plane it had sustained as much damage as the *Sangamon*. Fires raged for over four hours on the carrier before they were under control. The hanger deck, flight deck and bridge were completely wiped out. Somehow Schroeder escaped the bridge with only minor burns and clouded memories.

Donald Schroeder, USS Sangamon: *We lost 28 men that night. We had 115 men over the side. We had 117 wounded. I do remember the next day. When daylight came the captain was just sitting in a chair looking at the destruction. We only had one plane left, and it was missing a wing. But the plane's radio was operational and that's the only radio we had all the way back to the states. All our radio and radar was wiped out. There were bodies where there was no head and only parts of arms and legs left on them. The guys that were in the ready ammunition room had exploded shell casings in their ribs. We rolled them into canvas to bury them. Some men could only be* *identified by name the stenciled on their belts. I remember the smell of human flesh burning. I can smell it today. I'll never forget that smell.*

Shipmates shoveled debris over the side to clear a space for the burial services. "I'll never forget that service," recalled Schroeder. "We had a guy, a machinists mate, a big heavy-set man and he sang the Lord's Prayer. He did a good job." The Admiral came aboard and said, "You guys are going stateside." The *Sangamon* was going home. The engines could only muster 18 knots. Steering came from the secondary steering station on a catwalk. Survivors hoped the war was over them.

The war was far from over for sailors at Kerama Retto, the Okinawa landing beaches, or on the radar picket line. It was estimated that a destroyer's life on picket duty was about 10 days. Only 20 percent of them came away unscathed. The USS *Van Valkenburgh* was one of the lucky ones.

Harvey Fehling, Chief Water Tender, USS Van Valkenburgh: We survived, but there were so many of the other destroyers that went down and most of the guys are still laying on the bottom, north of Okinawa. They brought all the wounded destroyers into the Kerama Retto islands. They had repair ships and a floating dry dock. They'd patch them up and send them back into battle again. When damaged ships came into Kerama Retto they would have guys piled up on the deck in back like cord wood. About 100 destroyers got hit. They'd blow them almost out of the water with a single kamikaze and bomb. Nobody ever knew anything about this in the states. They never reported any of this news because they didn't want the Japs to know how bad they were beating us up with those kamikazes.

The USS *Hadley* was beyond patching up and going back to war. Once it was made seaworthy she was going to be towed home. A temporary patch was put over the massive hole in the hull. Water was finally pumped out to knee deep. A detail of six men was organized to go down and recover their dead crewmembers. Pharmacists Mate Jack McKim led the group down into the stench and tangled mess of the aft engine room. He was joined by volunteers, David Aerosmith and Eugene Wise. They were fellow snipes and knew the men down there. Plus, they could find their way around the engineering spaces with their eyes closed. Keeping their eyes closed would have been best. The mangled bodies had been trapped under water for two weeks. The recovery crew was given fabric breathing masks to help with the smell. This was an experience that would haunt these men the rest of their lives.

Gunners Mate 3/c Waymond Dean thought the Japanese pilot's body might be down below too. He had discovered a Jap's leg while cleaning up debris above the engine room. When he pulled it out of rubble the boot came off. The pilot's foot was so small, he wondered if he might be a girl. Dean was assigned the "head end" of the detail. He and a few other men were stationed at the deck hatch to the engine room. They lowered a line (rope) down to the recovery crew. Their job was to pull up the recovered bodies once they were secured on a line.

> ***Waymond Dean, GM3/c, USS Hadley:*** *Me and several other crew-members were responsible for pulling the bodies up from below and onto the deck. One body was particularly nasty. I vomited the entire time I was pulling the line. Someone took me off the detail and handed me a Springfield rifle. He told me to guard the deck. The next body came out and I retched so violently I threw the rifle down on the deck. It bounced about three times. I suspect the officer in charge thought I had had enough and gave me no more details with the dead.*

The engine and cockpit of the Japanese Zeke fighter plane were down there too. The pilot was still seated at the controls. There had been no major explosion or fire. The plane's bomb had been released prior to impact and exploded under the keel. Sea water put out any fires that may have started. The men died mostly from concussion, shrapnel and steam. Eugene Wise pulled the pilot out of the plane. He was wearing a parachute. *Hadley* crewmembers would ask, "Why would a kamikaze pilot have a parachute?" Wise presented the parachute to Captain Mullaney as a souvenir. Wise also found papers with Japanese writing and drawings in the pockets of the pilot's flight suit. He folded them up and put them in his own pocket. The bodies – including the Japanese pilot – were taken to a military cemetery on Kerama Retto island for burial. Waymond Dean did not stick around to see the rest of the Jap's body or help with his burial.

Now the *Hadley* could go into dry dock for more permanent repairs and the long tow home. The USS *Hugh W. Hadley* would eventually join the ranks of proud ships that were mothballed and scrapped. For the other battle weary crews of Task Force 58's invasion fleet, the kamikaze terror would go on for many weeks to come.

Chapter 12

Bache Reduced to Silence

O N 13 May 1945 - Mother's Day – 19 year-old George Riggs was sitting 75 feet above the water. He was in the Gun Director room of the USS *Bache* (DD-470). His ship was patrolling Radar Picket Station #9 about 50 miles southwest of Okinawa. His mom would not have been happy had she known his whereabouts.

In CIC (Combat Information Center) the air search radar operator had just picked up bogeys. He estimated the green blips on his screen to be three or four planes. Their range was 73 miles and closing from the west. Several more plots brought the raid to within 65 miles...then they vanished. Ensign Irv Clarke was the CIC officer in charge of air and surface radar. His radar provided early warning for the *Bache*, his supporting picket ships, plus the entire fleet at Okinawa. Hundreds of ships and thousands of sailors depended on him. *He was 21 years old.*

The air plotters in CIC dead reckoned the speed and direction of the raid and had it within 25 miles. Clark remembered something he was told in Tactical Radar School.

Irv Clark, Ensign CIC Officer, USS Bache: *I remembered something an instructor told us. He said if you get a disappearing bogey, don't*

ignore it, they might be flying down on the water. Acting on the pos-
sibility that the bogeys might have closed in along the dead reckoned
track, I vectored two CAP planes patrolling above us to intercept them.
A couple minutes later the flight leader reported sighting three planes.
Next report was, "Splash one Bogey." Then, "Splashing two more bo-
geys." My hunch was right.

The sun was setting. This was the most dangerous time for suicide
attacks. Planes were harder to see. By flying low they could sneak in
under the radar. Gunnery control personnel began spotting several
bogeys visually. They were taken under fire by the five-inch guns.
The two Marine Corsairs had just returned to RP #9. They were vectored out to meet this new threat.

Fire Controlman Riggs was the Range Finder Director during
General Quarters. He had already directed and fired the five-inch
guns at several attacking kamikazes. Two were destroyed. Now another attacker was approaching from aft of the ship with a Corsair in
hot pursuit.

George Riggs, FC3/c, USS Bache: We were on RP duty with another
DD and two LSM(R)s. Two Vals came in on our aft. Knocked one
down. A Marine Corsair made a pass between us and the Val. The
Captain ordered cease fire, friendly plane. I stepped out, looked at the
Val approaching and yelled, "Friendly plane my foot." I started fir-
ing again, but it was now 1200 yards away. Too close for our range
finder. All I could do is watch the plane keep coming at us.

The 40mm and other 20mm guns took over. Tracers tore into the Jap
Val and dozens of shells threatened to hit a Marine Corsair on his
tail. Marine pilot Lt. F.E. Warren braved the flak from *Bache* to within
500 yards. His attempt to stop the Val caused him to take AA hits
from the ship. Warren's Corsair was damaged in the right wing, forcing him to head back to Kadena Airfield. He almost made it back.

Warren bailed out over water and was rescued by artillerymen on a shore battery. He later received the Navy Cross for his valor.

The Val dive bomber continued its suicide attack. Two 500 pound bombs hung menacingly under its wings. Pieces of plane were ripping off from shell hits. One bomb separated and exploded in the water.

> *Irving Clark, Ensign CIC Officer, USS Bache: When the kamikazes attacked our ship I was watching a dial - which measured in yards - the distance from the ship to the target our main battery 5-inch guns were focused on. It was unnerving to see the dial spinning down. I watched in great suspense as the yardage rapidly decreased towards zero.*

The five-inch gun located at the rear of the superstructure had the best angle on the attacking Val. The nine man mount team was loading and firing at a furious rate of 22 shells a minute. Gunner's Mate second class, Al Everett was one of them. He was the trainer seated in the front right corner. His job was to control the mount's train angle or bearing. He could see the plane coming in through his sights.

> *Al Everett, GM2/c, USS Bache: I was the trainer in the number four 5-inch gun. When the Jap plane dove on us, the 40s and 20s were going right through him. I could see that plane coming.*

Third Class Electrician Mate, Mac Lockwood, was in the IC Room. That's where they repaired phones and maintained the Gyro Compass. The IC group had picked up the Jap plane on radar when it was still six miles out. When GQ sounded everyone in the room was ready.

> *Mac Lockwood, EM3/c, USS Bache: You know the GQ drill, run up forward on the starboard side and down aft on the port side. I ran*

*down to my station on the very aft fantail 20mm machine gun. Lester
Sterling had the gun ready for me to load. The best I can remember
was that the Jap plane came in low at 1 o'clock off the stern. We fired
when it was in range and I watched the tracers hit the nose of the
plane. It was only seconds when our gun jammed and the plane came
in just over our heads and into the depth charge racks next to us. We
all hit the deck.*

Ray DelSesto of Rhode Island had been in the galley cooking when
GQ sounded. He dropped a pan and raced to his station on the starboard 40mm gun. His job as first loader was to take a four round clip
from the 2nd loader and insert it into the gun.

Ray DelSesto, CK1/c, USS Bache: *At some point during the battle I
bent down to retrieve the clip from the second loader and he was not
there. I looked around and the entire gun crew was missing. They had
seen the plane coming right at our mount and ran to the opposite side
of the ship. When I saw the plane I hit the deck.*

Now every sailor on the deck watched their approaching doom.
Those last 500 yards are daunting for a kamikaze pilot too. The
Val dive bomber pilot was now in a steep dive which causes his
plane to lift. He fights the stick to keep from overshooting his target. Exploding shells and tracers are blinding him. Final thoughts
of family and friends might flash one last time. Then training reminders take over. "Don't look away. Don't close eyes. Strafe ship.
Pull up. Release bomb." Wings begin shaking at a 60 degree high
speed dive. The 500 pound bombs strapped underneath reduce
maneuverability. Pieces of the plane fly off from shell hits. Pulling
up too much - at the end of his dive - could cause a stall. G-force
yanks him out of his seat. He fights not to black out...then gives in
to his fate.

Irving Clark, Ensign: The dial went all the way down to zero...then there was a huge bang and the whole ship was jarred by the huge explosion of a 500 pound bomb. Lights went out and radio communications went dead.

H.E. "Bucky" Walters, LTJG, USS Bache: He came up low on the port beam with an F6F in pursuit. With our 40mm's and 20mm's we shot one of his bombs off and knocked him out of control. He slid into the ship, cut off the Number 2 stack and set the Bache afire with his residual fuel. The other bomb went off on the starboard side. It blew a hole in the main deck and the side of the ship above the waterline.

Most of the nearby ship's superstructure was wiped out when the wing hit the stack and the plane catapulted into the ship. Its bomb exploded seven feet above the deck spraying shrapnel the length of the *Bache*. The explosion penetrated amidships and destroyed almost everything in the forward engine room and aft fire room. Power was lost to both forward and aft engines. The ship was dead in the water. Live steam caused many casualties in the engineering spaces. All electrical and steam power were lost. Fires blazed amidships. The five-inchers and 40mm guns switched over to manual control and prepared for more attacks. Two more planes were knocked down by remaining CAP pilots. The number one 40mm opened up on a Dinah circling above. That plane was driven away by their fire.

Irving Clark, Ensign: No one in CIC was injured. Shrapnel which had penetrated the bulkheads of the captain's cabin and radio shack near us did not enter the CIC spaces. Our only CIC damage came from the continuous ringing of a bell. One of the phone systems had failed and had to be removed to stop the ringing. Now the normal operating sounds of a ship underway were reduced to silence.

The men in CIC had escaped unscathed. On deck the efforts to survive fire, explosions, and to rescue shipmates was chaotic. The blast lifted Ray DelSesto off the deck of the port side gun tub. It felt like a punch to the stomach. His leg was bloodied with shrapnel wounds. He pulled himself up and looked to the other side of the ship where his gun crew had retreated. The 40mm gun tub on the starboard side was gone. The plane had made a direct hit on the gun. It killed all the men stationed there plus the gun crew that had run to starboard side. Damage control parties were already fighting fires, helping wounded and jettisoning hot ammunition over the side. DelSesto was ordered to go to the mess hall and have cold drinks ready for the men. His leg got patched up. The punch to his stomach caused undetected internal bleeding that nearly killed him in the days that followed.

Mac Lockwood EM3/c: I recall someone stepping on my hand. The explosion pushed the fantail down in the water and our gun crew was soaked. My gun captain's life saver jacket was riddled with shrapnel. When I got up to see the damage I saw one of the starboard torpedo men running towards me. His scalp was blown off and covering his face.

At this point nobody knew if there had been an order to abandon ship. Flames were shooting up from midship. All power was out. The entire midship repair crew, including Chief Castleberry plus the 40mm gun mount crew were blown off the ship. Mac Lockwood joined a group of men at the 40mm gun magazine. They formed a line and passed hot 40mm shell ammunition over the port side.

Al Everett, GM2/c: The ship was on fire. We helped put out fires and threw shells over the side. My buddy, Ray DelSesto was injured when the plane hit and Bucky Walters was burned pretty bad.

Irving Clark, Ensign: I have a painful memory of stepping outside CIC where my feet encountered something on the open deck. My eyes had not adjusted to the total darkness so I asked someone nearby what that was. He replied the names of two of my radar crew. Their dead bodies were lying there on the deck. Apparently, when the firing began they had stepped outside to watch the fireworks.

Mac Lockwood EM3/c: A second plane, a twin engine bomber, was about to dive on our starboard side. Our power was gone. The 5-inch 38 and 40mm trained out and fired manually. I could only watch, as our gun couldn't fire in that direction. We drove the plane away, or the Jap decided we were going to sink. My prayers were answered.

Without power, *Bache's* firefighting hoses were useless. Men were battling huge flames with hand billies (water pump extinguishers). At 1900 *LCS(L)s 56* and *87* were joined by *LSM(R)-197* alongside *Bache*. They began pouring water on the flames and helping with wounded. There was flooding below in the engineering spaces caused by ruptured water intakes. The hull was not badly damaged. Flooding was controlled and eventually pumped out. Despite the ship being critically damaged, Captain McFarland announced *Bache* was not going to sink. They would not abandon ship.

George Riggs and the men in the Fire Control room had escaped death when the plane came in high and hit the smoke stack. As they regained their footing and assessed the situation, their telephone talker was scratching his belly.

George Riggs, FC3/c: My telephone talker said, "Man that's hot." He had a piece of hot shrapnel in his belly. It popped out and we looked all over for it, so he'd have a Purple Heart souvenir.

Irving Clark, Ensign: One of my responsibilities was to deal with the secret codes and other registered publications which were stored in CIC in a heavily weighted rectangular canvas container. I was supposed to drop it over the side if the ship was going to sink. There was great relief when the captain informed us the ship was not in sinking condition.

A section of the burning plane ended up on top of the torpedo tubes. The hot debris was shoved overboard. Then torpedomen tried to fire the torpedoes from tubes that weren't punctured. Several torpedoes remained in hot tubes. They could explode. With flames still licking at the tubes, Tom Morton climbed on top of the mount to jettison torpedoes over the side. He received a Navy Commendation Medal for his heroic action.

Dark sky was setting in when fires were finally brought under control. Damage reports were delivered to the captain...no steam, no power, no electrical, no antennas or communication. The helpless *Bache* was taken under tow for Kerama Retto, the graveyard of destroyers.

Now began the painful process of finding dead and wounded shipmates. The aft battle dressing station had been destroyed. Both pharmacist mates stationed there were killed. The officers' wardroom became the main battle dressing station.

Irving Clark, Ensign: When there was nothing to do in CIC I went into the officers' wardroom. Most of the wounded came or were dragged or carried to the wardroom. It was extremely crowded. Doc put me to work going around the room with a glass of water trying to get those who had been scalded by steam to drink. Some were unconscious or semi-conscious, so it was difficult to do. As I was trying to pour water into one unconscious sailors mouth, doc said to me, "Don't spend any more time on him – he's not going to make it."

Mac Lockwood, EM 3/c: I was called to the wardroom that was being used to help the wounded. A Lieutenant asked me to get more lights so they could care for injured men. I went to my spare parts locker and gathered up all the battle lanterns I could find and set them up as required. My next order was to get power to the ship. I went below decks to the diesel generator room and started it up...only to have it crap out. I opened and closed different circuits until it finally stayed on line. It worked all the way to Okinawa.

Care for the wounded, cleanup, and repair continued throughout the long slow tow to Kerama Retto. The dead were taken to the fantail for identification. One of Lockwood's fellow electrician mates was found in the aft engine room deck hatch. Many of the engineers in the destroyed engine and boiler rooms were burned and killed by the bomb and 600 pounds of super-heated pressurized steam. The next morning *Bache* was tied alongside a repair ship in Kerama Retto anchorage. There was little solace in the fact that other destroyers nearby – *Hadley, Evans, Aaron Ward* – were in worse shape than *Bache*. A final *Bache* casualty report showed 41 dead or missing and 32 wounded. The dead were transferred to another ship and funerals were held on shore.

Irving Clark, Ensign: I can picture in my mind the unloading of bodies after we were towed to the naval anchorage at Kerama Retto Island. Each body was on some sort of stretcher and they were stacked in a crisscross fashion on an LCVP that came alongside and took them to shore. A service ashore was led by a navy chaplain. Behind him were all of the bodies laid on the ground in neat rows, each covered by a white sheet.

The USS *Bache* had fought it last battle in this war. Guns, ammo and parts were stripped from the ship to be used on ships that could be repaired and sent back into battle. Temporary repairs were made. Metal plates were welded to the deck and hull. She sailed home on one engine and one screw. *Bache* arrived in New York Navy Yard on 13 July 1945. *Bache* was still being repaired when the war ended one month later. The USS *Aaron Ward* was also in the Navy Yard for her extensive repairs.

During the war, a group called "The Lambs – Servicemen's Morale Corps" had formed. They gave a weekly, invitation only dinner and party for units and wounded stationed near New York. On August 23, 1945, the officers and men of the USS *Bache* and USS *Aaron Ward* were invited to a "Gala Victory Night" at The Lambs Club. The program and menu listed the evening as the "170th Consecutive Weekly Function." Joseph S. Buhler, the Chairman of The Lambs had founded the Servicemen's Morale Corps in 1942. It presented 210 weekly entertainment nights for troops and served more than 50,000 dinners. The entertainment and business community donated their time, talent and money to keep this weekly morale booster afloat throughout the war.

Now the crews of two ships who had faced off with kamikazes would be wined and dined and entertained in a style most had never experienced. The menu listed dinner as "What the O.P.A. (Office of Price Administration) Allows Us." Food rationing was very strict by 1945. But they had plenty of Ruppert's Beer, compliments of New York's Jacob Ruppert Brewery and the Grand Piano was compliments of Steinway and Sons. Entertainment followed in the Theatre on the 3rd floor.

Irv Clark, Ensign: We were in New York when the war ended. We went down to Times Square. There were lots of free drinks. I remember we were invited to a very nice, big dinner with another ship too.

These sailors had survived the kamikazes and made it home.

The "Gala Victory Night" program was signed by dozens of musicians, singers and New York Club actors who performed on August 23, 1945. Many of these entertainers were well known in the 40's. The food, beer and entertainment was all donated to honor the crews of USS Bache and USS Aaron Ward. This was the 170th weekly event provided by The Lambs Servicemen's Morale Corps.

U.S.S. Bache (DD-470/DDE-470)

Commissioned - November 14, 1942
Decommissioned - January 27, 1946
Recommissioned - October 1, 1951
Aground and Sunk - Rhodes, Greece . . . February 6, 1968
Decommissioned - February 26, 1968

Neptunis Rex - December 14, 1943
Hit by Jap Plane - May 13, 1945

---

25 - Killed   22 - Seriously Injured
16 - M.I.A.   10 - Lesser Injured

World War II - Awarded 8 Battle Stars
Vietnam - Awarded 1 Battle Star

Credited With

January 8, 1943 - Class E. Assessment on Nazi Sub
October 24, 1944 - Sank Jap Battleship, Cruiser, Destroyer
February 28, 1945 - May 13, 1945 - 7 Jap Planes
May 11, 1943 - May 13, 1945 - 14 Pacific Invasions/Bombardments
May 3, 1945 - Picked up 69 Survivors of Sinking LSMR-95

This plaque honors the USS Bache and her crews. It is mounted on the Memorial Wall at the Pacific War Museum in Fredericksburg, Texas. Bache served until she became wrecked on the Island of Rhodes, Greece 6 February 1968. She received eight battle stars for her World War II service.

Chapter 13

Drexler Laying to Starboard

HAROLD Tatch was preparing ammo in the 40mm clip ready-room of the USS *Drexler*. The crew had gone to General Quarters at 0643. Tatch was probably the first man to be on his GQ station. He slept there. His bunk mattress was spread out right on top of cans filled with 40mm shells. The small clip room was dark, quiet, cozy and private.

A bogey was picked up 28 miles from radar picket station #15. The *Drexler* was patrolling one of the most dangerous RPs. It was located 50 miles northwest of Okinawa and directly in line with enemy planes from southern Japan airfields. Another destroyer, the USS *Lowry* (DD-770) and two "small boys" *LCS(L)-55* and *LCS(L)-56* accompanied *Drexler*. The *Lowry* vectored two CAP planes to intercept the intruder. The Marine pilots shot down one twin engine Nick bomber. More bogeys were still visible on radar. Tatch and his assistant filled each clip with four shells. They would need to re-supply both forward quad 40mm guns once the shooting started. These guns would be going through clips at a rate of 30 per minute per barrel. Over 200 clips per minute would be needed in a major battle. Tatch's bunk got shoved out of the way while they worked feverishly to load more clips.

Tatch was from Fredericksburg, Texas the hometown of Admiral Chester Nimitz. During high school, young Tatch worked as a bell hop at the Nimitz Hotel. When war broke out his older brother joined the Navy. As soon as Harold turned 17 he joined too. "When the Admiral of the Pacific Fleet is your neighbor, you join the Navy," Tatch would explain.

Harold Tatch, USS Drexler: May the 28th. That's when we were on picket station 15, East China Sea. That morning at 7 o'clock, six bombers came in. They were in for suicide. The first plane we shot down. Second plane, a combination of the Lowry and our guns shot it down. The third plane was heading for the Lowry, missed it and came in at us.

Drexler's skipper, Lieutenant Commander Wilson sighted the next enemy plane when it was out about 7 miles and approaching on the starboard bow. Nick bombers were known for speed in a dive and the amount of punishment they could take. The plane began his dive at the *Lowry* from an elevation of about 2,000 feet. Guns from both destroyers were sending flak and tracers into the attacker. The pilot pulled out of his dive too soon and passed right over the *Lowry*. He corrected and was now aimed for the *Drexler's* starboard side. *Drexler's* gunners had to hold their fire until the plane was out of *Lowry's* line of fire.

The gun captain on *Drexler's* starboard quad 40mm was Gunners Mate, Duke Payne. He was from Mississippi and before the war, had never left his home state. After Pearl Harbor was attacked he joined the Navy at age 17. It was one part patriotism, and one part wanderlust. Now he was watching a 9,000-pound twin engine plane screaming towards him at 330 miles per hour.

Duke Payne, Gunners Mate, USS Drexler: Combat was scary. When the heat was on and you were going into battle, you were scared. Then you would realize that SOB is trying to kill me, and you'd get mad. Then the adrenaline was flowing and you didn't think about it. After the action, you'd get scared again, and you'd throw up. You didn't want to talk to anyone, you just tried to find a quiet corner, and sit there and shake. Then the first thing you knew, you had to get up and do it again.

The bomber was too close now for the five-inchers to engage. It was up to the 40s and 20s to stop it. Payne's crew streamed hot shells from all four barrels into the nose of the plane. They maintained fire right up to the point of impact. The kamikaze smashed into the *Drexler* just forward of Payne's mount. The plane sprayed burning gasoline all over the mid-section of the ship. The bomb penetrated the hull and ruptured steam lines in the engine rooms. Everyone on Duke Payne's 10-man crew was killed except him. The explosion blew him out of his gun captain's hatch and onto the deck. Someone yelled "Jump overboard," so he did. Men were jumping over the side to escape the inferno on deck. Payne went under and came up sputtering oily salt water. He couldn't see a thing.

Duke Payne, USS Drexler: *When I surfaced, I thought I was blind. My face stung and I thought my eyes were gone. I yelled, "I can't see, I think I have shrapnel in my eyes." Someone nearby said, "You dumb SOB take your goggles off!" I did, then I could see. They were coated with oil. Truthfully, the goggles probably protected my eyes.*

Payne had found a very big, quiet corner. There was no time to talk and no time to shake. He had to start swimming. He didn't have a life preserver. It was too bulky to wear during battle. There was burning oil on the water. He had to swim away from the ship. *Drexler* had lost power and was slowing down. But her guns were still firing.

A plane was diving on the *Lowry*. Gunners on the *Drexler* switched to manual and hit the plane repeatedly. It crashed short of *Lowry's* stern. Another bomber was circling above. *Drexler* was dead in the water now. Fires raged amidships. She was taking on water and beginning to list.

Harold Tatch, USS Drexler: I knew right away something happened. I was in my clipping room, we opened the hatch to see what was going on. There was fire all over the place, guys were running, so I told the other old boy, I think maybe we better get back in that room. We went back in our room, closed one latch, and that's when the second plane hit us...midship, just behind the bridge, between the two stacks. My room was about 30 feet away. I'd just closed the latch and boy it flew open and there was steel and fire and everything where we were standing a couple of seconds earlier.

The second plane to hit *Drexler* began circling the ship at 10,000 yards. The Nick appeared to be lining up for a dead ahead attack on the bow. There were two F4U Corsairs on its tail. Both forward five-inch gun mounts were filling the sky with deadly bursts of shrapnel. The Marine pilots ignored the friendly fire while attempting to stop the Jap plane. One Corsair got hit and had to peel away for home while trailing smoke. The Japanese pilot was aiming for the bridge. His plane was being riddled with hits from the Corsair and bow guns on the *Drexler.* The plane was smoking. It veered off course. It appeared to be crashing, but the pilot recovered control, leveled off, and circled back for another run on the bow. He missed the bridge again, but his wing clipped the signal halyards and spun the plane into the superstructure deck. The bomber's load of explosives hit on top of the torpedo mounts. There was a massive explosion that rocked the entire ship and threw metal in all directions. Burning oil shot flames hundreds of feet in the air.

Harold Tatch, USS Drexler: When the second plane hit us, I stepped out again, me and this other boy. I was looking down the side of the ship and guys were going over the side. There was no announcement to abandon ship. We had no power. No way to communicate. I noticed the ammunition was falling out of our room. So, I picked up some of those clips. I looked down the side again and said "Hell, they're going overboard. I think we're sinking." We were laying to starboard side, so I threw the clips in the room and I told him, "Let's get the heck out of here." I went down the port side and the last thing I remember I was hanging on the side. Next thing I was about 50 yards away and the ship was sticking straight up in the air.

Tatch and other survivors saw their ship sliding down with the bow straight up. They started swimming away before being sucked down with her. Tatch had put on his life preserver after the first plane hit. He was a good swimmer. He helped another man without a life preserver find a raft. Just 49 seconds after the final plane hit, the *Drexler* was gone. Few men who were below deck had time to get out. They were trapped. Casualties on the *Drexler* were 150 enlisted and eight officers killed or missing plus 51 wounded.

Survivors of the sinking now faced survival in the sea. Many were injured. Most were covered in oil. Sharks were a common threat. Underwater explosions could cause internal injuries. Getting separated from the crew and lost at sea was the scariest of all. The LCS support ships had to make their way through fiery water that was strewn with debris to find the survivors. Tatch was in the water for three hours. When he and other survivors were picked up they were given old clothes, shoes and a bit of alcoholic beverage to warm them up.

Duke Payne, USS Drexler: *Inflatable belts didn't always work. All I had on were cut off jeans. While waiting to be picked up we had no problems with sharks. I received minor wounds but did not tell anyone. I wanted to go home for a 30-days survivors leave, not go to a hospital on Guam. We lost a lot of destroyers in the Okinawa* *campaign. Someone complained to Halsey about the losses and he said, "We got more destroyers than they got planes, so keep them out there." So, they did and honestly it was necessary. The kamikazes dove on everything in sight so the protection was essential.*

The USS *Drexler* was the 13th ship to be sunk on the radar picket line. The Navy's agony was far from over. The ground battle for Okinawa would go on for another 25 days. As of 28 May, U.S. troops had finally taken the first line of defense on Okinawa - the Suri line stronghold. But, the defending Japanese units had made an organized retreat in the dead of night. It would take 25 more days to break through the next two defensive lines and secure the whole island. Organized ground resistance would end on 21 June. But the threat from kamikazes would continue for six more agonizing weeks after a declared victory. Sailors couldn't understand why their enemy would choose to die for a lost cause. New tactics were needed to fight them.

Chapter 14

The *Barry* Decoy

QUARTERMASTER Floyd Bozman made several entries into the *LSM-59* deck log. It was 1600 on 21 June 1945. His ship was leaving the Kerama Retto anchorage. Following close behind was the sea going tug USS *Lipan* (ATF-85) towing a battered USS *Barry* (APD-29) . Their destination was the island of Ie Shima to the north of Okinawa. Their mission was to test some deceptive tactics on the kamikazes.

Bozman was just 18 years old. He had never traveled far from his home on the eastern shore of Maryland. Here he was, half way around the world on a mission that might save many sailors' lives. The *LSM-59* had been commissioned in 1944. It was an amphibious landing ship medium. Bozeman and his shipmates had trained at the Amphibious Training Base at Little Creek, Virginia. They had performed well during the invasion and landings on Okinawa. Now that Okinawa was secured, they had a new mission.

The destroyer graveyard at Kerama Retto was bursting with mangled ships waiting for repair. Many of them were beyond repair or salvage. The USS *Barry* was one of them. She had been attacked by kamikazes on 25 May while patrolling 35 miles northwest of Okinawa. One kamikaze crashed into the base of her bridge. The explosion from the plane's bomb ignited fuel oil in *Barry's* ruptured tanks. Fires below deck burned out of control. Fearing an ammunition magazine explosion, the ship was abandoned. It burned all night but refused to sink or explode. Crews re-boarded the next day and extinguished the last fires. The *Barry* was towed to Kerama Retto and declared unsalvageable.

USS *Barry* was a four stacker WWI vintage destroyer. She had been refitted and reclassified APD-29 (Transport Destroyer) in 1944. She was old and now burned beyond repair. She needed to be sunk. It was decided the *Barry* might make a good decoy. Why not let the kamikazes waste a couple of their planes and pilots on a ghost ship? One night, a kamikaze had been seen crashing into a diversionary raft of burning oil barrels. The pilot had mistaken this for a ship in distress. It was thought the same tactic might work with a decoy ship. And there were many other ships in the Kerama Retto harbor that could be reclassified as DDDs (Decoy Destroyers).

The *LSM-59* was assigned a group of electronic experts to design a system to fool kamikazes into attacking the *Barry*. These guys were the nerds of the 1940s. They called their unit the Beach Jumper's. Their job was to create diversions during a beach landing to draw Japanese defenders away from the invasion beaches. They used remote control devices for many of their diversions. For this mission, they first had to make the *Barry* sea worthy. They patched the hole in *Barry's* hull and filled her compartments with sealed empty oil drums. They wanted to keep her afloat after repeated hits by kamikazes. The *Barry* had already been stripped of anything useful. They needed a working gun. A dozen quality steaks were procured from the officers' mess and traded to an Army unit for a 50-caliber machine gun. It was mounted on *Barry's* deck. Smoke pots were rounded up and installed in *Barry's* smoke stacks.

The *LSM-59* was equipped with radio controlled (drone) planes. They were supposed to be used for AA target practice. At Okinawa, there were enough enemy planes for gunners to shoot at; anti-aircraft target practice was unnecessary. The control solenoids for the drone planes were removed and modified to operate the machine gun and smoke pots. Marine drone operators on the *LSM-59* would be able to control these clever deceptive devices. The remote control 50 caliber machine gun would be fired at night to give away *Barry's* position and attract kamikazes. Smoke pots would be fired up in daylight hours to give the appearance of a ship on fire. The effective radio range of the solenoids was about one mile. The *LSM-59* would just need to maneuver close by their *Barry* decoy to create the tantalizing appearance of an easy target. No fervent kamikaze pilot could resist crashing into a sitting duck destroyer. American ingenuity and resourcefulness was at work.

The three-ship flotilla chugged northward at seven knots. A tug is built for power not speed. It can do 12 knots when sailing solo. Towing the two-ton destroyer with partially flooded compartments was a slow go. Bozeman checked his charts and provided navigational information to the officer of the deck. They were nearing their ambush location. The control condition was noted as "Flash White Control Green." They were near a military airfield and friendly planes were in the area.

The island of Ie Shima had been invaded and secured in early April. It had a large airstrip with a division of Marine Corsairs that could provide air cover for their decoy operation. This obscure little island became famous when Ernie Pyle was killed there. Pyle was the famed war correspondent who had endeared himself to dog faced GIs all across Europe. He joined the GIs in the Pacific when Germany surrendered. Now he was buried alongside the boys who had shared their fox holes with him. They placed a monument with the inscription: "On this spot, the 77th Infantry Division lost a buddy, Ernie Pyle, 18 April 1945." The island was near the two most dangerous radar picket stations – RP #1 and RP #15.

No Jap planes were reported by lookouts until they neared Ie Shima. At 1837 two fighter planes were spotted approaching low on the water. They both had huge bombs strapped to their bellies. The 40mm gun on the *LSM-59* opened up first at 2,000 yards and then the 20mm guns followed. To the dismay of Floyd Bozman the first kamikaze was headed for him. The pilot bypassed the bigger, better decoy target to take out the smaller *LSM-59*. Despite taking repeated hits the plane crashed through the tank deck, went into the engine room and through the bottom of the hull. All electrical power and both engines were knocked out. The ship was in immediate danger of sinking.

The second kamikaze circled and was taken under fire by *Lipan's* 40s and 20s. It barely missed the tug as it aimed for the *Barry* trailing slowly behind. The kamikaze pilot had an unimpeded attack run at an unmanned ship. The pilot was probably thanking the gods for giving him a slow-moving target with sleepy gunners. The plane crashed into the superstructure of the *Barry*. The bomb blast opened a new hole in the hull.

The stern of the *LSM-59* was engulfed in flames. The fires were put out quickly, but flooding was severe. The ship began to settle, stern first. The captain gave the order to abandon ship. At 1854 the bow sank from view. Two men were killed and eight others were burned. Floyd Bozeman was one of the injured. He was severely burned over 75% of his body. But Bozeman would survive to marry and raise a family.

The empty oil drums in the hull of the USS *Barry* kept her afloat through the night. She finally sank the next day. One kamikaze pilot had sacrificed himself for a decoy ship. But another ship was sacrificed in return. Not a good trade off. There would be no more decoy missions. On 21 June an American victory on Okinawa was declared. Japanese General Ushijima of the 32nd Army would take his own life in the accepted Samurai tradition. Despite the formal end of hostilities...there would be continued kamikaze attacks.

Chapter 15

The Cruelest Kikusui

ADMIRAL Ugaki had planned for ten massive "Floating Chrysanthemum" (Kikusui) attacks. The first one began on 6 April 1945. The mass attacks continued every seven to ten days for the next two and a half months. A final launch of kamikazes was scheduled for June 21 and 22. It would not be massive. Fewer than 100 planes and pilots were at Ugaki's disposal. Only 58 would reach the fleet at Okinawa. Many were shot down, some had to ditch in the ocean due to mechanical problems and others simply aborted their mission. Kikusui had become synonymous with a Samurai warrior who fought to the death against overwhelming odds to honor and protect the Emperor. Hundreds of Japanese pilots and crews were being sent to their deaths the same way. In terms of military value, their missions were useless.

Vice Admiral Ugaki's Diary, Commanding Officer 5th Air Fleet:
Even though it becomes impossible for us to continue organized resistance after expending our strength, we must continue guerilla warfare under the Emperor and never give up the war.

Ugaki was aware Okinawa had fallen. General Ushijima, commander of the beleaguered 32nd Army, had already sent his farewell message to Imperial Headquarters. Kamikaze pilots would now deliver symbolic death and destruction. Their sacrifice was meant to show resolve in Japan's fight to the end. That same resolve was not shared by all the pilots. The original kamikaze units were made up of all volunteers. Now many of the pilots had been volunteered by their unit commanders. Some had been on one or more missions that aborted due to weather or mechanical problems. Many of the newer recruits would return to base with the excuse of "I got lost." Kamikaze pilots were losing their eagerness to make the supreme sacrifice for a lost cause. One kamikaze pilot wrote, "I say frankly, I do not die willingly, I die with regret. My country's future leaves me uneasy." Preparing for your known death is difficult once. Having to do it two or three times is nearly impossible.

Kikusui 10 included six of the manned rockets called Ohka bombs. Betty bombers with seven man crews were required for launching each Ohka. The bombers were slowed by the rocket's weight. Most were in poor repair and easy targets for the Combat Air Patrol. Two of these mother planes were shot down before reaching Okinawa. Two of the Ohkas launched but missed their targets and crashed into the sea. Two other Ohka rockets failed to release from the mother plane.

Ohka pilot, Keisuke Yamamura was on his third mission. His first was aborted due to mechanical problems. Bad weather sent him home on the next. He was no longer the ardent, idealistic young man who volunteered to be a Thunder God hero. Yet he prepared again by writing his farewell note and sealing a lock of hair in an envelope. On this morning, he was both sad and angry.

Keisuke Yamamura, Ohka Pilot: *I'm going to die. I'm going to die. Hurry up kill me. Get it over with.*

When he reached the target area Yamamura climbed dutifully into his tiny coffin. He placed a photo on the dashboard, took a deep breath and yelled, "Ready" into the speaker tube. A red light began to flash to alert him that he was about to be released. His mouth went dry as he grabbed the controls and waited to fall away from the plane above. Nothing happened. He was still attached. He screamed in anguish and rocked back and forth attempting to disengage the Ohka. Nothing worked. He was still attached to the Betty bomber so he climbed back up into the plane. Yamamura had been cheated of a divine death once again.

On 21 June, the sailors at the Kerama Retto destroyer graveyard were getting ready for another night of mayhem. Kamikazes would usually arrive just after sunset. Navy intelligence had warned the fleet that another Kikusui attack was imminent. Smoke pots were being lit, sailors on night watch were issued weapons, and AA guns were readied for battle. *Hadley* shipmate James Reaves SM3/c from Alabama was on board the USS *Curtiss* (AV-4). He had been transferred to the seaplane tender for temporary duty. They needed a signalman. The *Hadley* was still tied alongside a repair ship and had little need for Reave's abilities. He was probably glad to have a change of scenery. The *Hadley* still smelled from the death and destruction it had endured on 11 May.

A single kamikaze came in low with the setting sun behind him. Nobody saw the plane approaching in the glare of sunlight. Not a single gun was fired. The pilot had his pick of stationary anchored targets in the harbor. He chose *Curtiss* and crashed into the superstructure where the signal bridge is located. There was a huge explosion. Now the entire anchorage erupted into gunfire. Tracers, shell bursts and fire on the *Curtiss* lit up the night sky. Throughout the night, jumpy gunners continued shooting at anything that moved. The *Curtiss* suffered 38 killed and 21 wounded. James Reaves was among the dead. He had survived one of the biggest kamikaze battles of the war aboard the *Hadley*. Now he was killed by a single plane on a non-combatant ship. Reaves was the 30th man killed in action from the *Hadley* crew. His shipmates learned of his death the next day. It's what one sailor called a "dirty break."

A movie projector was being set up after sundown on 21 June. The crew of *LST-534* had docked on a pontoon pier at the Hagushi landing beach on Okinawa. Their ship had been anchored in Buckner Bay for several weeks with hundreds of other transport ships. They all awaited their turn to unload supplies and get some much-needed shore recreation. The borrowed movie would be shown on the ship's tank deck that night.

Enemy planes had been picked up on radar throughout the day. General Quarters was on more than it was off. The crew was hoping for a respite from GQ so they could enjoy the movie. Ensign Alex Fiedler, the engineering officer, had seen the movie in New York. It was a good one so he talked it up. The first reel was wound into the projector. The movie was being shown on a white sheet.

Alex Fiedler, Ensign, LST-534: *We had this movie we were showing out on the tank deck. As soon as it's all clear you go ahead with the movie. Anytime there is an alert we shut down and blackout. This 33mm movie was a six reeler. Changing each reel takes a bit of time. Probably would take three hours to watch the movie.*

GQ sounded before the first reel was finished. When all clear was reported, the crew gathered again and the movie continued. This went on throughout the night. At 0400 they still hadn't seen the final sixth reel. It was decided to keep everyone in suspense until the next night. The crew needed some sleep.

Nobody got more than an hour of interrupted bunk time that night. By sunup the unloading activity resumed. *LST-534* was carrying 40 barrels of high octane aviation gas, 50 barrels of calcium carbide, hundreds of barrels of crude oil, containers of ammunition and a small LCS boat. They were a floating fire bomb. They wanted this stuff off their ship before the kamikazes returned.

James Miller from New York was a Pharmacists Mate 1/c. Because of his specialty rating he never had to chip paint or pull garbage details. His GQ was in the officers' ward room. This is where the officers dined and held meetings. It doubled as a medical emergency room during battle. It was a nice GQ station.

James Miller, PhM1/c, LST-534: I was in the ward room. I was listening to Tokyo Rose. She was playing good music. Music of the 40's and she was telling us…why are you out there or why aren't you home with your sweetheart. I said to her, "Keep quiet and play more good music." So, she did and all of a sudden whamo! I knew we were in action when the twin 40s went off.

Norris Long, QM2/c was an elder among the enlisted crew. He was 35 years old. Long had a camera and enjoyed photography. His GQ was on the bridge, so he had a great view of a kamikaze circling the ship while being chased by a Corsair. He watched it being shot down. Somebody asked him why he didn't grab his camera and get a picture of the action. He said, "Well I'm saving my film for the plane that hits us." Sailors didn't expect their ship to leave Okinawa unscathed.

Norris Long, QM2/c, LST-534: For some reason, I picked up my camera and stepped out. Maybe because those Marine pilots were nailing them. Here comes a kamikaze around and I thought he was a long way off but I'll try to get a photo. So, I followed him around as he went past our stern. Thought I might have gotten the shot, he was pretty close. Next thing I know whoomph, the darn fool turned around, came back and hit us from the other side. I hadn't paid a bit of attention to him after he turned.

Yeoman Willie Gunn was at his damage control station watching the kamikazes circle. He had followed the plane when it was first spotted coming in over a mountain that was inland. There was a small gun boat about 150 feet off *534's* starboard side. It was supposed to be providing fire support while the *LST-534* was unloading. The gun boat had a crew of six manning a twin 50 caliber machine gun. The plane leveled off and appeared to be heading for the gun boat.

Willie Gunn, Yeoman, LST-534: I saw the LST gunners pointing at the plane. The men thought they were about to be machine gunned, so they did the best thing. They jumped overboard. It was almost humorous. Then I was really surprised beyond belief when I saw him do the most magnificent roll. His plane went a little to the right and then he dipped it down just perfectly and when he dipped his wing down he came right in at a thirty- degree angle. He disappeared from my sight, but I knew he hit right below one of our 20mm gun tubs. I was totally sure that everybody on the gun had been killed. The ship shook violently, went up into the air and sank into the sand.

The kamikaze's bomb exploded in the tank deck. It blew a huge hole through their flat-bottomed hull. The ship sank immediately in 12 feet of water and became grounded in the sand. It was low tide so the ship was only half under water. Men who were in the forward gun tubs were catapulted out onto the pier, into the water or down into the hole made by the bomb. Fortunately, none of the crew was on the tank deck. The bow doors and ramp were wide open. Seabees were doing the unloading and most were on the pontoon pier.

Alex Fiedler, Ensign, LST-534: The interesting thing was that we were in the process of unloading and the bow doors were open, the ramp was down and a lot of people on the pontoon deck were working. The force of an explosion will seek its easiest path. With that door being open the big force of the explosion went right out the bow.

Two officers were standing side by side just outside the open doors. They were blown 30 feet off the pier. One was killed by shrapnel. The other stood up and brushed himself off, uninjured. Most of the serious injuries occurred to Seabees out on the pier. That is where the full force of the blast hit. Damage control teams ignored flooding in the damaged compartments. Hatches had been secured for GQ which kept most of the ship dry and protected from fires that broke out. The ship had already sunk as far as it would go until high tide. Rescuing wounded and fighting fires were the immediate concerns. Several gunners who had landed in the bomb hole had to be rescued from spreading fires. Ammunition on deck was tossed over the side. Barrels of flammable materials were stored below. Keeping the fires from igniting the barrels was critical.

Pharmacist Mate James Miller discovered many of the injured had been shot by 20mm shells. Their sister ship *LST-1022* was anchored 500 yards away. The kamikaze had come in low on the water right between the two ships.

> *Alex Fiedler, Ensign, LST-534: The 1022 was in a position maybe 500 yards to our port, lined up parallel to us at the pontoon pier. The kamikaze was a Zeke fighter. They were getting desperate. They didn't have many kamikaze pilots or planes left. At this point in the war they were converting every plane that would fly into a suicide plane. One of their techniques was to fly down between two ships. If the gunners on both ships were shooting at him, they're also shooting at each other. The 1022 started firing at this kamikaze when he was off our stern. They raked all the way across our deck. This caused some casualties.*

It took until 2100 hours that night to bring all the fires under control. The crew was exhausted. The ship was in shambles. Most of the crew went to shore for the night. After the shock of battle, anger and grief set in. The next day Ensign Fiedler looked over at the *LST-1022* and couldn't believe his eyes. They had painted a Jap flag on their bridge to show they had shot down an enemy plane. What they had shot down was the *LST-534* along with several of the shipmates. Fiedler strapped on his 45-caliber gun and grabbed three crewmembers. They took a small boat over to *LST-1022* and found the officer of the deck. Low ranking Ensign Fiedler - who was commissioned as a 90-day wonder - ordered the officer to paint over the flag. It was painted over while they watched.

The *LST-534* was patched, pumped and floated but never fully repaired. It was eventually towed out to sea and scuttled. Ensign Fiedler had to tell the crew how their movie had ended. The sixth reel was destroyed by the kamikaze.

Kikusui #10 was a waste of men and machines on both sides of the battle. Over 100 kamikaze pilots and crewmembers were sacrificed. They only scored hits on six ships. They sank the *LSM-59* and *Barry* decoy. They damaged the *Curtiss, Halloran DE-305, LSM-213, LST-534* and killed some sailors. The Jap fighter escorts shot down a few CAP planes. The battle for Okinawa was over. Now every young man killed at Okinawa – Japanese or American - was getting the cruelest of dirty breaks.

Chapter 16

Callaghan Unluckiest DD of All

IT was like Christmas in July, according to Radarman Don Ball. The USS *Callaghan* (DD-792) had just received word that they would be replaced on picket duty in two days. They would be heading eastward towards San Francisco. They were finally going home after 18 long months at sea. Nobody slept that night. The excitement was too much. Ball was thinking about his family back home in Oregon.

The *Callaghan* was patrolling RP station #9A on 27 July 1945. They assumed the Fighter Director role and led their formation 70 miles west of Okinawa. *Callaghan* was accompanied by the destroyers *Pritchett* and *Cassin Young* plus three LCS(L)s. The ground battle on Okinawa was over. Japanese troops were surrendering in numbers never seen in previous campaigns. But the Navy still had their hands full due to smaller kamikaze attacks. These were more dangerous than the massive Kikusui raids. Hundreds of planes were easily detected on radar and intercepted by CAP squadrons. These smaller raids would attack after dark. They could sneak in under radar and strike at any time. Japan's air attacks had taken on a form of guerilla warfare.

It was 5 February 1944 when a newly built USS *Callaghan* sailed from the West Coast. She had been named in honor of Rear Admiral Daniel J. Callaghan. He was killed on the cruiser *San Francisco* at Guadalcanal. *Callaghan's* new crew went right into action with the fast-striking 5th Fleet. They screened and supported raids on the Palau islands, Yap, Ulithi, Woleai and Hollandia during their first year of the war. In 1945 they participated in raids on Formosa, Indo-China, Hong Kong and now Okinawa. The embattled picket line at Okinawa had proven to be the most dangerous duty of all. But now the end of war was near. The Japanese fleet had ceased to exist. The torpedo racks on a destroyer had become useless armament. Torpedomen Sam Elrod and Jehu Frasheur were reassigned to an aft 20mm gun mount for GQ. Elrod was the talker who communicated through headphones with the bridge. Frasheur was a loader. There was no need for these men to stand ready at the torpedoes. They had nothing to shoot at on the water…but just above the water was another story.

Shortly after midnight on 29 July, radar picked up a contact thirteen miles away and closing. The blip was small and moving slowly, at about 130 miles an hour. It was too small and slow for fighters or bombers. The bogey's course changes made it difficult for radar to keep the bearing and range. Bill Benton had just come off his watch on the helm when GQ sounded again. Before heading for his gun-station he grabbed a wad of cotton. The concussion from the five-inch guns was enough to burst ear drums. Benton wet his cotton and screwed it deep into his ears and headed aft. The five-inch guns opened when the slow-moving attacker was within range. Shell bursts with proximity fuses should have been visible if near a metal plane, but none were seen.

Bill Benton, USS Callaghan: *I had just been relieved from my watch station on the helm. The weather was clear and the sea calm. Radar had reported a contact thirteen miles out. I kept thinking, 13 is an* *unlucky number. We started taking evasive zig zag action. We had seen several torpedo planes use a slow course changing tactic before launching their torpedoes or bombs at very low altitude. But this attacker turned out to be an old Willow bi-plane trainer. The plane was virtually impossible to pick up on radar because it was constructed of wood and silk.*

The construction of a Willow trainer made it invisible to the five-inch proximity shells too. These high-tech shells were designed to explode when metal was detected. The plane's wooden and cloth fuselage made the shells ineffective. When the bi-plane came into view it was driven off by well-aimed 20mm fire. But the pilot circled and dove into the main deck on the fantail. A 250-pound bomb exploded in the after-engine room.

__Bill Benton, USS Callaghan:__ All hands in the engine room were killed instantly. The hull of the ship was split wide open and the stern was engulfed in flames. A second explosion followed when burning gasoline from the plane flowed into the magazine of No. 3 gun and set off the powder bags. Suddenly I was preparing to go in the water.

The second explosion came about 10 minutes after the plane hit. The rudder was now jammed to starboard and the stern was going down. The fantail was in chaos. Crews on surrounding ships saw the blast and were certain everyone on board had been killed.

__Jehu Frasheur, TM, USS Callaghan:__ Smoke was so bad no one could see. I was waiting for my buddy Sam to say something. I yelled for him a couple of times. But he didn't answer. I found where the head phones were plugged into the bulkhead and started tracing back to the phones. As I inched my way along, I kept yelling for Sam because the fantail was becoming awash. When I reached out again my hand went into his chest and rib cage. Something large had hit Sam square in the *chest. Death must have been immediate. I checked on Sam one more time before abandoning ship. Sam went down with his ship where he had died.*

The *Cassin Young* took over Fire Director duties and defense of the RP while *Pritchett* and the LCS small boys came to aid of *Callaghan*. This had not been a lone plane sneak attack. There were now eight or more of the Willow bi-planes circling and strafing the ships at RP #9A. The sea was all lit up from the blazing fire on *Callaghan*, making ships easy targets. *Cassin Young* gunners splashed one bi-plane that was headed for *Callaghan* plus another plane a couple miles away. *LCS(L)-125* moored their ship alongside *Callaghan*, poured on water and fought off planes. The bow of *Callaghan* kept rising as fires on the stern raged. A prepare-to-abandon ship order was passed. Most of the crew had gathered on the bow for safety. They helped one another secure life jackets. There were reminders of abandon ship protocol. Remove helmets, cross your legs and fold arms. A strapped helmet could break your neck when hitting the water. Hitting debris in the water with legs spread wide was even scarier. The bow was now 30 feet above the water. When the abandon ship order was given, nobody jumped overboard. Everyone was looking for someone to lead the way. Finally, Benton yelled, "Oh shoot" and jumped in. Everyone followed. Benton swam frantically to get away from the sinking. When he stopped, he was all alone.

Bill Benton, USS Callaghan: *When I hit the water, I started swimming away from the ship. I really must have been crazy, as I was singing as I was swimming. Why? I don't know. I was by myself and scared as hell. I was already about a hundred yards away from the ship when I turned around and looked. The Callaghan was in bad shape. She was burning with great intensity and the stern was low in the water. It was quiet, then I heard a splash, splash, "Help, help, I can't swim." It was a colored Stewards Mate. He was in trouble. I took off my life* *jacket and we both held on. I asked him how he got out so far if he couldn't swim. He didn't know. I thought, he must have been so scared he ran on water. When the ship finally sank, there was a huge explosion under water. The hot boilers blew when cold water hit them. The concussion felt like a firecracker going off in my rectum. Very painful.*

Benton and his companion joined up with a group of other shipmates. One guy had a flashlight. He flashed it trying to get someone to see their group. It worked. A Willow bi-plane swung low on the water and strafed them. Bullets splashed all around the group. Nobody was hit but they didn't flash the light anymore. They just hung on to one another and watched the show overhead. Marine night fighter pilots were on the scene in their Black Widows. Tracers would streak across the sky exploding bi-planes into balls of fire. Another Willow attacked a ship from a position between his target and Benton's group in the water. Shell bursts from the ship flew over their heads and splashed all around. Benton dove deep to escape the friendly fire. He came up with a nose bleed. With enemy planes circling, the rescue ships could not stop to pick up survivors. They laid smoke to hide ships and the men in the water. Finding them in the dark and under a blanket of smoke would be harder.

It was four and half hours before Benton and the others were found and rescued. They were too tired to climb the rope ladder. Sailors hauled them up and gave them a bottle of liquor. They were allowed two drinks to warm their innards. No more.

Bill Benton, USS Callaghan: *We were covered with black crude oil, head to toe. The Steward's Mate started laughing at me and said he thought I was his brother. I looked just like him.*

USS *Callaghan* (DD-792) was the 15th ship sunk on Okinawa radar picket line. She has the dubious honor of being the last ship ever sunk by a kamikaze. Unfortunately, she wasn't the last U.S. ship sunk in the war. On the very next night, 30 July 1945 the cruiser USS *Indianapolis* was heading for Leyte in the Philippines. She had just delivered the atom bomb to the B-29 airfield on Tinian. Either due to the secrecy of the mission or oversight, *Indianapolis* was not escorted by a destroyer with sonar. The Japanese submarine *I-58* intercepted *Indianapolis* and fired six torpedoes. Two of the torpedoes hit her and the ship sank in 12 minutes. Their SOS was never received. Over 800 men struggled to survive in the water for the next five days. Only 316 crewmen were lucky enough to still be alive when a navy patrol plane accidentally discovered them.

Ironically, the *Indianapolis* had delivered a weapon that would end the war and save thousands of American servicemen. Their mission was two weeks too late to save 47 sailors killed and 73 wounded on the *Callaghan*. With the end of the war just 15 days away, young men would continue to die needlessly.

Chapter 17

Kill with Silence

THE ground war at Okinawa was over by July of 1945. U.S. carriers, battleships and cruisers moved north to find new targets. Parachute rigger T.P. Oswald on the USS *Bennington* (CV-20) was delighted to be in waters off northern Japan. "Boy, it feels so good to be cold again," he wrote in his diary. "We're hitting airfields around Tokyo. Pilots say that no enemy planes were in the air. Flak over the target was heavy to meager. Lost one TBM (torpedo bomber) over target with no survivors."

Germany had been defeated. Japan's war machine was gasping. It appeared the war was nearly over. For those men who had survived kamikaze attacks, island invasions, or bombing missions over Japan, they hoped their luck wouldn't run out. About 200 Americans were still dying daily and not always from enemy fire. To die in the final weeks, days or hours of the war seemed so senseless.

T.P. Oswald, PR1/c, USS Bennington: July 1945 diary entries. A deck hand was putting air in a tail wheel tire when it blew up and tore the left side of his face off. We don't expect him to live. First hop preparing to takeoff today when a man on flight deck walked into a prop and was killed. A plane was given the cut to land signal, but something went wrong and the pilot gave throttle to take off, he pulled up too steep and stalled, fell over into the ocean on one wing and crashed; breaking into three pieces. The pilot was thrown clear but the crewman was trapped and went down with the plane.

Japan expected the next U.S. attack to be in late fall on the southern tip of their homeland. They were correct. General MacArthur's invasion of Kyushu was scheduled for November 1st. Japan's geography made this the obvious choice. This island provided a natural base of operations for the Americans. There were three very good landing beaches, several good harbors, and many airfields. Knowing this, Japan's Imperial Army would be able to accurately build a defensive plan. They also knew it would take months for American war planners to prepare for an invasion this large. Time was on Japan's side. The mindset of a militaristic society with no word for surrender was horrifying. American sailors and soldiers shuddered at what they'd be facing in Japan.

Emperor Hirohito announced an official policy called Ketsu-Go. It outlined how every man, woman and child would be called upon to defend Japan...and fight to the death. Marines had captured Jap code books at Iwo Jima. American code breakers – they called themselves "Magicians" – had decoded the entire Ketsu-Go Plan. It called for a total defense of Kyushu. Japan still had two million soldiers in the homeland, 32 million militia and 10,000 planes in hiding for use as kamikazes. Kamikaze attacks would avoid well defended battleships and carriers. Instead they would target supply and troop transport ships that would be easier to sink. Children were being trained as suicide bombers and women were armed with bamboo spears. Ancient canons, muskets and even bows and arrows would be used in defense. Thousands of troops were building bunkers and defenses all along their southern coast line. Their remaining warships would be beached or docked to provide artillery platforms that couldn't be sunk. They had several hundred midget subs that could be launched in harbors. Thousands of small craft would be converted to suicide torpedo boats. It would be a war of attrition. Japan hoped it would become too costly for Americans to endure.

Japanese Slogans, summer of 1945: *The sooner Americans come, the better…one hundred million Japanese die proudly.*

MacArthur's estimate of U.S. losses during the invasion of Kyushu was 106,000 casualties. His numbers were based on the averages taken from the last four years of war. After the carnage endured at Okinawa, most planners considered this to be conservative. All U.S. casualties for the Okinawa campaign totaled over 49,000. It took three months to secure the 463 square-mile island that was defended by 110,000 Japanese soldiers. In contrast, Kyushu covers fourteen thousand square miles and would be defended by millions of Japanese soldiers, militia and civilians. A more realistic estimate for conquering all of Japan was set at half million dead and 4 million wounded. If this were true, it would be a greater loss than all American's killed and wounded in the previous four years of war. Ending the war without a ground invasion was critical.

General Curtis LeMay was making every effort to bomb Japan into submission. His fire-bombing tactic was brutally effective. Hundreds of thousands of civilians had been killed and millions were homeless. LeMay's B-29s were based on airfields at Tinian and at the Saipan group of islands 1500 miles south of Japan. Marines had captured the islands in August of 1944. By the end of July target planners were telling LeMay, "There are no more targets within range of our B-29s." So, he extended their range by reducing weight. All their defensive guns were removed except one tail gun. The Flying Fortresses had become cargo planes for incendiary bombs.

T.P. Oswald, PR1/c, USS Bennington: Aug. 5, diary entry. Our losses on Benni were not good on July 28 with six planes shot down. We haven't had another strike in 7 days now. It seems we are in the way of the Army's B-29s. We hit too many places at the same time and cause too much smoke. The B-29 pilots can't see their target. So, we are wasting time out here right now.

President Truman was briefed on Ketsu-Go and casualty estimates for Operation Downfall. He had sent the Potsdam Declaration to Japan. It warned of "prompt and utter destruction." There had been no reply. There is a Japanese word used for contempt. "Mokusatsu" does not translate well in English but the best attempt is "to kill with silent contempt." Truman seethed with Japan's refusal to respond. B-29s were ordered to fly over the city of Hiroshima on 3 August. This was one city that had not been bombed yet. It was very flat, had no known POW camps and was headquarters for over 40,000 soldiers. It was a good target. When the bomb bay doors opened, thousands of 4x8 sheets of paper floated out. They read in Japanese, "Civilians, evacuate at once. Your city has been targeted for destruction."

Again, there was no response from Japan. Truman considered the American lives that would be lost if the war continued. His decision is easy. He gives the order to use the Atom bombs. Two bombs have already been delivered to the air base on Tinian. A third is being built. He leaves the time and date up to the military. On 6 August, Colonel Paul Tibbets pilots the *Enola Gay* over Hiroshima. The Atom bomb is dropped from 31,000 feet destroying the city 43 seconds later. News of the successful bombing flashes around the world and is received with shock, horror and elation. For some, all the emotions were interwoven. But for U.S. troops facing a blood bath in Japan, it's elation. "Thank God for the bomb," is the most common refrain. Everyone thinks the war is over. It's not.

Truman sends another ultimatum to Japan. He warns of "total destruction." Japan is silent. Plans to drop a second A-bomb move forward. Kokura is the next target. Major Chuck Sweeny's *Bockscar* uses the entire runway before lifting off on the second A-bomb mission. This five ton bomb is bigger and heavier than the first. It's also live. It had to be armed while still at Tinian. Ground crews are thankful to see *Bockscar's* cargo disappear into the night sky. Kokura is lucky. Cloud cover and smoke from B-29 fire bombings mask the city. Sweeny is forced to divert to an alternate target. Nagasaki is home to Mitsubishi Steel where they produce firearms and torpedoes. It's close enough to Hiroshima that some survivors from the first bomb have found refuge in Nagasaki. On 9 August 1945, this city is destroyed too. The killing continues.

Truman must decide if he should drop a third atomic bomb. The next target is going to be Tokyo. He wants Japan to surrender. But is willing to do whatever it takes to save American lives. Truman tells Winston Churchill, "When you have to deal with a beast you have to treat him as a beast." In Russia, Joseph Stalin sees the end is near for Japan. He wants more spoils of war. Russia declares war on Japan and invades Manchuria.

Japan is now fighting on two fronts. They face total annihilation from the new weapon. In Tokyo, Hirohito addresses his cabinet. With tears in his eyes he tells them "It is now necessary to bear the unbearable." The morning of 10 August 1945 Truman receives communication from Japan through neutral Switzerland. Japan will accept the Potsdam Declaration with one condition. His Majesty, Emperor Hirohito, must remain in charge. That's not acceptable. Truman makes a counter offer. Hirohito can remain on the throne but must answer to the Supreme Commander of Allied powers. The amended declaration is delivered by air drop. Thousands of Potsdam Declaration leaflets rain down on the bewildered populace of Tokyo. The surrender terms can no longer be ignored. But silence from Japan continues.

T.P Oswald PR1/c, USS Bennington: Aug. 14 diary entry. There has been word that the Japs have had enough of our atom bombs and are ready to quit if they can keep the emperor. We heard that was OK if the EMP took orders from us. They have not done any more about it so we will keep on bombing the hell out of them. I hope they use a lot of atom bombs in the next few days. We are getting a blue jacket party (dress blues) ready if Japan gives up. This looks like a deal all the way through. My name is on the list of men for this party.

News of possible surrender has filtered down through the rank and file of U.S troops. Celebrating has already begun. Some believe the war is already over. For three days Truman waits for Japan's response. He's frustrated and angry at their contempt. The third atom bomb is not ready. He orders General LeMay to, "Give 'em everything you got."

The B-29 air crews on Tinian, Saipan and Guam have already been celebrating the expected war's end. Some are drunk or hung over when they are ordered into briefing rooms. They are shocked to hear they will be part of a massive bombing mission involving 828 planes. Their targets will be over 1,500 miles away. One target is Japan's last working oil refinery located on Akita Island at the northern tip of their homeland. It will require flying 3800 miles round trip and 17 hours in the air. This will test the endurance of both men and planes. Other distant military targets were identified all over Japan. They'd be lightly defended because Japan considered them beyond the range of B-29s. Target planners had determined the stripped-down B-29s could reach these targets and return... but just barely. They'd be joined by 186 fighter planes at Iwo Jima. These fighters would provide some defense for the nearly defenseless bombers.

Over 9,000 airmen would be involved in what became WWII's last raid over Japan. All of them thought their war was over. All of them knew the average loss rate for recent missions was about one percent.

The probability was high for at least eight planes to be lost due to mechanical problems, human error, or being shot down. Running out of gas was an added risk on this mission. They began taking off at 0500 on 14 August 1945. Pilots were told they might be called back if surrender terms were accepted. The code word to abort the mission would be "apple."

Dallas Bowman, 2ⁿᵈ Lt., Army Air Corps: The bomb had just been dropped on Nagasaki, but the Japanese did not respond. Expectations were high that the war was over. It was just word of mouth. There was no TV back then. No personal radios, the only thing we got was word of mouth, by telephone and short-wave radio.

An Imperial Message was broadcast as the B-29s were flying toward Japan. It announced that acceptance of the Potsdam Declaration would be coming soon. Unfortunately for thousands of Japanese citizens (and American aircrews), the message was too ambiguous. Japan's leaders continued to put more precedence in "saving face" than saving their people. The B-29s would not be called back.

Emperor Hirohito recorded his message to Japan that night. The recording and a signed document were hidden in a safe at the Imperial Palace. His recording would be broadcast on radio. Newspapers were given this news release to insure all of Japan would be listening to the radio at noon the next day. The Emperor's lack of urgency nearly extended the war indefinitely.

Militant rebels of the Imperial Japanese Army were in revolt. They took over the Imperial Palace the night of 14 August in hopes of stopping the surrender announcement. They searched all night – in the dark - for the Emperor's recording. They were hampered by a black out. The B-29s heading for Akita Oil Refinery passed directly over Tokyo. Fearing another atom bomb, the city was blacked out until morning. Hirohito and his staff were locked safely away in his bomb shelter. B-29s obliterated the Akita Oil Refinery as Japan's warlords searched the palace with flashlights. Their attempt to continue the war ended when loyal Palace Troops overtook the revolt in the morning. The Emperor's recorded broadcast shocked his nation. The rest of the world rejoiced.

B-29 crews heard a special bulletin during their return flight. The Emperor would issue his acceptance of the Potsdam Declaration later that day. Crews whooped and hollered. One normally "by-the-book" pilot pulled his plane into a series of wild maneuvers. Aircrews were ecstatic and relieved. They'd never have to test their luck over Japan again.

This was a war that began as a fight for oil and ended only when Japan's supply ran out. The war was finally over. But not for Japan's warlords who considered surrender worse than death. Some committed a ritual suicide called Hari Kari. Others were determined to go down fighting. This was the mindset Truman had feared.

Ernie Pyle's last column was found in his pocket the day he was killed near Okinawa. The famous war correspondent had spent two and half years with GI's in Europe. He saw the senseless death and misery continue after Germany was beaten. Now he worried that Japan would continue to fight for honor while men died in vain. These are the last words he would ever write.

> **Ernie Pyle, War Correspondent:** *We hope above all things that Japan won't make the same stubborn mistakes that Germany did. You must credit Germany for her courage in adversity, but you can doubt her good common sense in fighting blindly on long after there was any doubt whatever about the outcome.*

The Emperor's message was confusing. It never used the word surrender. His sentences rambled in an Imperial dialect many did not understand. "We have decided to effect a settlement of present situation by resorting to an extraordinary measure." This wording left many citizens asking what it meant. For the radical warlords, it meant one thing. They'd go down fighting. Orders to lay down arms had not been received yet. Navy Captain Kozono addressed his air group. He told them surrender means the end of our national essence. To obey will be treason. Join me to destroy the enemy. His men shouted back their famous war cry, "Banzai."

At the Oita Naval Air Base in northern Kyushu a similar scene was unfolding. Vice Admiral Matome Ugaki had commanded the naval kamikaze units. He was resolved to die fighting. He had sent thousands of young men to certain death in kamikaze attacks. "I must pay for it," he said. Ugaki was preparing for the final kamikaze mission. He ordered three planes to be readied. He wrote a farewell in his diary and called for vengeance. Ugaki arrived at the air base carrying a Samurai sword and wearing an airman's uniform with no insignia. When he arrived at the air base there were 11 Judy bombers and 22 crewmembers waiting for him. He asked the men if they were all willing to die with him. Every hand went up. He joined a two-man crew and they took off for Okinawa. Four of the planes developed mechanical problems and returned. At 1925 hours Ugaki radioed back that his plane was diving toward a target. Nothing more was ever heard from the remaining seven planes.

No reports of successful kamikaze attacks showed up in any action reports that night. It's likely they were all shot down by anti-aircraft fire or night fighter planes. The following morning a landing craft crew found a plane crash on the shore of a small Ryukyu island. The smoldering remains of a cockpit held three mangled bodies. A short sword was found nearby.

At Okinawa, there were Japanese troops hiding in caves and fighting a guerilla war. They never heard the Emperor on August 15th. They had no access to radio communications. That night they watched a fireworks display. Tracers and shell blasts lit up the night sky over the U.S. fleet. Scouts came back and reported the Americans were celebrating a victory. They saw soldiers drinking beer and shooting their guns in the air. Without orders or a command structure, Japanese guerillas would continue to fight for years after the war.

At a POW camp on Kyushu there were 16 captured B-29 crewmen. Japanese soldiers loaded them on a truck and drove them up to a wooded hill. They were told to strip off their clothes. Then they were led into the woods one by one and beheaded.

On 15 August 1945 the USS *Heermann* (DD-532) was on radar picket duty 200 miles southeast of Tokyo. Machinist Mate 3/c Norman Halverson was up on deck watching the sun come up over an ocean that was finally at peace. Several hours earlier the *Heermann* learned the war was over. The official date/time for the end of WWII was 14 August at 2300 hours. They had received an announcement to end all hostilities.

The *Heermann* had barely survived two years of war. She had been attached to the *Taffy-3* Escort Carrier group during the Battle of Samar in October of 1944. Their light force of destroyers and six "baby flattops" were surprised by the powerful Japanese fleet that included the battleship *Yamato*. *Heermann* and three other destroyers made a suicidal torpedo charge through a hail of shells. They disrupted the Jap attack enough to allow the carriers to escape. *Heermann*, though damaged badly, was the only destroyer that wasn't sunk. Her Captain received the Navy Cross.

Now Halverson was hanging out with some buddies on the port side near the five-inch mount. Everyone was relieved the war was finally over, and they had survived. Halverson thought about getting back home to his family in Sioux Rapids, Iowa. Radar picked up a suspicious bogey and they went to general quarters. A plane emerged from a cloud bank and began a dive toward the *Heermann*. It was a kamikaze. Alert gunners spotted the plane and several guns opened up. Puffs of exploding shells surrounded the plane. It kept coming. Now 40mm tracers started ripping at the fuselage. The plane tipped and crashed into the ocean.

Norman Halverson, MM3/c, USS Heermann: I could see the pilot of the plane very clearly. I think I was more scared after the plane crashed. We were all relieved it was the pilot and not us.

The *Heermann* is credited with firing the last official shots of the war. There were many Japanese units on remote islands that did not receive any word yet. And there were warlords and guerillas who planned to fight on. The Russians continued the fight in Manchuria for a couple more weeks. A global conflict the size and scope of WWII doesn't turn off like a faucet. It would continue to drip and people would continue to die.

The *Heermann* probably splashed the last kamikaze. It was a Japanese weapon developed out of desperation when a nation had their backs to the wall. The fervor of the young pilots is something sailors found difficult to understand. The pilot who attacked *Heermann* might have shared the feelings of Hisao Horiyama.

Hisao Horiyama, Kamikaze Pilot: "I couldn't hear the radio announcement on the radio very well because of the static. One person started crying loudly. That's when I knew we had lost the war. I felt bad that I hadn't been able to sacrifice myself for my country. My comrades who had died would be remembered in infinite glory, but I had missed my chance to die in the same way. I felt like I had let everyone down."

On the USS *Bennington*, Thomas Patrick Oswald made a couple of final entries in his war diary. In all caps he wrote, "THE END OF WORLD WAR II" But at the bottom of the page was one more entry.

T.P. Oswald, PR1/c, USS Bennington: Aug. 15, diary entry - It seems that there is always some son of a gun that doesn't get the word. Today, after the war was over we were under attack by Jap planes, which of course were shot out of the sky. The Rising sun is now Sunk.

Thomas Patrick Oswald was aware of the historic significance of his time aboard the USS Bennington. He kept a detailed diary. Had his diary been discovered it would have earned him a hearing at Captains Mast and certain punishment.

Thomas Patrick Oswald from Chicago, joined Division 82 on the USS Bennington 1 April 1944. He began keeping a diary that same day. As a parachute rigger, he had close contact with pilots and may have been involved in debriefings. His diary entries included many details of torpedo plane mission results.

This last photo of Vice Admiral Matome Ugaki was taken before he led a final kamikaze attack. He wore a simple uniform with no insignia and carried a Samurai Warrior sword.

Chapter 18

It's Over

EMPEROR Hirohito's recorded radio address was broadcast throughout Japan's empire. Few of his citizens had ever heard him speak. His high-pitched voice and use of an archaic form of the Japanese language left many citizens shocked and confused. He asks them to bear the unbearable and help pave the way for peace. He never says they were surrendering. But eventually it sinks in and the national mourning begins. Hundreds of military leaders commit suicide. POWs are executed in one last act of rage and terror. Government offices begin burning files to cover up war crimes.

The rest of the world breaths a collective sigh of relief and begins celebrating. Horns honk, bells ring, and guns are fired in the air. In cities and towns and military bases, everyone is out in the street whooping and hollering. In bars the drinks are free to anyone in uniform. People are cheering, laughing, hugging and kissing. When one sailor sees a nurse on Times Square, the hugging and kissing becomes legendary.

George Mendonsa and the crew of *The Sullivans* had been in the Pacific for two years. On 11 May 1945 they rescued 166 sailors from the *Bunker Hill* after it was hit by kamikazes. Soon after, *The Sullivans* was ordered home. Mendonsa's ship steamed into San Francisco

Harbor in early August 1945. Mendonsa went on leave and headed for home to Newport, Rhode Island. While home he was introduced to his brother-in-law's niece. She was 20 and Mendonsa was 22. He was immediately smitten with her.

George Mendonsa, QM1/c, USS The Sullivans: The niece was beautiful. I kept in touch with her by phone. On my last day of leave I went to New York and met the niece there. I made reservations and we went to Radio City Music Hall to see The Rockettes. Late in the day, all the people out on the street started pounding on the door. We're in the theatre wondering what is going on outside. They stopped the show, put the lights on and said, "The War is over. The Japs have surrendered."

Everyone ran out onto the street. Mendonsa and his date went down to Times Square. They went into Childs Bar, just a few blocks away. The bartenders had glasses lined up all along the bar. They kept filling them up. "I downed quite a few drinks," George says. Then he and his date went back out to Times Square. At Seventh Avenue and 44th Street, George caught sight of a woman in a nurse's uniform. It reminded him of the nurses on the hospital ships at Okinawa. He had seen the nurses helping the wounded sailors from the *Bunker Hill.*

George Mendonsa, QM1/c: Everyone was hitting the booze and I had been too. Finally, after a while it was getting close to my flight time, to fly out of New York and go back to Frisco. We left Childs Bar and I'm going down Times Square to get on the subway and I saw a nurse. When I saw the nurse...I remembered back to seeing what nurses on the hospital ships had done for the sailors on the Bunker Hill. I always remembered how those nurses helped those wounded men. Now the war is over and I had drank quite a few drinks. I was half bombed. So, I saw this nurse walking and I grabbed her instinctively and kissed her. After I kissed her she went her way and I went mine.

Mendonsa headed down to the subway, kissed his date goodbye and promised to stay in touch. Neither of them were aware that photographer, Alfred Eisenstaedt, had seen him kiss the nurse and captured the moment on film. The picture ran in Life Magazine. It became one of the most iconic photos of WWII. When the photo published again on the cover of a Life Magazine special issue, Mendonsa realized he was the sailor. His date, now his wife, can be seen behind him in the photo. The nurse was identified as Greta Zimmer.

The Times Square crowd was estimated at over two million that day. First word of the Japanese surrender had been flashed as a headline on the Times Square news ticker. The big ticker billboard was called the "Zipper." It read, "Official: Truman Announces Japanese Surrender."

In Washington D.C. thousands lined the fence outside the White House. They chanted Truman's name until he stepped out on a balcony. He didn't try to speak. Nobody would have heard the words. He just held up two fingers in the "V" for victory sign. Confetti poured out of office windows. When that ran out goose feathers from pillows were used.

In Chicago, the Mayor had planned for this day. By prior arrangement all taverns in the city were ordered closed when the surrender was announced. A half million sober revelers jitterbugged down State Street. They were drunk with joy.

In San Francisco, one of the largest Navy towns in the country, no such precaution had been taken. Navy enlistees, who had never served in a war zone, turned the celebration into a three-night orgy of drunkenness and rioting. A third of the USS *Hadley* crew had recently arrived in Frisco on a troop ship. Bob Bell, Perry Camp, and Tex McCreight, joined hundreds of other petty officers assigned to Shore Patrol. The city was so out of control they just watched in disgust. There was nothing they could do without becoming one of the statistics.

Worshipers by the thousands flocked to churches to pray and give thanks for the war's end. Families who had lost loved ones mourned their sacrifice. Young men found themselves treated like heroes for doing nothing more than being in uniform. Eighteen year-old Carmon Howe was home on leave when the war ended. He was on a train heading into Milwaukee when he heard the news. By the time he got downtown the celebrating had already begun. Everywhere he went people wanted to buy him a drink. There was no drinking age for sailors in dress whites that day.

Howe would be joining the crew of the USS *Rotanin*, a cargo ship that became a troop transport after the war. The first sea story he heard was how his shipmates celebrated at war's end. "They were three days out from Pearl Harbor when the war ended," said Howe. "The supply officer broke out some five-inch ammo. He made sure no other ships were in range. Then he fired a 21-gun Presidential salute to the moon."

While the folks in the states celebrated wildly, those in the Pacific and those who had just returned were more subdued. The USS *Aaron Ward* had limped home under her own power. On 14 August she was on keel blocks in dry dock number two of the New York Navy Yard. Suddenly, every siren, bell and horn in the shipyard was blasting in celebration of the surrender. The *Aaron Ward* was high and dry with no boiler steam of her own. She did have one steam hose coming through the shore lines. A shipmate ran up to the bridge and gave the whistle a couple of good healthy toots. That honored the memory of the men who didn't return with them. Some of the *Aaron Ward* shipmates were still in Okinawa buried under white crosses.

On the night of the surrender, troops at Okinawa put on a huge pyrotechnics display. Ships fired their guns into the sky until they were ordered to shut down. Commanders feared casualties from all the friendly fire. But on VJ Day all the guns at Okinawa spoke one last time. Every gun on every ship and shore battery all fired one joyous shot at an appointed hour. It shook the entire Ryukyu chain of islands.

Marines and GIs who had fought from fox holes on Okinawa were simply relieved. Many were stunned and in disbelief that they had survived. They no longer had to prepare for an invasion of Japan. These men didn't feel right about celebrating while camped at Okinawa. Many of their units had suffered over 50 percent casualties. It would have been like throwing a beer party in a cemetery. That's what Okinawa had become.

On *LSM(R)-198* there was no celebration at all. They had been sent out on radar picket duty 100 miles south of Japan. Kamikaze attacks were still being reported. They were on high alert. Then they received orders to do an about face and head for Hawaii. They found out the next day the war was over. What a relief. There would be no more RP duty. No more watching the skies and waiting for kamikazes to crash into their ship.

Navy corpsman Charles Daniel was aboard the hospital and troop transport ship USS *Rixey*. Their orders were to pick up the half dead American POWs in the Philippines, and then the many wounded soldiers from Okinawa. Daniel had dug bullets out of the bloodied bodies of soldiers all across the Pacific. He'd seen more burials at sea than he could count. When the *Rixey* announced that Japan had surrendered the reaction of the crew was "calm." Daniel went topside and smoked a cigar. As he looked over the ocean, for the first time in the war he could see lights on ships. They were no longer darkened to prevent submarine attacks. His thought turned to his wife and the one month old daughter he had not yet met. The words of a big band tune by Vaughn Monroe streamed through his mind.

"When the lights go on again all over the world. And the boys are home again all over the world. And rain or snow is all that may fall from the skies above. A kiss won't mean Goodbye, but Hello to love."

On VJ Day, sailor George Mendonsa celebrated famously on Times Square. Seeing a nurse made him flash back to Okinawa. He remembered how nurses cared for the burned sailors from the Bunker Hill. The kiss was in gratitude. The photo, by Alfred Eisenstaedt, was in Life Magazine. Mendonsa would be immortalized as "The Kissing Sailor."

George Mendonsa, QM1/c, USS The Sullivans aka "The Kissing Sailor"

Chapter 19

LSM(R)-411 Saved
by the Bomb

IN the spring of 1945 the final push of the Pacific War hit full speed. Amphibious craft were being launched at Charleston, Virginia shipyards at a record pace. High school boys training for the "gator" crews were under the command of officers who were called "90-day wonders." Most of the men in these crews had never been to sea.

One young sailor was laying on a bottom bunk aboard *LSM(R)-411*. He inhaled a cigarette and held the smoke in a couple of seconds longer than the drag before. He choked when he exhaled a noxious plume. The bunk above - just eighteen inches over his nose - was blurry. He felt nauseous. To get sick would be embarrassing, because his legs felt too rubbery to make it to the head.

Seaman Robert Veesenmeyer was learning to smoke. Lying down was the only way he could inhale and keep from falling down. At age 17 the lanky young man weighed all of 120 pounds soaking wet in his dress blues. Smoking didn't agree with him. But he was determined to learn. Veesenmeyer wanted to appear older. He needed to fit in and gain the trust of his shipmates. They all needed to be confident about the guy next to them. The *411* was heading for the invasion of Japan.

Just seven months earlier Veesenmeyer was a first semester senior at Schurz High School in Chicago. He had a best girl, best buddy, part time job and a love for big band music. He was bored with learning. School was secondary to having fun. He would cut school to go see Tommy Dorsey or Glenn Miller play downtown. His dad gave him an ultimatum... go to school or join the Navy. So now he learned to chip paint, swab decks, take orders and smoke.

The *LSM(R)-411* (Landing Ship Medium Rocket) was an amphibious rocket ship. This new class of ships was designed specifically to fire aircraft type rockets. A dozen other LSM(R)s were already serving with the fleet at Okinawa. These "Interim" LSM(R)s had been converted from standard LSMs. They proved their worth during landings on Okinawa and the surrounding islands. Kamikazes had already sunk three of the interim LSM(R)s. Those ships needed to be replaced. Many more would be needed for the next campaign. The Navy designed a new "Ultimate" LSM(R) Class from the keel up. Forty-eight of these rockets ships would lead the way during landings on Kyushu beaches at the southern tip of Japan.

The *411* was commissioned in Charleston Harbor on 23 May 1945. For the sailors stationed along the east coast, the Pacific war was 9,000 miles away and still a distant thought. During the spring and summer of 1945, Veesenmeyer was busy growing up and learning the ways of the Navy. He discovered life aboard ship was hard work. What he learned each day was critical to his safety and the survival of his ship. He'd write his girlfriend, Shirley, most every night. His letters showed a homesick boy, who was becoming a man.

Robert (Bob) Veesenmeyer, SM2/c, LSM(R)-411: *(Letter dated May 22, 1945) Well Shirley, tomorrow we get in our whites and they are going to christen our ship. They are going to waste a whole bottle of champagne. I don't think it's worth a coke! But as soon as it is* *launched we change into our dungarees and start loading supplies and food. We start at 4 pm – and this is the truth – we work all night loading that stuff. So I guess I'll be pretty tired.*

Veesenmeyer went through boot camp at Great Lakes during January and February of 1945. On day one he was issued a sea bag of uniforms, and gear that weighed half as much as he did. He had to drag it across the drill field to his barracks. After eight weeks of marching, conditioning and classes he was glad to be sent to the Amphibious Training Center at Little Creek, Virginia. He'd never traveled much beyond Chicago. While on the east coast he saw New York, Washington D.C., Charleston and the infamous navy town of Norfolk, Virginia. Now training had more of a purpose. Becoming part of a specialized crew gave these men some pride. The amphibious ships were capable of landing right up on a beach. Crews called themselves "gators." They'd be subjected to mortars, machine guns and small arms fire during an invasion. The bigger warships never experienced this type of close-up action.

Navy planners realized early in the war that beach landings would be required for invading foreign shores. For it to be successful, landing large numbers of troops and equipment while under fire, required specialized training. The order first went out to build an amphibious force in 1942. Carrying the war to Europe and the Pacific would require landing tens of thousands of men and their equipment on beaches. The Amphibious Training Command (ATC) was created in March of that year. It began with an eight man staff, no equipment or even office space. The Little Creek Amphibious Base became a beehive of activity throughout the war. Over 360,000 navy, Marine and army personnel passed through the training center. Most training techniques were developed from scratch. By 1945 Little Creek had trained an amphibious force for 60,000 vessels.

The British developed the original landing craft designs for commando raids against Germany. The need for different kinds of landing craft soon became obvious. The most critical need was for large armored craft capable of crossing the seas. This new class of ships had to deliver many men and heavy equipment while under fire. The LSM (Landing Ship Medium) was born. Training for these "gators of the Pacific," became the primary focus of the amphibious base at Little Creek.

There were four ship types using the base for training... the LSM (Landing Ship Medium), LCU (Landing Craft Utility), LCI (Landing Craft Infantry), and LCVP (Landing Craft Vehicle Personnel). Veesenmeyer learned he'd be assigned to the new LSM(R) rocket ships being built at Charleston Ship Yard. His 203-foot ship carried a complement of 6 officers and 137 enlisted. It also carried ammunition for 15 gun mounts and 20 rocket launcher tubes. It was often called a mini-battleship due its firepower. Veesenmeyer called it a floating bomb. His bunk was over the rocket magazine. One bomb, one torpedo or one kamikaze could blow one of these ships right out of the water. Its mission was to escort landing craft up to an invasion beach and fire mass salvos of rockets. This would keep defenders hunkered down long enough for infantry to disembark and get a beach foothold. The LSM(R) mission was extremely dangerous duty.

Robert Veesenmeyer, SM2/c: (Letter dated May 24, 1945) I am aboard our little ship and is it ever crowded. I'm in a compartment that has nine bunks in it,(stacked three high) and I've got the bottom bunk which is 5 inches from the deck and has 18 inches between my bunk and the bunk above me. So you can see it's kind of hard to move around.

Top bunks were no roomier than a bottom. The overhead (ceiling) was a maze of fuel transfer piping, vent ducts and hanging electrical wires. The ducts provided outside air coming from fans on the main deck. During inclement weather, ducts had to be closed to keep sea water out. It was hot and stuffy in crew compartments. The largest sleeping compartment was amidships. It billeted 60 sailors. Racks were stacked four high with 30-inch wide aisles. Each rack was 72 inches long. Guys over six feet tall hung over. They slept head-to-feet to cut down on germ transfer. Sleeping below a 6 foot 2 inch sailor meant smelling his feet all night. No room for chairs or tables. Relaxing in this compartment meant standing or laying down.

A 30-inch square hatch and ladder provided access to other compartments. While going up the ladder, Veesenmeyer learned the hard way not to hit his head on the hatch cover. "The ship is awfully crowded. It's so darn small. It's hard to get used to running up and down those hatchways without falling down or bumping your head." He was amazed by the old salts (guys in their 20s with two years at sea) who could run up a ladder with a cigarette in one hand and coffee in the other!

Robert Veesenmeyer, SM2/c: (Letter dated May 25, 1945) After the ship was christened yesterday we started to load the gear and we worked from 3:30 to about 11:30 p.m. and boy am I tired. And then today we went to the armory and loaded ammunition from 10 a.m. to 4:30 p.m. and that was steady work. The only time we had off was 20 minutes for chow. That ammunition is really heavy too! I was down in a little hole below deck loading it. I never worked so hard in all my life and that is the truth. I'm sore all over.

Work was hard aboard ship. There were no days off. But men were fed well. Navy chow is something a sailor either loves or hates. There is no in between. Veesenmeyer liked the navy chow. He never understood why guys complained about creamed chipped beef on toast, named "SOS" to those who loathed it. He liked it – even for breakfast. "The chow is really good, and you get a lot of it," he wrote. Each morning would begin with the shrill whistle from the boatswain's pipe. "Good Morning Rocket Ship Sailors. Reveille at 0600. Breakfast for the crew. Sweepers man your brooms, give the ship a clean sweep down fore and aft, sweep down all lower decks, ladder backs and passageways, empty all trash on the fantail... now sweepers." Despite close quarters the *411* crew was soon learning to function as a unit. But at the end of a work day it was every man for himself.

When in port, the *411* would "Secure from Work," at 1545 hours (3:45 PM). The first liberty boat to shore would leave at 1600 hours. The first 20 guys on the quarterdeck would make the liberty boat. It was a mad scramble. They raced to turn in tools, shower and shave. Pulling on dress uniforms meant fastening 13 buttons. Veesenmeyer complained of sore fingers from buttoning his dang trouser flap. The Navy put 13 buttons on the flap - a 175-year-old navy tradition intended to honor the 13 original colonies. Veesenmeyer learned the ropes. Liberty on base or in town was fun for a 17 year-old.

With thousands of navy and Marine personnel at the training center, the town of Little Creek and the amphibious base became their playground during off hours. A weekly newsletter called the "Gator" provided base news and entertainment information. The "Gator' issue of 10 March 1945 announced the three year anniversary for the Amphibious Training Center. Navy celebrations of this type meant Admiral inspections. Every vessel and sailor would need to be spit-shine ready on Friday. Gator crews looked forward to letting loose that night. An article in the "Gator" issue, was headlined "Gala Fight Show in Norfolk To Mark ATC Anniversary." On Friday night a ten man team of amphib boxers would meet opponents from Camp Bradford. Tony Zale, the middleweight champion of the world and amphibious base boxing instructor, would referee the bouts. All servicemen in uniform got in free. Veesenmeyer sent home a photo of Zale and wrote, "I've seen him every day so far and he is one swell guy." The newsletter carried war news and photos. There were stories from sailors who'd seen action in Europe and the Pacific. A full page of Navy humor provided only those jokes clean enough to send home to parents and girlfriends. Coming events listed nightly movies in the Rec Hall that included "Here Come the Coeds" with Abbott and

Costello and an all hands dance on Thursday night. The Gator Girl photo of the week was movie star Esther Williams in her swim suit.

The "Gator" newsletters were designed to keep men informed, entertained and build morale for their branch of the Navy. Unfortunately, the amphib sailors were looked at with a bit of disdain by the crews of battleships and cruisers. A transfer to the amphibious branch was considered a demotion by many officers. Sailors who screwed up on capital ships were often reassigned to the amphibs. To address this feeling of inferiority an amphibious patch was designed to be worn on dress uniforms. The LSM(R) crews didn't need to feel special. They already knew their ships had a special mission. They'd be on the tip of the spear for the invasion of Japan. Instructors in training classes told them that heavy casualties were expected. The LSM(R) crews wore their Gator patch with pride and a bit of swagger.

The original LSM was a flat-bottomed ship with a bow that opened and a ramp that could be lowered onto a beach. It could land five manned tanks or vehicles, retract off the beach and return with more men, equipment and supplies. They were armed with 20mm and 40mm guns. During the early Pacific invasions, the first wave of Marines suffered very high casualties. Heavy shore bombardment from battleships, cruisers and destroyers had to be lifted when landing craft were still several hundred yards from shore. More firepower was needed to keep defenders' heads down while Marines hit the beach. The idea of a rocket ship was conceived.

The LSM hull was the best available platform for the close-in rocket support. Aircraft type rockets could deliver a massive amount of firepower on enemy positions at close range. This would enable infantry to disembark and gain a foothold on landing beaches. The first 12 LSM(R)s were converted from LSMs already being built. Bow doors were welded shut and rocket launching platforms installed. These "Interim" rocket ships were needed immediately for the invasion of Okinawa. Their crews earned praise from Marines who walked ashore after devastating barrages on the Ryukyu islands.

Destroyermen gained respect for the LSM(R) sailors too. The rocket ships provided valuable anti-aircraft support on the picket line and came to the rescue of many destroyers hit by kamikazes. Their performance at Okinawa convinced the Navy they needed more of these ships for the invasion of Japan.

The new "Ultimate" LSM(R)s were built as rocket ships from the basic LSM hull and up. They were armed with 30 caliber, 50 caliber, 20mm and 40mm guns. They had four 4.2 inch mortars and a five-inch dual purpose gun mount. The ten, twin tube continuous loading rocket launchers could fire 240 five-inch rockets in one minute. Each rocket carried the explosive force of an eight-inch shell fired from a heavy cruiser. A rocket barrage could rain down total devastation on a small geographic target. Marines could land more safely. Charleston and Houston shipyards built this new group of 48 LSM(R)s. Workers dubbed them the "mighty midgets." These ships were being laid down, built and launched within 30 days.

Robert Veesenmeyer, SM2/c: (letter dated May 27, 1945) I didn't write last night because I was pretty tired and turned in early. We were out all day on a trial run firing all our guns. Some of the fellows got pretty sea sick and were hanging over the side getting rid of their morning chow. For some darn reason I didn't get sick, but probably will some other time. There were about eight porpoises following us. They were fun to watch. The largest was about 12 feet long.

The flat bottomed LSM(R)s were a rough riding ship. They drew only seven feet of water forward and nine feet aft. The twin screws were recessed into the bottom of the hull so the ship could run right up on the beach. These ships were incredibly tippy. Crews joked that their ship rolled when somebody shifted from one foot to the other. Sea sickness was common.

The invasion for Japan was scheduled for 1 November 1945. Throughout the month of June, LSM(R) crews trained on gunnery every day. They'd bombard deserted islands with rockets, mortars and five-inch shells. Planes would pull target sleeves past their ships for anti-aircraft practice with 40mm and 20mm guns. Instructors taught tactics used by kamikazes and how to defend against them. General Quarters drills were held day and night. Every man trained for damage control and fire-fighting. Training was intense. The thought of going to war was real now. The *LSM(R) 411* crew was building confidence and pride in their abilities.

Robert Veesenmeyer, SM2/c: (letter dated June 7, 1945) We've been firing all day at some little island. My ears were really taking a beating. I got two direct hits out of five, so the skipper was well pleased. I think our ship has done the best firing out of all the ships so we feel pretty good. From now on my mail will be censored. So I can't send any more kisses or anything that looks like code – that's what some guys do I guess. I've been listening to the news and it sounds like the Japs are really getting it. Boy I hope it's over soon so we can get together again.

The crew of *LSM(R)-411* participated in competitive shore bombardment exercises with all units of the division. They scored high in gunnery. Battle problem training was designed to resemble an actual landing. As the ship neared its target area the loudspeaker blared. "Secure the Chow line. Muster on Station. The ship expects to set Condition One Rocket at 0800."

Everyone had a job. They practiced daily because there was no room for error in combat...or live shell exercises. Gunner's Mates would be getting the rocket launchers ready for the day's mission. They would test the firing circuits and the phone circuits. Covers were removed from their guns. Men in the ammunition handling room opened ammo cans and loaded racks with clips or shells. In the engine room men checked fuel and oil gauges. The quartermaster pulled out his charts. Cooks and mess cooks cleaned up after chow and headed to their GQ stations. Down in the rocket handling rooms men are loading rockets. Each finned shell weighs about 50 pounds. It's a hot sweaty job while wearing full battle gear. When the rocket ships are lined and ready, they let loose with a barrage of 240 rockets. The sound, the smoke, the sight of hundreds of rockets created the biggest 4th of July finale crewmembers had ever witnessed. As rockets devastated the beach *LSM(R)-411* would do a 180 and head back out to sea. The beach was so covered with smoke, fire and explosions no one knew what damage had been wrought. There'd be some time to relax before they reloaded and led the way for another mock landing.

Veesenmeyer had finished passing rockets one morning. He'd had the mid-watch the night before. He was hot and tired. He took off his helmet, sat down on it, leaned back on a rack of rockets to take a short nap. The ship turned, the waves chopped, somebody shifted their foot and the ship rolled. So did an unsecured rocket. It landed on Veesenmeyer's head and bounced several times across the deck. Veesenmeyer was knocked out. An alert gunner's mate grabbed the rocket and threw it over the side. Others carried Veesenmeyer to the emergency ward room.

When Veesenmeyer came to he was chewed out for removing his helmet, taking a nap, and leaving a rocket unsecured. His throbbing head was a sufficient learning tool. This never happened again. Constant drilling eliminated mistakes. The *411* was nearly ready for war. Veesenmeyer already had a war story. He took a direct hit to his head with a five-inch 50-pound rocket and survived. He got plenty of extra duty and lost some liberty time as punishment.

Robert Veesenmeyer, LSM(R)-411: (letter home June 9, 1945) We got in last night about 6:30. I was on the wheel. And brought the ship all the way in. No sooner I'm off the wheel watch and I had a watch on the gangway so I didn't get a chance to write. When I get liberty again,

I'll go to the canteen. I always play the jukebox. There is one song I play every time. I never miss it and that's "Anywhere." It reminds me of you Shirley.

The LSM(R)s passed their shakedown cruises. The *411* crew had become a well-oiled machine that took pride in their ship. They were ready. Orders came to steam to San Pedro, California by way of the Panama Canal. It was a trip of about 6,000 miles. With a top speed of 13 knots, they'd be at sea for several weeks. Now it was real. They'd be heading for the war in the South Pacific. Veesenmeyer knew he wouldn't see home again until the war was over. Music was his escape from thoughts of war and the fear of not returning home.

Robert Veesenmeyer, LSM(R)-411: *(letter home June 13, 1945), I learned that from now on I can't take a shower every night. I can only take one every three nights, and you have to be through in 3 minutes! Right now I'm listening to the Hit Parade. I wonder if you are. This is the first I've heard it in about three weeks. They are playing "All my life" and now they are playing "Candy". Oh, how I wish we were dancing together. Here's one of my favorite songs. "Dream." Boy does that bring back memories of that seven day leave we spent together.*

It was August before the *LSM(R)-411* reached San Pedro. There had been several ports of call for fuel and supplies plus a stop-over in Panama. Training and drills continued while en route. Additional gunnery practice was possible on towed target sleeves. Kamikaze attacks would be their greatest threat when they reached Japan. Final preparations were being made for the next leg of their voyage. Crewmembers never knew where they were going until they were out to sea. They were constantly reminded that "loose lips sink ships," and were never trusted to know their destination. Rumors and conventional wisdom told them their next stop would be Pearl Harbor. That was exciting. Most of the crew had never been there.

On 7 August they heard about a powerful bomb being dropped on Japan. Three days later another one was dropped. It was hard to believe these single bombs wiped out entire cities. Japan's possible surrender was a hot topic on the rumor mill. After several more days they learned that massive B-29 bombing raids over Japan had resumed. Also, the Russians invaded Manchuria. The war was still on. On the morning of 14 August, *LSM(R)-411* joined a convoy of ships headed for Hawaii. Veesenmeyer looked back at the Los Angeles skyline and wondered how long it would be - or if ever - before he'd be back.

Later the next day an un-coded message was received on the *411*. Japan had surrendered. The war was over. Ships sounded horns, rang bells and fired a few shots. The anxiety of leaving the states was suddenly gone. They were all going to survive the war. Now they worried if they'd still get to go to Hawaii. Orders are orders. The *LSM(R)-411* went on to Pearl Harbor. They arrived on 23 August and stayed until October.

Honolulu was fun. The post war mood was joyous. Those men shipping out were headed for occupation not invasion. Those heading back to the states were going home for good. Veesenmeyer knew of several buddies from Chicago who were anchored on other ships at Pearl. They got together for good times. They'd grown up a bit. A year or two ago they were a bunch of high school kids just goofing off.

The September 7th issue of "Yank" magazine had an article about VJ Day in Honolulu. On the night of 14 August 1945 the local radio station received an Urgent Message regarding Potsdam. At 0245 hours, word came that Japan had accepted the Potsdam Declaration. The War was over. The station immediately cut into the music and broadcast the news.

Hickman Field had been the first to be attacked by Japanese Zeroes on December 7, 1941. Now they were first to start the victory celebration at Pearl Harbor. Army Air Corps crews had kept planes flowing with supplies 24 hours a day since the war began. At three in the morning the night shift woke up six members of the Army Air Force band. They started a parade up Fox Avenue with jeeps and trucks honking their horns. Forty other assorted musicians joined in playing "Hail, Hail The Gangs All Here." People poured out of the barracks. The celebration continued throughout the next day.

At wars end over 12 million men and women were in uniform. Now they all wanted to go home. Servicemen who had been counting their days to the likely invasion of Japan were now counting up their points to the "Magic Number." Points were given for each month of service, each month serving overseas, each year of age, battle stars or awards, and dependent children. The magic number when the war ended was 85. Veesenmeyer had about ten. He wouldn't be going home anytime soon. In October, the *LSM(R)-411* sailed back to California. His ship would cruise up and down the west coast for the next nine months. He'd make stops in L.A., San Francisco and Seattle, Washington. Training for war was now replaced with maintaining the ship. Paint one day, chip it off the next. It was a way to keep sailors busy.

Robert Veesenmeyer SM2/c, LSM(R)-411: (letter dated Mar. 5, 1946)
I was on a work party this morning to load supplies. This afternoon I had to paint the head white. I sure had a lot of paint on myself again, I wish I wasn't so careless when I'm painting. Honestly, I think I have more paint on myself than anywhere else.

The military was processing and transporting a million people a month. They called it Operation Magic Carpet Ride. Battleships, carriers, transport, every ship capable of carrying people was converted into troop carriers. In addition, the Navy had thousands of ships that no longer had a mission. They were being moth balled, scrapped or sold to other countries. The 48 "Ultimate" LSM(R) Rocket Ships had never been in combat. It was decided an invasion the size and scope that had been planned for Japan was unlikely in the future. The Navy would soon put most of them into their mothball fleet.

The Magic number was eventually reduced and Veesenmeyer had enough points for discharge. On 5 July 1946 he boarded a train for Great Lakes. His last letter home said, "Homeward bound. By the time you get this letter I'll be on my way home. I'll call you when I get to the Lakes."

Buffalo, NY, September 19, 2015 – Jeffrey R. Veesenmeyer: I'm thinking about my dad's life after he was discharged. He married his best girl Shirley. They would become my parents and raise three children. Robert W. Veesenmeyer became a well-known and respected manufacturer of custom made, handcrafted jewelry in Chicago's downtown. He came home from his war time service and witnessed two more generations of his family. I served in the Navy Air, earned a degree in journalism, married, raised a daughter, and authored books. My sisters became teachers, got married and raised their own children. Dad lived long enough to see six grandchildren come into the world. There were so many others of his generation that never had these opportunities.

I'm standing on the main deck of the USS *The Sullivans* (DD-537) at the Naval and Military Park Museum in Buffalo, New York. The USS LSM-LSM(R) Association is touring *The Sullivans* during their annual reunion. I've joined this group to learn more about my dad's ship, the USS *LSM(R)-411*. For the moment, I'm staring at a plaque mounted on a bulkhead of *The Sullivans*. It reads, "Honoring Joseph, Francis, Albert, Madison and George Sullivan who were lost in the USS *Juneau* 13 May 1942." All five brothers were killed when their ship was torpedoed and sunk by a Japanese submarine at Guadalcanal. This was the greatest single loss for any one American family during WWII. Five branches of this family tree never had the opportunity to grow. Their mother sponsored the ship and it was commissioned on 30 March 1944. The tragedy inspired a movie "The Fighting Sullivans," released in 1944.

I especially wanted to tour USS *The Sullivans* while in Buffalo. This destroyer's crew saved 166 of the *Bunker Hill's* sailors after they were hit by two kamikazes on 11 May 1945. That was the same day my uncle Louis Veesenmeyer was killed by a kamikaze on the USS *Hadley*. His brother, my uncle Elmer Veesenmeyer, was serving aboard the hospital ship *Bountiful*, at Okinawa. I have a picture of *The Sullivans* alongside the *Bountiful* and the *Bunker Hill*. Both warships are transferring wounded sailors to the *Bountiful*. I find the connection to these ships and my family's history, truly amazing.

I had the privilege of interviewing one of *The Sullivans* most famous crew members, "George Mendonsa, aka "The Kissing Sailor." Mendonsa was the helmsman who steered his ship to *Bunker Hill* sailors who were struggling to survive in the water after abandoning ship. *The Sullivans*, transferred *Bunker Hill* survivors to hospital ships where nurses tended to their burns and wounds. It was a scene that Mendonsa would remember on VJ Day in New York. He'd be photographed while thanking a nurse for her compassionate service – with a famous kiss.

Veterans of *The Sullivans*, hold "field days" each year to help maintain their ship. I marvel at how well the ship has been preserved. Shipboard life is portrayed showing mannequin sailors at work. I step inside the five-inch gun mount. Twelve men worked inside this mount. During battle, they'd be loading, aiming and firing each shell at the rate of 20 per minute. It had to be cramped, hot and ear splitting work. I head up to the bridge and enter the wheel room. Now I am standing on the same spot George Mendonsa stood during the rescue of the *Bunker Hill* sailors. He would have been looking out over the bow and steering in close enough for deck hands to toss lines to men struggling in the waves.

Museum ships like *The Sullivans* provide a real-life glimpse of how sailors lived and fought during WWII. This ship has so much history.

It underscores the importance of preserving the museum ships and telling their stories. It has brought me closer to my family's history. I'm glad for the opportunity to tour the ship.

The Navy veterans with me have all served on LSMs or LSM(R)s during WWII, Korea or Vietnam. Several of the reunion attendees served on *LSM(R)-409*. This ship is identical to my dad's. It was built and commissioned at about the same time as his *LSM(R)-411*. The stories and information shared about this unique class of ships has broadened my understanding of my dad's service during WWII.

Later that day I attended the LSM-LSMR Banquet. My wife and I sat with shipmates from the *LSM(R)-525*. Like my dad's *411*, this ship missed WWII. It was commissioned on the same day Japan surrendered. It avoided mothballs and saw combat in Korea and again in Vietnam from 1966 to 1969. These men are my age. They served during the Vietnam War. They shared photos and stories of their tour. I see a similar camaraderie between these amphib veterans that is evident with all the tin can sailors I've met. Their ships were small. They knew most of the men aboard and felt a brotherhood with all their shipmates.

Most of the navy veterans who attend ship reunions share a bond that goes beyond everyday shipboard life. These men faced death. They have memories of combat or sea disasters that are difficult to talk about. The reunions provide a safe place to share stories and remember those navy buddies who didn't come home.

A ships bell rang out at the LSM-LSMR banquet. The room became quiet. One member announced, "This is the moment of reverence we dedicate to the memory of our departed LSM/LSMR shipmates." He began reading a list of names; members of their group who had taken their last voyage in the past year. The list was long. This association gets smaller each year. Ray Olley, a WWII vet who served on *LSM-311* came up to the microphone. He was in his dress blues uniform. He sang a moving rendition of, "America the Beautiful." It was a fitting tribute to all the sailors who have sailed, fought and died for the United States of America.

The USS LSM(R)-411 was commissioned on 23 May 1945 in the Naval Shipyard, Charleston, South Carolina. She was one of 48 new rocket ships needed for the invasion of Japan. Her complement included 6 officers and 137 enlisted men.

L-R: Seamen, Santure and Veesenmeyer were both from the Chicago area. They remained good friends for many years after the war.

The Gator newsletters from the Amphibious Base at Little Creek, Virginia were among the navy memorabilia saved by Robert Veesenmeyer. Other items include the Blue Jacket Manual and a Lookout Manual.

This plaque is mounted on a bulkhead of USS The Sullivans. It lists the five brothers who all died during the sinking of the USS Juneau and the service history of The Sullivans.

The museum ship USS The Sullivans is moored at the Naval and Military Park in Buffalo, New York. The ship is beautifully maintained by shipmates who served on her through 1952.

These salty dogs attended the LSM-LSMR Association Reunion September 2015 in Buffalo, New York. They proudly wore their dress blue uniforms to the banquet. L-R: Ron MacKay Jr., Rick Bahrenburg, Raymond Olley and Frederick Bahrenburg Jr.

Chapter 20

Epilogue

WORLD War II was the most devastating event in our global history. Over 60 million people were killed. That number equaled nearly half the population of the United States in 1940. During the six years of war, an average of 27,000 people would be killed each day throughout the world. Europe and Asia took the brunt of it. Russia lost 20 million and 15 million were slaughtered in China. Yet it was the ferocity of war with Japan that changed the world forever.

The blood bath at Okinawa became a brutal dose of reality for war planners. American losses totaled 12,520 dead or missing and 36,631 wounded. Overall casualties were listed at 82,000. This included non-combat injuries, disease and shell shock. Combat fatigue was at the highest level of the war during the Okinawa campaign in 1945. American naval losses were greater than the previous four years in total. Thirty-six ships were sunk and 368 damaged. The number of sailors killed (4,907) exceeded the wounded (4,824). This statistic underscored the lethal impact of kamikazes.

The kamikazes were a deadly and destructive weapon. They failed to sink the biggest warships in the allied fleets. The fear kamikazes created made up for that shortcoming. Nothing was more terrifying than watching the death dive of a kamikaze heading into a ship. Every sailor who looked into the eyes of a kamikaze pilot, felt that pilot was aiming his plane directly for him. No other naval weapon could create that fear. Artillery shells, mines, bombs and even torpedoes were seldom seen until they exploded. But a plane could be seen approaching from several miles away. Once a kamikaze was a few hundred yards from crashing into the ship, a sailor could count the seconds he had left to live.

Japan created the Kamikaze Special Attack units to sink American warships and transports. They hoped to cut off ground troops from resupply and support; then they'd starve the invaders into surrender. Their plan was to make Okinawa so painful that Americans would no longer have the stomach for an invasion of Japan. Part of their plan worked. Okinawa had been very painful. And war planners expected American casualties to be ten times greater when they invaded Japan. Every alternative to the invasion had to be considered. President Truman chose an alternative.

Japan made Truman's decision an easy one. They had ignored the Potsdam Declaration and warnings of total annihilation. They had already endured six months of conventional bombing and fire bombing raids on their cities. Over 400,000 people had been killed and 67 cities destroyed. Japan's Emperor Hirohito had ordered every man, woman and child to fight to the death. Defending their nation's honor was more important than life itself.

General LeMay had run out of bombing targets for his B-29s. Most of the large cities that didn't have known POW camps had already been incinerated. Nearly 20,000 American POWs were being worked to death as Japan's slave laborers. If Japan was invaded, these POWs, who had somehow survived, would be executed before they could be liberated. The invasion fleet would be sitting within range of 10,000 kamikaze planes, thousands of suicide boats and hundreds of midget subs. The terror created by these weapons made the thought of invasion a nightmare. The loss of more American lives made the alternative decision an easy one for Truman. The killing could only be stopped with a weapon of terror greater than the world had ever seen.

On 6 August 1945 the first ever atomic weapon was dropped on Hiroshima. Three days later the second bomb was dropped on Nagasaki. The face of war changed forever. Over 100,000 people were killed in an instant. Their deaths saved many more Japanese citizens and probably hundreds of thousands of American servicemen also.

When the war ended, one word summed up the feelings of all Americans. Relief! Remarkably, many of the Japanese shared the same feeling. They were tired of the war and angry at their government. Relief was felt by many Japanese who had already accepted death as inevitable.

On Okinawa, there were still many Japanese soldiers hiding deep in caves when the war ended. Thirty Japanese crewman emerged with a white flag after hearing American loudspeakers announce Japan's surrender. They were attached to a kaiten suicide boat unit. These men were surprised to be so well treated by their captors and felt happy to have survived.

A school girl from a small village near Hiroshima had been training to fight. Her class was taught how to kill Americans with a sharpened bamboo spear. To miss her training class would bring arrest to her and dishonor to her family. She lost many friends in Hiroshima, yet she was deeply grateful for the bomb. She felt it gave her leaders a way out of the war. Her life was saved and now she had hope for a future.

Many years later, Paul Tibbets, the pilot of *Enola Gay*, met a famous Japanese fiddle player. Tibbets and his B-29 crew were in Branson, Missouri for a reunion. They were attending the famed Shoji Tabuchi Theatre. The musical extravaganza had become a phenomenon at Branson. The star, Shoji Tabuchi, came up to Tibbets after the show and shook his hand. Tabuchi was a child when the bomb was dropped on Hiroshima. His family escaped the fall-out by heading up into the mountains. He thanked Tibbets for saving him and his family. Tabuchi's father believed if the war had continued, all of them would have died." He told his son, "The lives of men, women and children all over Japan were spared by the atom bomb."

General George Patton once said, "No bastard ever won a war by dying for his country." The kamikazes couldn't win the war or even end it with their sacrifice. But they did create terror. A much greater terror was required to bring it to an end.

Chapter 21

Scuttlebutt and Salty Tales

WITHIN a decade of this book's publication (2017), there will be very few eyewitnesses to WWII. Every man, woman and child born before 1939 has some recollections of how the war affected them. Those who served in uniform will be a century old if still alive. It's crucial to our history and the memory of those who served to preserve stories about the WWII experience for future generations.

The following stories are from sailors who served during WWII. These memories of the war years are still fresh in their minds 70 years later. They provide more insight to their war experiences. The tales were gleaned from the shipmates' interviews, oral histories, published articles and information from their families.

Each story is written in first person, but they are not direct quotes. They've been edited and arranged for ease of reading. The stories do reflect each shipmate's personal memories. These are the scuttlebutt and salty tales they've shared with family, friends, and shipmates. Now they are saved for one and all.

USS *Aaron Ward* (DM-34)

Lefteris "Lefty" Lavrakas
The *Aaron Ward* was hit by more kamikazes than any other ship. We took a beating topside. We went into a place called Kerama Retto for repairs. The Captain called me up to his cabin and said, "Lefty, I just got word that we've been assigned to Brooklyn Navy Yard for repairs." That was a hell of a long way to go for repairs. He knew I was engaged to a lovely blond back in California. So he sent me back as advance repair agent to Brooklyn. What a decision from wonderful Bill Sanders. I bummed rides on Navy Patrol planes across the Pacific. When I got to Pearl I called my dear lass and said, "Chances look good that we might get married." I flew to Oakland and thumbed to L.A. We got married quickly. I took her to Brooklyn for our honeymoon. While waiting for my ship to return we saw every show on Broadway. When I bought tickets for Carousel I pronounced it Carousal. I'd never heard the word carousel. The blond debutante ticket taker corrected me with a smirk. I went from a one dollar officer to a one cent recruit.

Eddie Gaines
I was a steward on the *Aaron Ward*. I worked in the chow hall and officers' ward room. My duties were to feed and serve the officers. There was racism at that time in the Navy. Even though they were hating the color of my skin, I didn't hate them. That's the way they were raised and there's nothing they can do about it. During the battle I helped the doctor by mixing the plasma used to save the lives of those wounded men.

USS *Bache* (DD-470)

Ray DelSesto

I joined the Navy in 1942. My girlfriend and I wrote to each other. I never proposed. In one letter, I said we would get married when I got home on leave. She didn't know when that would be, but she was ready. Marie and I got married during the final days of 1944 while on leave. I was 23 and she was 21. We spent New Year's Eve at Copley Plaza in Boston. We have a folder with the tickets and coat-check stubs from that night. There is a bill for the wedding dress that included alterations, which cost $22.45. Our honeymoon ended too soon. I caught a train back to the ship docked in California and rejoined WWII. One day we were in a rough sea and I was cooking pork chops on the stove for dinner. The pan slid off the stove and spread pork chops all over the deck. I picked them up, rinsed them off, put them in a large roaster, coated them with Worstershire sauce and put the pan in the oven. The crew complimented me on how good they were. From that day on one of the guys called me "pork chop."

H.E. "Bucky" Walters

In 1944 the *Bache* left Oakland for Pearl Harbor. We were loaded for war including the new teardrop-shaped depth charges. A young gunnery officer thought we should test the new depth charges. The manual for this test required a ship speed of 12 knots and depth setting of 50 feet. I informed the LT. that the new teardrop-shaped charges would sink faster than the old cylindrical cans. The test requirements were not appropriate and would result in early detonation causing damage to the *Bache*. Unfortunately, the captain followed the advice of the gunnery officer. The shock from depth charges destroyed the steering engine and ruptured every tank on the ship. We limped into Pearl Harbor steering manually and leaving an oil slick for miles.

Jeremiah Tuttle

In November of 1944 I was detached and sent to Washington D.C. for advanced Fire Control training. When I told my mother, she commented that it must be awfully hot down in the engine room. I had to explain that Fire Control is how we automatically aimed and fired the guns. There were four of us in a room below the analog computer. I monitored a switchboard that controlled range, elevation, ship movement, speed, direction and temperature in the magazine. All these measurements can change the ballistics.

Al Everett

They took all kinds of things off *Bache* before we left Kerama Retto and headed for home. They took off our five-inch guns, took all our torpedoes and depth charges. We limped back on one engine and one prop. Sonar picked up what they thought was a submarine. We had some old depth charges we hadn't taken off. We dropped those old depth charges on the sub sonar-contact. We brought up a whale. When we got back to the Navy Yard in New York we did a 21 gun salute for a memorial of our lost shipmates. But we fired the gun 22 times. I was the gunners mate. My Lieutenant said, "Hey, can't you count?"

George Riggs

I started working on iron ore ships in the Great Lakes when I was 16. I worked as the cook's helper. I peeled many potatoes on the fantail, swabbed decks, cleaned cabins. When I joined the Navy, I went straight to Great Lakes Training Center from the Cleveland recruiting office. I had 13 weeks of boot camp and 16 weeks of Fire Control training. Those scoring 85 or better in FC School would get promoted to third class immediately. I got an 85.4 and never had any more KP duty. The *Bush* crew had some fun liberty in Sidney, Australia. We had about 10 to 20 days there. I met a girl. Next time I was in town I had no way to contact her. So, I'm standing on a street corner and she walks by with another sailor. She saw me. Ten minutes later she came back without him.

USS *Bunker Hill* (CV-17)

Dick Lillie

In San Diego, I'd go to lunch down on the docks, and watch the ships coming in from Guadalcanal. You could stand by the gangway and look into the eyes of the wounded and survivors. They'd have that 1,000 mile stare. They'd been through Hell. So, I take my hat off to those guys who fought in the early war. When I got out there the war had turned. They never licked us again. We just pushed them and pushed them fast. When the *Bunker Hill* got hit, I went into the water and got picked up by *The Sullivans*. The first thing I did, because I was a torpedoman, was go to the torpedo shop and get a drink of torpedo juice. I was in the destroyer's torp shop and George Mendonsa (aka The Kissing Sailor) was down there too. I was still soaking wet when I first met him.

Phillip "Pot" Wilmot

During Marine flight training I was doing my usual hot rod pilot thing. For gunnery, they'd pull a target sleeve of white canvas, tied to a long line on the rear of a plane. I was having trouble getting hits. We needed 10 hits out of a hundred rounds to qualify for gunnery. I got real close to the sleeve, maybe 10 yards when I fired. My bullets were out ahead of the sleeve and I cut the tow rope. The sleeve slid over my wing. The rope wrapped around the hub of my prop. The guys started calling me Dilbert, the cartoon guy who screws up. My last name is Wilmot so they changed it to Dilpot and then shortened it to "Pot." That's how I got my nickname.

On the *Bunker Hill*, we nicknamed our squadron major, "Handsome Harry." His wingman was Ray Smally. They were chasing a kamikaze that was diving on a ship. Navy guys can't distinguish between Jap and friendly planes in the heat of battle. Smally shot down the kamikaze that was diving on the ship, but this ship's gunners shot down Smally and he had to bail out. "Handsome Harry" made the Captain of the ship paint a Corsair on the gun mount of their five-inch gun.

Wesley Todd

When my squadron of 16 Corsairs returned to the *Bunker Hill* on May 11th we saw the smoke. Then we saw men jumping overboard and in the water. We would zoom down over groups of men in the water so destroyers would see where they were and go pick them up. We couldn't land on the *Bunker Hill*. When we got low on gas we landed on the *Enterprise* and spent the night there. Next day, somebody decided "these fellas have been out here long enough," and we got Class 2 Priority to go home. We were ordered to deliver our planes to the Marines at Yontan Airfield on Okinawa. This would be our last day in our planes over a combat zone. One of the guys suggested that we hit the Jap held island of Amami on our way. We decided not to do it. Why take a chance of losing somebody on our last day? So, we landed on a coral runway at Okinawa and gave them our airplanes. We had to wait a few days before we could arrange transportation back to the *Bunker Hill.* She was heading for Guam. So, they put us on a DC-3 to Guam. Before we could board the plane, we had to be deloused. Anybody who had been on Okinawa had to be deloused. They squirt you all over your body to kill the lice.

USS *Bush* (DD-529)

Jim "Okie" Reeder

I was a Radioman Third Class on the *Bush.* My station was the emergency radio room. I'd send Morse Code messages at 35 to 40 words per minute. I went to radio school at the University of Wisconsin – Madison. They taught us how to type at radio school. I could pick up news from AP, UPI and even Tokyo Rose in my radio room. I was a pretty good typist. I decided to publish a newspaper. I called it the "Daily Twig." So, I typed up the news that came over the radio, and passed copies out to the men. Tokyo Rose wanted us to think we were losing the war. That old girl was quite a talker. She'd report that they were winning the war, so the Japs would keep fighting. One time we went into a beachhead and bombarded the landing area. We got about three hundred yards from the beach and started shooting. Then the Marines on board loaded a Higgins boat and headed for shore. When they landed they saw a big sign. It said, "Welcome U.S. Marines, signed "Navy Frogmen."

USS *Drexler* (DD-741)

Duke Payne

When you are in war and face death it makes you realize how important life is. That is one reason so many WWII veterans are still married. We appreciate life. Every minute of every day we were thinking of getting home. I really appreciate home and family. Remember the last scene in "Saving Private Ryan." In the background was his entire family. Think about that. By one small mishap his family wouldn't have been there. To this day, we still have annual reunions on the anniversary of the sinking of our ship the *Drexler*. About a hundred have attended reunions which include the descendants of the crew. They are really family affairs. We can still "Pitch Liberty" at reunions.

Harold Tatsch

After the *Drexler* sank I got a 40-day survivor leave. The war ended right after I got back. I had hoped to be assigned to a new ship. Instead they sent me to an ammunition depot in Algiers, Louisiana. I had to get out of there, so I went down to the main office and asked about re-enlistment. I told them I'd re-enlist in the regular Navy if I'd get destroyer duty. I liked sea duty on a destroyer. They said, "Oh heck yes. We'll give you sea duty." I re-enlisted. I got another 30-day leave for re-enlisting. When I came back they shipped me to California. Then they put me on a transport to Guam. In Guam they put me on shore patrol for the next 18 months. When I finally got back to the states I told them to give me my discharge.

USS *Hugh W. Hadley* (DD-774)

Doug Aitken

The *Hadley* needed to be towed all the way back to San Francisco. We had no engines. We left Okinawa hooked to a sea-going tug boat. Weather reporting wasn't good back then. There was a typhoon brewing and we didn't know it. So, we went through the edge of the typhoon under tow. If you can picture going into the swells, you have to be very careful as the tow line stretches and contracts. The tow line must never come out of the water. If it does it would snap. There is a big catenary – an arch in the cable - down in the water that takes up the give. In order to keep from losing the *Hadley* in the storm our tug captain extended that catenary a long way. We rolled way beyond our survival rate, up to 57 degrees at one point. Much of our damaged top weight had been removed. We had extra metal plates on the hull so our center of gravity was lowered. We survived the typhoon. During the rest of the two-month tow we sailed though much calmer waters. That's when our tow line broke…nine times!

Tom English

While attending the 50th Anniversary *Hadley* Reunion in San Diego, Gene Wise handed me a packet. Inside the envelope were documents, notes and items – all written in Japanese. Wise had been on the detail that went down into *Hadley's* flooded engine room to recover our dead shipmates in 1945. He found the kamikaze plane's cockpit and pilot down there too. Gene went through the pockets of the Jap's flight suit, removed the items and put them in his own pocket. He kept them in his personal possession for 50 years. At the time, my son Christopher worked for a company who bought and sold TV programs. There were two Japanese women who worked with him. We asked them to translate the documents and items. They were returned after several months with some very interesting translations. There was a leaflet dropped by American bombers and notes that had anti-government messages. I gave the items to Doug Aitken who turned them over to the Nimitz Museum (Museum of the Pacific War – Fredericksburg, TX) for display in the *Hadley* Room. (see documents at end of chapter)

A.W. Hodde Jr.

I was not the most popular gunners mate on the *Hadley*. I entered the Navy in July 1943. I was originally stationed in New Orleans as a student at Tulane University in the V-12 program. I became disillusioned with the courses I was taking and so was sent to boot camp. I made a very high score on an IQ test and was given the option of radio, electrical or gunners mate. Since I am an avid hunter, I chose gunners mate school. I graduated as valedictorian and was immediately promoted to GM3/c. I skipped Seaman 1/c because of my number one rank in the class. They also made me an instructor at the naval gun range at La Jolla, CA. I spent six months there instructing people on the operation of the 40mm. When the crew of the *Hadley* was being assembled, they wanted someone familiar with the 40mm to help train the crew, especially the two quad 40s. But the Chief Gunner's Mate told me he'd be doing all the instructing on the weapons. When gunner's mates had questions, they'd come to me. This irritated the higher ranking men. I never got a promotion until after the *Hadley* was decommissioned.

Dell Burt Hall

I joined the Navy in 1943. After boot camp, they sent me to Watertenders school to learn how to maintain ship's boilers. Then I was assigned to the A.P.A. Ferry Crew #2. Our small crew would ferry newly launched attack transport ships to the east coast where they would be finished and fitted out. During 1943 and 1944 I helped deliver seven new ships. They were the USS *Clay*, USS *Catoctin*, USS *Alderamin*, USS *Baxteen*, USS *Sabiz*, USS *Cecil*, and USS *General Harry Taylor*. My time aboard these ships was very short – from five days to about a month. But by the time I was assigned to the *Hadley*, I was already a plank owner on seven other ships. I don't think the Captain had that many on his service records.

James Gibbs

On September 22, 1942, at age 20, I enlisted in the US Navy at the Naval Reserve Station in Charleston, West Virginia. My first assignment was aboard the USS *Iowa* (BB-61). On November 27, 1943 the *Iowa* crossed the equator while bound for South America. This being my first crossing, I was considered a Pollywog. I was initiated that day into the Solemn Mysteries of the Ancient Order of the Deep and became a Shellback. This tradition of the Line Crossing Ceremony dates back to the British Navy in the early 1800s. My next assignment was aboard the USS *Hugh W. Hadley*. I was wounded on May 11, 1945 during the kamikaze attacks on Radar Picket Station #15. I received the Purple Heart and the American Area Campaign Ribbon. I was incredibly proud of my granddaughter when she joined the US Navy and served on the USS *Nimitz*.

Waymond Dean

I joined the *Hadley* in November of 1944. I was assigned the No. 1 gun position as gun captain on the portside 20mm. My mount immediately spotted and shot down the first two planes during the 11 May 1945 battle. I had my gun ready very quickly. There was no time for thoughts or feelings while focusing on the job. After we were ordered to abandon ship a Marine Corsair pilot made a slow pass and we waved at each other. I helped two wounded men while we were in the water. Another destroyer picked us up. When they hauled me out of the water I asked for drink to warm up. The only alcohol they had was a bottle of aftershave. I took a swig of that…it was not a good idea.

Ted Davis

I enlisted in the Navy during January of 1944 at age 17. I already had enough credits to graduate from high school. My mom said "no" I couldn't enlist. She wanted me to finish my senior year. My dad said I could make my own decision. I trained at Great Lakes and became a Signalman. When I joined the *Hadley* crew I became good friends with the bakers. I went in the Navy weighing 157 pounds and came out two years later weighing 205.

Marty Weibel

I enjoyed being in the Navy. I should have stayed in. Food was good on the *Hadley*. We had a bunch of real-good cooks. Our skipper didn't believe in powdered milk. We had fresh milk when he could get it. Captain Mullaney took care of the enlisted men. We'd get to go on liberty before the officers. My navy experience was a good one. We learned how to work together. The Navy made me a better person. I tend to watch over other people now. After the war, our new skipper wanted me to re-up. I could have gone to Norfolk and attended school. I should have done it.

LSM-57

Fred Lee

We celebrated the 4th of July 1945 at sea by firing our machine guns at boxes we threw overboard. We made a lot of noise anyway. The lead ship in our column sent back a message. "Happy Fourth of July!" We replied, "Same to You." It broke the monotony of steady steaming at sea. We crossed the Equator, which was a big deal to the crew, but for an old salt like me, it was my third crossing. Once we reached our destination we were tied to a dock, and it was handy to get ashore. We could get ice cream, cokes, and see movies and not be stranded without a boat. Saw the movie "Salome Where She Danced," no good. Two good ones, "Diamond Horseshoe" with Grable, "the shape", and Tracy and Hepburn in "Without Love." I had to buy some new clothes, two shirts and two pants that cost $11.00. Seemed like a tremendous expenditure, but my old clothes had rotted away. We were in Saipan Harbor when the war ended. All the ships in the harbor were blowing their whistles in celebration. All we did after that is sit and collect discharge points. Out of 60 men, only one man was eligible for discharge on *LSM-57*. Officers needed 49 points and I only had 41. We were only getting a half point for each month service at that time.

LSM(R)-190

Lyle Tennis

After the *190* was sunk they put us on an APA transport and took us directly to the States. We never even stopped in Hawaii. We got to San Francisco and we all looked like a bunch of vagabonds. We didn't have decent uniforms, hadn't shaved in 10 days. All our possessions went down with our ship. I was the ranking officer for the crew now. I went to the Red Cross to see if they'd get us some clothes, lend us some money. They gave us a shaving kit and tooth brush and a comb. That is all. We went to the ship's store to cumshaw some clothes. Being an officer, I had to buy my food. I had no money to eat with. I took off my officer's insignia and snuck into the Chief's mess. That's the only way I could eat on base. After the war ended I decided to stay in the Navy Reserve. I retired after 28 years as a Commander. I've been very active in the Navy Club of America in Racine, Wisconsin. The only other organization I belong to is the LSM-LSM(R) Association, the big one. I go out to schools and tell them about the war, show then my Purple Heart and Navy Cross. They are all bug-eyed. They can't believe what we went through.

LSM(R)-191

John Stavola

They were sending experienced LST Petty Officers to Little Creek, Virginia to help train new rocket ship crews. They were forming crews and exercise was part of the training. The prize fighter, Tony Zale, was the Chief Phys Ed instructor. We all had to participate. He is up on the platform shouting directions for the obstacle course and I got tired. I just stood there. He says, "Hit it." You had to hit the wall and climb over. He said, "What the *blank* is the matter with you?" I told him, what you are teaching us for exercise is a waste of time. The ship I'm going on is 203 feet long, it's cramped. There is no room for this kind of exercise. On my LST, which was bigger at 345 feet long, I had a punching bag for exercise. I had it welded, up high on the gun tub. I hit the bag every day for exercise. He didn't believe me. I told him I had a new bag and gear I would be using on the rocket ship. He said, "I don't believe you, go ahead and get your gear." I showed him my boxing bag and gear. He said, "Okay, you don't have to go through the maze." Tony Zale and I got along fine after that.

LSM(R)-198

Henry Kalinofsky
On Good Friday, two days before the invasion of Okinawa, we were served a big turkey dinner. The meal was real fine, but being a Catholic I thought, "My God, I'm not allowed to eat meat on Friday. Boy, I'm going to hell." Anyway, the invasion was in progress on Easter Sunday and our guns are firing. We are firing our guns at kamikazes and the concussion of one blast knocked a sandwich out of my hand. That's all I had to eat that day. I'm eating the darn thing and lost it. I thought, "Well that's my punishment."

LSM(R)-411

Robert (Bob) Veesenmeyer
Shipboard life relaxed a bit after the war ended. On hot days and with a calm sea the captain would stop so we could swim. We'd dive

off the side while men with machine guns kept watch for sharks. Most of us were kids with a few months of sea duty. The old salts were always trying to prank the young guys. They'd hand a guy a rope and tell him to rig a "chow line." Or somebody would announce that a "sea bat" had been caught and it could be seen back on the fantail. Guys would be sent for bulkhead remover, buckets of prop wash or keys to the sea locker. But I liked going on liberty with one of the older guys. He'd put on a show at each bar by betting he could eat a glass or photo flash bulb. He'd get us free drinks. He'd also end up getting another tattoo every time he got drunk. Next morning he'd ask me to check his back to see if there was a new tattoo. There always was.

USS *Rotanin* (AK-108)

Carmon Howe

When the war ended, my ship the *Rotanin* - we called her "Rotten Annie" - was converted from cargo to troop transport. We took occupation troops to Japan and brought thousands of troops home to be discharged from service. I was able to get liberty in Japan. We were restricted to several parts because of the bombed-out areas. We could see the destruction in the distance. One day several buddies and I spotted some Japanese children. We called them over and gave them chocolate bars. The kids were excited to have been befriended by Americans. Through sign language they invited us to their home for dinner. Their parents welcomed us. We joined the family for a traditional Japanese meal; seated on the floor around a table that was about eight inches high. None of us had a camera, but we asked them for a photo of the family. They gave us a photo from their album. It was a memorable experience. I bought a scarf from a street vendor.

It was embroidered with the words…"A Friend, USA." It seemed the Japanese people were grateful to have American troops occupying their country.

USS *Van Valkenburgh* (DD-656)

Harvey Fehling

In early August of 1945 the *Van Valkenburgh* was anchored in Buckner Bay at Okinawa. One night at 10 pm all hell broke loose. The sky lit and everybody was shooting. We didn't know what the heck was happening. Thought we were under attack. But some guy got the word that Japan had surrendered and he passed it along. They started celebrating prematurely. We hadn't even dropped the Atom bombs yet. Finally, the generals and admirals got their units to cut it out. There wasn't any peace yet. When they did drop the bombs, we had no idea what they were. Just some big mysterious bomb. Right after the accepted surrender on 15 August the *Van Valkenburgh* led a squadron of destroyers and two hospital ships into the harbor at Nagasaki to pick up our POWs. That's where the second bomb was dropped. We had a Jap pilot on board to guide us through the minefields. We got to the inner harbor. Nobody was on the docks. The harbor area was still intact. The town and surrounding hills were flattened. The prisoners started arriving by train in open boxcars. When those guys saw our destroyers tied up with American flags flying they went crazy. We hooked up hot water lines so we could wash them off a little. They were just filthy skeletons. We stayed there about a week. I got to go ashore. I walked right around in the devastation and radiation. We didn't know any better.

—ɯ—

These were some of the stories returning sailors would share with their families and friends. They were the memories that were easy to talk about and provided some insight into their war time experiences. Many of the other stories were never discussed. They were difficult memories. Nobody who had been in combat wanted to be that guy who bragged about his war experience. They all felt that the real heroes were the ones who didn't come home. They knew that they couldn't communicate what it had really been like. Even if they could, no one would truly understand. The *Enola Gay* pilot, Paul Tibbetts, had an explanation for it. If you walked into a bar after the war and some guy was telling heroic war stories, you knew he had never seen combat.

It was decades later before some of the stories started to come out. Ship's crews started to have reunions. They were meeting up with buddies they hadn't seen in over 20 years. One guy would bring up a shocking memory and that would lead to another. It felt okay to tell these stories with men who had shared the same experience. They understood, because they were there. The reunions have served as therapy for some. These men gather, not just to tell stories, but to be with comrades. These are people who acted their best while suffering and sacrificing together. Fortunately, WWII veterans are finally talking. Many museums have started oral history collections. Through books, films and historical projects, the worst event in human history is now being archived. Hopefully the knowledge from these efforts will keep it from ever happening again.

The USS Bache served the Navy for 25 years. Thousands of sailors walked her decks. Tom Erb from Desota, Wisconsin is one of them. He honored the ship he called home for 33 months by building a model of her. The four-foot long model is 1/96 scale. The hull is made from planks on a WWII Fletcher kit frame. Above deck is all scratch built out of acrylic. Fittings came from numerous model suppliers. It took Erb five winters of research and work. He proudly displays it at Bache reunions and Tin Can Sailors events.

Japanese Arisaka Type 99 rifle was their primary battle weapon throughout the war. Though crude in appearance it had one of the strongest receiver/actions of any military bolt action rifles. This rifle was brought back home from Okinawa by Elmer Veesenmeyer. He was a shipmate on the hospital ship USS Bountiful. Thousands of these captured weapons became souvenirs of GIs and Sailors.

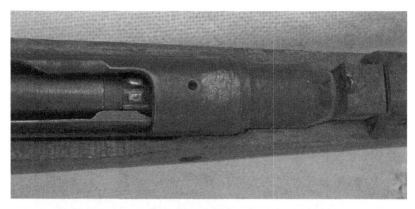

The receiver of each Arisaka Type 99 rifle was stamped with a mum - the imperial symbol of the Japanese Emperor. The 16 petal chrysanthemum markings were ground off by surrendering Japanese troops. It was considered a disgrace to hand over a rifle that was the property of the Emperor. The symbol on this rifle receiver was filed off before being surrendered.

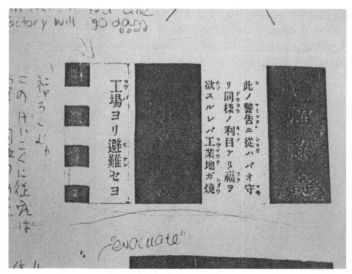

American B-27 bombers dropped millions of leaflets warning Japanese citizens of bombing raids. This one was found on the Japanese pilot that crashed into the Hadley. It reads…

"Evacuate the factories. If you obey this warning you will be in luck. If you are greedy the factory will go down in flames."

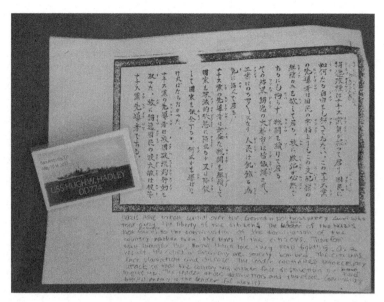

This anti-war message was found in the flight suit of a kamikaze pilot by Eugene Wise. The plane had crashed into the engine room of the USS Hugh W. Hadley. It was translated 50 years later. The message is a stunning attack on Germany's war. It probably resonated with the pilot's own destruction. It reads in part…

> *"Nazis have taken control over the German political party who took away the liberty of the citizens. The leader of the Nazis looks forward to the continuation of the domination of the country, rather than the lives of the citizens. The leader chose destruction and therefore Germany's biggest enemy is the leader of the Nazis."*

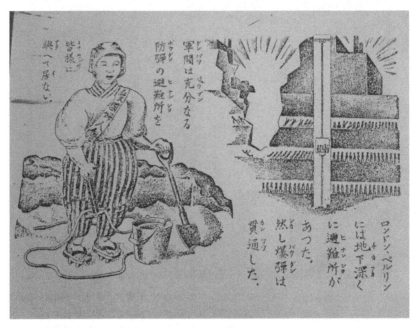

A propaganda leaflet aimed at the governments of England and Germany. It shows a bomb shelter being destroyed. This was also found with the kamikaze pilot in the Hadley's engine room. The translation reads...

"London and Berlin had fall-out shelters but the bomb penetrated through the ground. The army/military were not providing the people with enough safety."

The surrender of Japan took place aboard the USS Missouri on 2 September 1945. Official photographers lined the rails. Many ships were in Tokyo Bay that day. Representatives from those ships came aboard the Missouri to witness the surrender. T.P. Oswald from the Bennington got this unofficial picture that was taken from above MacArthur's signing table. It was found among Oswald's navy memorabilia.

After the war, this Japanese family invited several sailors to dinner in their home. Carmon Howe and his shipmates were on liberty from the USS Rotanin. They had befriended these children who then brought them home for a typical Japanese meal. Howe asked the father if they could have a photo of the family. This photo was taken from the family album and presented to the sailors. Howe of Cambridge, Wisconsin treasures this memory and the photo.

Appendix 1

Japanese Aircraft Code Names

FOR the purpose of identification and simple reporting, all operational Japanese planes were assigned Allied Code names. They were given male or female names. Tony, Zeke, Betty and Sally are referred to often throughout the book.

Male names were given to Army and Navy fighter planes as well as Navy reconnaissance float planes. Female names were assigned to all others, which included bombers, dive bombers, and transports. Trainers were also being used as kamikazes towards the end of the war. They were given code names of trees as in Hickory, Willow and Pine. There were 61 Japanese planes listed in the Photographic Interpretation Handbook published in April of 1945. Only those commonly used as kamikazes or those mentioned in this book are listed below.

BOMBERS AND TRANSPORTS		FIGHTERS AND FLOAT PLANES	
MAVIS	Navy Patrol Bomber	NICK	Army Fighter
EMILY	Navy Patrol Bomber	ZEKE	Navy Fighter (Zero)
BETTY	Navy Land Attack Bomber	TONY	Army Fighter
NELL	Navy Land Attack Bomber	FRANK	Army Fighter

SALLY	Army Medium Bomber	OSCAR	Army Fighter
PEGGY	Army Medium Bomber	JACK	Navy Fighter
FRANCES	Navy Torpedo Bomber	TOJO	Army Fighter
DINAH	Army Recon	JAKE	Navy Recon Float
KATE	Navy Torpedo Bomber	PAUL	Navy Dive Bomber
JILL	Navy Torpedo Bomber	PETE	Navy Recon Float
VAL	Navy Dive Bomber	NORM	Navy Recon Float
JUDY	Navy Dive Bomber-Recon	REX	Navy Fighter
BABS	Navy Recon	GEORGE	Navy Fighter
GRACE	Torpedo Bomber	NATE	Army Trainer
CHERRY	Navy Patrol Bomber	DAVE	Navy Recon Float
BAKA	(Idiot) Manned Rocket	WILLOW	Army Bi-Plane Trainer

Appendix 2

Glossary of Naval Terms and Slang

AFT (AFTER)	rear areas of ship
AIRDALE	carrier sailor
AOL	absent over leave
AWOL	absent without leave
BATTLEWAGON	battleship
BEACH	any shore location
BELLY ROBBER	cook
BELOW	downstairs
BOATS	boatswain's mate
BOOT	below a Seaman
BOW	front of ship
BRIDGE	command center for steering/communication
BULKHEAD	interior walls
DECK	floors
DEEP SIX	throw away overboard
DOG WATCH	2-hour watch during evening chow
ENLISTED	general work force
FANTAIL	rear of ship

FAST	snug or secured
FLANK SPEED	top speed
GALLEY	kitchen
GQ	General Quarters (battle stations)
HAND BILLY	hand pump extinguisher
HATCH	doorway
HEAD	toilet
JARHEAD	Marine
KNOT	1 nautical mile
LADDER	stairs
LAYING	laying starboard means ship is leaning right
LEAVE	authorized vacation
LIBERTY	permission to go ashore
LIFELINE	deck lines to prevent falling overboard
LINE	any length of rope
MIDSHIPS	middle area of a ship
MIDWATCH	most dreaded watch from midnight to 4 a.m.
MUSTER	roll call taken a 0800 each morning
OVERHEAD	ceilings
OIL KING	kept daily measure of fuel oil
OUTBOARD	outside the ship's hull
PASSAGEWAY	hallway
PLANK OWNER	crewmember on newly commissioned ship
PORTSIDE	left side of ship
RACK	bed or bunk
RATING	job specific title
SCREW	ship's propeller
SCUTTLEBUTT	gossip and rumors
SECURE	stop work
SHAKEDOWN	testing for seaworthy and battle ready
SKIPPER	Captain (any rank) who commands ship

SKIVVY WAVER	Signalman
SNIPE	anyone in the engineering department
SP	security police
SPARKS	radioman
STARBOARD	right side of ship
STERN	aft or rear of ship
STRIKER	apprentice in job training
SWAG	sonar's wild ass guess
TBS	Talk Between Ships on short range radio
TIN CAN	destroyer
XO	Executive Officer (2nd in Command)

ENLISTED MEN'S RATINGS

Boatswain's Mate – supervises ship maintenance and seamanship

Coxswain – helmsman who steers the ship

Damage Controlman – fights fires and makes emergency repairs

Electrician's Mate – maintains electrical equipment and power

Fire Controlman – operates computer for aiming guns

Fireman – maintains engine room equipment

Gunner's Mate – operates and maintains all gunnery equipment

Machinist's Mate – maintains the engineering equipment

Pharmacist's Mate – administers medical assistance and treatment

Radarman – monitors air search and ground search radar

Seaman – works on deck crews and ship maintenance

Signalman – uses flags or lights to send ship to ship messages

Sonarman – operates submarine detection equipment

Steward – serves officers (only rate for Negros in WWII)

Torpedoman – maintains and operates torpedo launchers

Watertender – maintains the boilers and steam lines

Quartermaster – assists with navigation and steering of the ship

ENLISTED MEN'S RANKS

S – Seaman
PO – Petty Officer
CPO – Chief Petty Officer (most experienced man on ship)

OFFICERS RANKS

ENS – Ensign is the lowest rank of an officer
LTJG – Lieutenant Junior Grade
LT – Lieutenant
LCDR – Lieutenant Commander
CDR – Commander
CPT – Captain
RADM – Rear Admiral
ADM - Admiral

SHIP DESIGNATIONS

CV	Aircraft Carrier
CVE	Escort Carrier
BB	Battleship
CA	Heavy Cruiser
CL	Light Cruiser
DD	Destroyer
DE	Destroyer Escort
DM	Destroyer Minelayer
LST	Landing Ship Tank
LSM	Landing Ship Medium
LCS	Landing Craft Support
LSM(R)	Landing Ship Medium Rocket
ATA	Auxiliary Ocean Tug

AK	Attack Transport
APD	Attack Personnel Destroyer
SS	Submarine

COMMON NAVY ACRONYMS

AAA	Anti-Aircraft Artillery
A/C	Aircraft
BUPERS	Bureau of Naval Personnel
CAP	Combat Air Patrol
CIC	Combat Information Center
CINCPAC	Commander In Chief Pacific
CNO	Chief of Naval Operations
FIDO	Fighter Director Operator
NAVY	Never Again Volunteer Yourself
OOD	Officer of the Deck
PBY	Amphibious Plane
UNREP	Underway Replenish
USS	United States Ship
WAVE	Women Accepted for Volunteer Emergency Service

Appendix 3

U.S Ships Sunk by Kamikazes at Okinawa

April through July 1945

Bush (DD-529)	destroyer, 94 killed on 6 April
Colhoun (DD-801)	destroyer, 35 killed on 6 April
Emmons (DMS-22)	destroyer, 60 killed on 6 April
Hobbs Victory	ammunition ship, 11 killed on 6 April
Logan Victory	ammunition ship, 12 killed on 6 April
LST-447	landing ship tank, 5 killed on 7 April
Mannert L. Abele (DD-773)	destroyer, 65 killed on 12 April
LCS(L)(3)-15	landing craft support (large), 4 killed on 12 April
Pringle (DD-477)	destroyer, 65 killed on 16 April
Swallow (AM-65)	minesweeper, 2 killed on 22 April
LCS(L)(3)	landing craft support (large), 15 killed on 22 April
Canada Victory	ammunition ship, 1 killed on 27 April
Little (DD-803)	destroyer, 30 killed on 3 May
LSM(R)-195	landing ship medium (rocket), 8 killed on 3 May
Morrison (DD-560)	destroyer, 159 killed on 4 May
Luce (DD-552)	destroyer, 149 killed on 4 May
LSM(R)-190	landing ship medium (rocket) 13 killed on 4 May

LSM(R)-194	landing ship medium (rocket) 13 killed on 4 May
Bates (APD-47)	high speed transport, 21 killed on 25 May
LSM-135	landing ship medium, 11 killed on 25 May
Drexler (DD-741)	destroyer, 158 killed on 28 May
William D. Porter (DD-579)	destroyer, no casualties on 10 June
Twiggs (DD-591)	destroyer, 152 killed on 16 June
LSM-59	landing ship medium, 2 killed on 21 June
Barry (APD-29)	high speed transport, no casualties 21 June
Callaghan (DD-792)	destroyer, 47 killed on 29 July

Appendix 4

A Navy Custom

Poem by Edgar A. Guest

They've a custom in the Navy, which I think is very nice,
There's no ice cream on destroyers, for those ships are short of ice.

So, the men upon a carrier, when a plane has been downed at sea,
And the pilot and his comrades are reported to be.

In the breeches buoy, which brings them, (What a gracious thing to
do)
They put ice cream in containers for the skipper and his crew.

The destroyer boys don't ask, with the rescue they're content,
But the lads upon the carrier, have a touch of sentiment.

And although for days or longer, they may have to do without,
They have a stock of sweet refreshment, and they gladly dish it out.

In the breeches buoy returning, hence this bit of verse I pen,
They send "chocolate" and "vanilla," for the skipper and his men.

To The Men Of Bombing "82"

From the diary of Thomas Patrick Oswald, PR1/c, USS Bennington

Many are the times we had together,
Pitching liberties in all kinds of weather;
Fights we've had quite a few,
But from each one more friendships grew.

We've slept beside one another,
And when death claimed one of our crew;
Sorrow was deep in the heart of each man.
And when this war is won,
We'll look at each other and say "Well Done."

And maybe someday once more we'll meet,
With our civvies walking down the street.
Walk in a gin mill and order up,
And drink together from the friendship cup.

Reminiscing of days gone by,
We'll take a sip and breathe a sigh.
And say to the bartender bring another,
For each one here is like a brother.
C.A. BROWN
L.R. WITT
T.P. OSWALD

Appendix 6

Dear Santa

By Earl H. Bickett Jr., SF1/c, (and buddies)
Sixth Naval Construction Battalion

December 1, 1942
Dear Santa Claus,
This month when you're down in the Solomon Isles,
Give your reindeer a rest and stop in for a while.
To help you to pack a small list I will give,
Of what Seabees want just as sure as we live.

Give the Second-Class Seamen the privilege to bitch,
And hope for a raise 'ore they finish their hitch.
To the First-Class Seamen, dear Santa a raise in rate,
And relief from the work that they've done up to date.

Third-Class Men want something in their line of work,
Where they won't be as seamen, in their minds a jerk.
To the cooks a cookbook, something they really need,
So our food sometimes tastes like the can label reads.

Our Commander a small slip of paper that reads,
Your battalion's accomplished what Uncle Sam needs.
Take them home for a rest – Santa, please be a pal,
And get us the hell off Guadalcanal.
Your little friends,
The Sixth Battalion Seabees

Bibliography

BOOKS

Baldwin, Hanson W. *Battles Lost and Won:* New York: Konecky & Konecky, 1966

Block, Leo. *Aboard the Farragut Class Destroyers in WWII:* Jefferson, NC: McFarland & Co. Inc. Publishers, 2009

Bradley, F.J. *No Strategic Targets Left:* New York: Turner Publishing Co., 1999

Bradley, James. *Flyboys:* New York: Little, Brown and Company, 2003

Becton, F. Julian. *The Ship That Would Not Die:* New Jersey: Prentis-Hall, 1980

Burt, Ron. *Kamikaze Nightmare:* Corpus Christie, TX: Alfie Publishing, 1995

Chant, Chris. *Aircraft of World War II:* New York: Metro Books, 2015

Dana, Mitchell. *Illustrated Story of WWII – Hold that Line or Die:* Readers Digest, 1969

Darman, Peter. *World War II Stats and Facts:* New York: Metro Books, 2009

Deutermann, P.T. *Sentinels Of Fire:* New York: St. Martin's Press, 2014

Dupuy, Trevor Nevitt. *The Naval War in the Pacific – On to Tokyo:* New York: Franklin Watts, Inc., 1963

Feifer, George. *Tennozan – The Battle of Okinawa and the Atomic Bomb:* New York: Ticknor & Fields, 1992

Gailey, Harry A. *The War in the Pacific:* Novato, CA: Presidio Press, 1995

Goodenough, Simon. *War Maps World War II:* New York: Crescent Books, 1982

Grahlfs, F. Lincoln. *Undaunted:* St. Louis: F L Grahlfs, 2002

Green, Bob. *Duty:* New York: Harper Collins Publishers Inc., 2000

Hastings, Max. *Inferno – The World at War 1939-1945:* New York: Random House, 2011

Jennings, Peter and Brewster, Todd. *The Century:* New York: Doubleday, 1998

Leckie, Robert. *Okinawa – The Last Battle of World War II:* New York: Penguin Books USA, 1995

Lee, Fred S. *Naval Memories and Adventures of World War II 1942-1946:* Self Published, 1995

Lord, Walter. *Day of Infamy:* New York: Henry Hold and Company, LLC, 1957

Lott, Arnold S. *Brave Ship Brave Men:* Annapolis, MD: U.S. Naval Institute, 1964

MacKay, Jr. Ron. *The U.S. Navy's "Interim" LSM(R)s in World War II:* Jefferson, NC, McFarland and Co. Publishers, 2016

Miller, Donald L. *The Story of World War II:* New York: Simon & Schuster

Miller, Nathan. *The U.S Navy – An Illustrated History:* American Heritage Publishing Co. Inc., 1977

Morison, Samuel Eliot. *Victory in the Pacific 1945:* Boston: Little, Brown and Company, 1975

Naito, Hatsuho. *Thunder Gods - Sure Hit Sure Death:* New York: Kodansha International, 1989

Newcomb, Richard F. *Abandon Ship! – The Saga of the USS Indianapolis:* New York, Harper Collins Publishers, 2001

North, Oliver L. *War Stories II:* Washington DC, Regency Publishing Inc., 2004

Olson, Michael Keith. *Tales from a Tin Can – The USS Dale:* Minneapolis: Zenith Press, 2007

O'Reilly, Bill. *Killing the Rising Sun:* New York: Henry Holt and Company, LLC, 2016

Overy, Richard. *The New York Times – Complete WWII:* New York: Black Dog & Leventhal Publishing, 2013

Porter, Colonel Bruce R. *ACE! – A Marine Night-Fighter Pilot in World War II:* Gladstone, MO: Pacifica Press, 1985

Reilly, Robin L. *Kamikazes, Corsairs and Picket Ships- Okinawa 1945:* Drexel Hill, PA; Casemate, 2008

Sears, David. *At War With The Wind:* New York, Kensington Publishing Corp., 2008

Sledge, Eugene B. *With the Old Breed – At Peleliu & Okinawa:* Novato, CA, Presidio Press, 1981

Sloan, Bill. *The Ultimate Battle – Okinawa 1945:* New York: Simon & Schuster, 2007

Smith, Rex Allan and Meehl, Gerald A. *Pacific War Stories:* New York: Abbeville Press Publishers, 2004

Staton, Michael. *The Fighting Bob:* Bennington, VT: Merriam Press, 2001

Stern, Robert C. *Fire from the Sky:* Barnsley, Great Britain: Seaforth Publishing, 2010

Stevens, Michael E. *Letters from the Front:* Madison, WI: State Historical Society of Wisconsin, 1992

Toland, John. *The Rising Sun:* New York: Random House Inc., 1970

Van der Vat, Dan. *The Pacific Campaign – World War II:* New York: Simon & Schuster, 1991

Veesenmeyer, Jeffrey R. *Kamikaze Destroyer – USS Hugh W. Hadley (DD-774):* Bennington, VT: Merriam Press, 2014

Ward, Geoffrey C. and Burns, Ken. *The War – An Intimate History:* New York: Alfred A. Knopf, 2007

Wheeler, Keith. *The Road to Tokyo – World War II:* Alexandria, VA: Time Life Books, 1979

Yahara, Colonel Hiromichi. *The Battle for Okinawa:* John Wiley & Sons, Inc., New York, 1995

VIDEOS

AHC, *Ultimate Warfare*

AHC. *Okinawa:* American Hero Channel, 2014

American Pride Productions USA, *USS Hadley – 100 Minutes in Hellfire:* Chuck Pride, 2016

Battleline. *WWII Kamikaze Story & Battleline Okinawa 1945:* U.S. and Japanese War films, 1964

Combat at Sea. *The Destroyers:* Columbia Tristar, 1992

History Channel, *The Kamikazes*

Modern Marvels, *The Fletcher Destroyer:* History.com

National Archives, *The Fleet That Came to Stay:* Sherman Ginsberg Production

Victory at Sea. *Suicide for Glory:* National Broadcasting Company.

ARTICLES & PUBLICATIONS

Air Force Magazine. *The Year of the Kamikaze:* by John T. Correll

Alligator Alley. Newsletter of the USS LSM-LSM(R) Association

Alligator Alley. *Saga of the LSM-59:* by Floyd Bozeman Jr.

Authorhouse, *Gunship Sailor:* by M. Edward Arnold, March 2003

Bache Newsletter, *From the Quarterdeck:* Tom Blaszczyk, 2009

Destroyer History Foundation. *The Champion Kamikaze Killer:* By Capt. Doug Aitken, 2000

Gator - Amphibious Training Base. Vo. 11 No. 3, 4, 5, March 1945

Mission: History. *1945 The Deadliest Duty:* April 2000, Vol. 2, Number 1

National Geographic, *Okinawa – Threshold to Japan:* by David D. Duncan, October 1945

NBC Network. *Your Navy Interview with Commander Mullaney:* May 20, 1945

New York Herald Tribune. *Destroyer, Most Gallant Fighting Ship of All:* by John Steinbeck, 1943

Online Posting, *Life on a Fletcher Class Destroyer in the 1950's:* by Captain George Stewart, USN (Retired), July 31, 2013

The Quarterdeck, *A Brief Bache History:* Captain H.E. Bucky Walters, 2008

Proceedings. *Nobody asked me either, but...:* Commander Bruce R. Linder, U.S. Navy

Real for Men: *Tin Can Ace of Okinawa:* by Harrison Forman, 1960

Sea Classics 30th Anniversary issue. *Radar Picket Station 15:* by Robert Sinclair Parkin

Sea Classics. *Deadliest Ships Afloat:* by Richard Hillyer, November 2010

The Lower Deck Newsletter. *Last Destroyer at Okinawa USS Callaghan:* Number 33, Sept. 2003

The Tin Can Sailor. Quarterly Newsletters: Terry Miller, Editor

The Tin Can Sailor. *A Tin Can Sailors Destroyer History – USS Drexler:* July 2005

U.S. Naval Institute. *U.S. Destroyer Operations in WWII:* by Theodore Roscoe

Victory in the Pacific 1945. *Ten Go Gets Going:* by Samuel Eliot Morison, 1975

World War II Magazine. *Laffey Attacked off Okinawa in WWII:* by Dale P. Harper, March 1998

Yank-The Army Weekly. *Kamikaze Pilot:* by Sgt. Robert MacMillan, November 30, 1945

DECLASSIFIED DOCUMENTS

Action Reports. USS *Bunker Hill*, May 1945

Action Reports. USS *Hugh W. Hadley:* Office of Naval Records and Library, 15 May 1945

Action Reports. USS *Bache:* Okinawa Operation March to June 1945

HyperWar: Battle Experience. *Commander U.S. Navy Secret Bulletin No. 24 - Radar Pickets,* July 1945

Log Book. *Of the* USS *Hugh W. Hadley:* Department of the Navy, 25 Nov 1944 to 15 Dec 1945

Navy Dept. Office of Public Information, Ship Section, 1945

ORAL HISTORIES

Bob Bell. USS *Hadley* Interview: by Richard Harden for National Museum of the Pacific War,

Donald Malcolm, USS *Hadley* interview: by John Strupp 2002

Doug Aitken. USS *Hadley* Interview: by National Museum of the Pacific War, 2005

Duke Payne. USS *Drexler*: auto bio by Duke Payne for Costoffreedom.org

Frank Boffi. USS *Hadley* Interview: by National Museum of the Pacific War, 2012

Henry C. Fehling. USS *Van Valkenburgh* interview: by Wisconsin Veterans Museum Research Center, 1996

Harold Tatsch. USS *Drexler* interview: by Nimitz Education & Foundation Center, 2005

Jim B. Reeder. USS *Bush* Interview: by John Weingandt, Wisconsin Veterans Museum, 2006

John J. Stavola. USS *LSM(R) 191* interview: by Richard Misenhimer, National Museum of the Pacific War

Kenneth Kalhagen. USS *Bush* Interview: by James McIntosh, Wisconsin Veterans Museum, 1999

Lefteris "Lefty" Lavrakas. USS *Aaron Ward* interview: by Richard Misenhimer, National Museum for Pacific War, Feb. 2007

Lyle Tennis. USS *LSMR 190* Oral History Interview: by John Driscoll, Wisconsin Veterans Museum, 2003

Marty Weibel. USS *Hadley* Interview: by National Museum of the Pacific War, 2012

Norris Long. Edgar Overstake, Alex Fiedler, Frank Frame, Willie Gunn. *LST-534* interviews: by Audio Visual Management Group, Inc.

Perry Camp. USS *Hadley* Interview: by Richard Harden for National Museum of the Pacific War, 2005

Tom English. USS *Hadley Interview:* by National Museum of the Pacific War, 2012

Wesley Todd. USS *Bunker Hill* Interview: by Wisconsin Veterans Museum Research Center

PERSONAL INTERVIEWS

USS *Hadley* Shipmates & Family: Doug Aitken, Bob Bell, Frank Boffi, Tom English, Dell Burt Hall, Marty Weibel, Leo Helling, Phillip Goeble, Terry Stokes, John Shephard Jr., Leo Polek, Waymond Dean, Ted Davis

USS *Bache* Shipmates: Irv Clark, George Riggs, Al Everett, Ray DelSesto, Mac Lockwood, Jeremiah Tuttle

WWII Navy Veterans: Fred Lee, F. Lincoln Grahlfs, George Mendonsa, Dick Lillie, Phillip Wilmot, Carmon Howe, Norman Halverson

DIARIES & LETTERS

Jack Garska, Thomas Patrick Oswald, A.W. Hodde Jr., Hunter Robbins, Robert Veesenmeyer

WEB SITES

ASCFUSA, www.ascfusa.org
Destroyer History, www.destroyerhistory.org
Destroyers Online www.destroyersonline.com
Elephants Forever, www.elepahantsforever.com
History Net, www.historynet.com
Ibidlio, www.ibidlio.org
Kamikazes, www.kamikazeimages.net
Naval History and Heritage Command, www.historynavymil/foia. html

NavSource Online Website, www.navsource.org/archives
Pacific War Online Encyclopedia, www.pwencycl.kgbndge.com
Today's History Lesson, www.todayshistorylesson.wordpress.com
The Smithsonian, www.Smithsonian.com
USN History, www.history.navy.mil
USS *Bache* (DD-470), www.USSBache.com
USS *Bush* (DD-529) Website, www.USSBush.com
USS *Colhoun* (DD-801) Website, USS Colhoun.com
USS *Hugh W. Hadley* Memorial Website, www.USSHadley.net
USS *Laffey*, www.usslaffey.org
USS *LST 534* www.lst534.com
USS *Robley Evans* Website, www.USSEvans.com
U-Boat and Allied Warships, www.Uboat.net
War Damage Report, www.destroyers.org
Wikipedia, www.wikipedia.com

FACEBOOK PAGES

Kamikaze Destroyer
Remembering LSM and LSMR
USS *Hugh W. Hadley* (DD-774)
Tin Can Sailor II
Destroyers: Greyhounds of the Sea
USS *Laffey* (DD-724 – (DD-459)
USS *Bache* (DD-470)
USS *Bennington*
USS *The Sullivans* (DD-537)

MUSEUMS

National Museum of the Pacific War - Fredericksburg, TX
Patriots Point Naval & Maritime Museum - Charleston Harbor, SC

Buffalo and Erie County Naval & Military Park - Buffalo, NY
Wisconsin Veterans Museum - Madison, WI
Cambridge Historic School Museum- Cambridge, WI
Wisconsin Maritime Museum - Manitowoc, WI

About the Author

JEFF Veesenmeyer earned a degree in Journalism at Northern Illinois University. He had a successful career in the publishing, printing and direct mail industries. He worked for several newspapers and magazines in Illinois and Wisconsin.

Veesenmeyer's interest in naval history developed from his father and other family members who were navy veterans. His uncle was killed on the USS *Hugh W. Hadley* during WWII. Veesenmeyer authored "Kamikaze Destroyer - USS *Hugh W. Hadley* (DD-774)," to learn more about how his uncle died. Veesenmeyer served in the Naval Air Reserve for six years. He attained the rank of PT2/c in Photographic Air Intelligence.

Veesenmeyer lives with his wife Joy in Cambridge, Wisconsin. They enjoy traveling to Navy reunions to meet with the veterans he writes about. Many friendships have developed through the stories these men have shared. Veesenmeyer serves on the board of directors for the Cambridge Historic School Museum. He manages the *Hadley* website and Facebook page.

Web page: www.USSHadley.net
Facebook/USS Hugh W. Hadley (DD-774)
Facebook/Kamikaze Destroyer